Piercing the
Illusion

To Billie Andrews

Let's keep the torch
of Liberty burning.

John Baptist Kotmann Jr.

GALATIANS 5:1

Piercing the
Illusion

Setting straight the misrepresentations that have in one way or another deprived American citizens of their Individual Liberties for the past one hundred and forty-one years.

By:

John Baptist Kotmair, Jr.
Fiduciary of the
Save-A-Patriot Fellowship

First Edition, Registered Number ___ −159− ___

Library of Congress Cataloging-in-Publication Data

Kotmair, John Baptist, Jr., 1934 -

Piercing the Illusion: Setting straight the misrepresentations that have in one way or another deprived American citizens of their Individual Liberties for the past one hundred and forty-one years / John B. Kotmair, Jr.
    p.cm.
Includes bibliographical references and index
    ISBN 0-9719339-7-9
    1. God's plan for government— Bibical tax plan 2. United States Constitution—Constitutional money—Constitutional taxing authority 3. Sedious activity 4. Spiritual struggle—Political action—United States. I Title
Editors: Dick Greb, James Kerr and Bonnie Nobile

                                    2002096402

Published in the United States by
Save-A-Patriot Fellowship
12 Carroll Street
Westminster, Maryland 21157

Visit us at www.save-a-patriot.org

Printed on acid-free paper
Manufactured in the United States of America

Dedication

First, this book is dedicated to the service of _Our Lord_ and _Saviour_, may _His Will_ be done.

Then to my wife _Nancy Loretta_ who has suffered my extreme patriotism for this Constitutional Republic these last forty-six years. _For her price is far above rubies._

To my children, grandchildren, and great-grandchildren may they see the end of intrusive government and flourish in the _Liberty_ of its absence.

To the _Patriots_, past and present, who have labored, suffered loss of property, incarceration, and their lives for the cause of _Liberty_.

And last but not least, to the suppression of the budding police state, the dismantling of all unconstitutional government agencies and activities through peaceful educational means—so help us _God_.

Contents

Introduction

As far back as I can remember, I hungered for knowledge about the history of the American Revolutionary period, and was very disappointed that I was not taught more about it in school. Of course, this hunger was enhanced by being indoctrinated as a very young boy by the propaganda that was emanating from everywhere during World War II. It was truly an extremely patriotic time in America. The atmosphere was so patriotic, that I feared the consequences of anyone not appearing to be so.

In that same era, I was exposed to political activity, having an uncle who was a political office holder in Baltimore, Maryland, a grandfather who was very influential in the Stonewall Democratic Club in South Baltimore, and a grand-uncle who was very influential in the Shamrock Democratic Club in Southwest Baltimore. I felt very much at home in this political environment, but due to my youthful inexperience I did not see or understand the evils of the New Deal era in which I grew up. All that you heard at that time was that President Roosevelt had saved us from the depression and would lead us to victory over Hitler, Hirohito, and Mussolini.

I was a proud eighteen-year-old, serving during the Korean "War" (Conflict) in the Air-Wing of the United States Navy, and it was not until eleven years later, serving as a Baltimore City police officer, that I became disillusioned when examining the cause of the failure of the Bay of Pigs invasion in Cuba. Being a Navy veteran, I knew it was no mistake that the ammunition issued to the Cuban Freedom Fighters, as they embarked on the landing craft, did not fit their weapons, and that the promised air support was withdrawn at the last minute—leaving those helpless Freedom Fighters to be rounded up on the beach by Castro and incarcerated in Cuban prison camps.

A year later, after reading the book, *Conscience of a Conservative*, by Senator Barry Goldwater, I was led to and eagerly joined the John Birch Society. My patriotic zeal seemed to fit right in, and I rose through the ranks of the Birch Society to become a Section Leader. It did not take but a year or two to realize that the program was not, whether intentionally or unintentionally, designed for success. The historical education about the Communist conspiracy was second to none, but not really having any effective way of putting it to use, the members quickly become disillusioned, despondent, and quit.

After leaving the Birch Society, I became involved with some members of the Minutemen (an organization started by Robert Depew), and some Lithuanian and Cuban Anti-Communist Freedom Fighters. Having a very active experience in both the Barry Goldwater and George Wallace presidential campaigns, I became one of the state organizers of the American Party, which was started by George Wallace. This gave me first-hand experience of the election fraud used to try to keep the socialists and pseudo-conservatives in office. In the meantime, I left the Baltimore City Police Department and went into housing construction as a carpenter, and in 1968, started a very successful home building business called Freestate Home Builders.

At the very same time, I became aware of Mr. A. J. Porth, a building contractor in Wichita, Kansas, who contended, and reasonably so, that an Internal Revenue Service income tax return, Form 1040, could not be filed without waiving one's 5th Amendment Right. Already being aware of the evils of the Federal Reserve Bank and Federal Reserve Board, this was, in my opinion, tailor-made to combat them. I envisioned it as much more effective than anything I had experienced so far.

In 1973, I took the plunge, stopped filing tax returns and withholding taxes from the wages of my employees, and gave the IRS notice that I was doing so. That same year, I organized the

Maryland Committee of Correspondence and became its chairman. The Committee of Correspondence grew, and I began holding meetings on a weekly basis.

In 1975, in order to get more exposure, one of the members of the Committee and I decided to challenge the Baltimore District Director of the Internal Revenue Service and the United States Attorney for Maryland to a public debate over what was being taught at that time at the Committee meetings. We chose the beginning of the tax-filing season to go public with our plans. This, of course, caught the news media's attention, and one of the local TV stations offered time for the debate. All that occurred was my being interviewed, because the District Director and U.S. Attorney declined the TV station's invitation. This was followed by another media event—this time covered by all three local TV stations, at which a very large audience watched as we buried a black coffin with *IRS* painted in white on its sides. We realized that putting on such a display would invite retaliation, and it came not too long after.

On April 15, 1976, two special agents of the IRS appeared at my door. The conversation started off with one of them reading me my 5th Amendment Rights in accordance with the Miranda Decision of the U.S. Supreme Court. I thanked them, explaining that I have been trying to tell them that I had such Rights, and they left. Five years later, I was indicted by a federal grand jury, which charged me with two misdemeanors. After a month-long trial, the story of which could fill another book, I was convicted and sentenced to the maximum sentence that could be given.

During this period, an effort was made to organize all the tax Patriot groups meeting all over the United States. In that effort, I was chosen to be one of the directors, and I immediately embarked on a journey the length and breadth of the United States, organizing for the Patriot Network. This organization evolved into the National Patriot Association, for which I performed the same duties until I was ordered to report to the federal prison camp at Maxwell

Air Force Base in Montgomery, Alabama, on August 24, 1982.

Having a difference of opinion of the purpose and function of the National Patriot Association, I founded the Save-A-Patriot Fellowship one month after my release from the prison camp (February 28, 1984), and became its fiduciary, a title I hold today.

Over the years, while working with the Internal Revenue Code, Regulations, and Manual, knowledge was gained which, regardless of whether the forced filing of a tax return would violate the 5th Amendment, revealed that American citizens were not even subject to a liability for any tax on their domestically earned income. This discovery of the proper application of the federal and state tax laws has truly *pierced the illusion* that just about every American citizen holds on the subject, and led to other discoveries such as the federal government's lawful jurisdiction within the union of States.

So much was learned that, in 1993, as the Fiduciary of the Fellowship, I challenged the Commissioner of the Internal Revenue to prove wrong the facts that were being disseminated by the Fellowship. As you have probably already guessed, the results of this challenge turned out to be the same as the challenge to the District Director and U.S. Attorney—they declined. Then on December 10, 1993, the Fellowship was raided by the IRS, and they confiscated all the computers and paper files. But this time, the results were different, to the IRS's dismay. The Fellowship has weathered internal and external attacks, and is the only Patriot organization that has successfully prevailed after being attacked by the IRS.

The knowledge gained through serving the Fellowship members these past 18 years must become public knowledge if our Constitutional Republic is to be saved, and to that end, this book is dedicated. My experiences as the Fiduciary of the Fellowship have proven to me that this effort is within the Will of God, and He would not have revealed this knowledge to me, and then not expected me to pass it on.

Yes, He has Blessed the Fellowship for the stand that we have taken. He has additionally Blessed me with an understanding and equally Patriotic wife and family, who have been immensely helpful in the efforts that have been made on His behalf. And rightly so, for it is written that we should: *Stand fast, therefore, in the liberty with which Christ hath made us free, and be not entangled again with the yoke of bondage.* Galatians 5:1.

Part I

THE FRAMERS' INTENT

Chapter 1

GOD'S GOVERNMENTAL
PLAN for MANKIND

Not distracted by any electronic-age gadgetry, entertainment media, sports event, or such other type of activity, the Founders had to rely on themselves for entertainment. Their main forms of entertainment were reading, fellowship with friends and family, and church activities, the church being the center of most community events. Wherefore, unlike today, interest in education was even more meaningful than the mere possibility of monetary gain.

The knowledge of this social culture was reflected throughout the history of colonial and post-revolutionary America. An example of the average intellect of that day is found in *The Federalist Papers*. In this collection of essays, James Madison, John Jay and Alexander Hamilton made a successful effort to explain the intent and extent of the proposed new federal Constitution. *The Federalist Papers* were published for the consumption of the state legislatures and the public in newspapers within the several States for the purpose of securing consent for the ratification of this proposed United States Constitution by the legislatures of the several States. A random computer grammar check of these essays reveal that they were written in the average grade level of 24 years of education. It is an established practice today that all daily newspapers throughout the United States are written at the 5th-grade level. This alone should justify all the clamor being made about the inability of our modern public schools to teach our children.

Further evidence of our intellectual decline is exhibited in the 18th-century entrance examination for Princeton University. One of the requirements was that the prospective enrollee would be required to read a book written in Latin aloud in English. Today colleges, out of necessity, are routinely giving extended courses in reading. *Johnny can't read* has become the intellectual norm. Is this happening naturally? If so, why? I contend not.[1] Through the ages, government schools have always been a political tool in the hands of unscrupulous demagogues. Franklin Delano Roosevelt said:

> *In politics, nothing happens by accident. If it happens, you can bet it was planned that way.*[2]

From their writings, it is evident that the *Founders*[3] and the *Framers*[4] had a vivid knowledge of the Bible, history in general, and the intricacies, attributes and faults of all forms of governments. They were scholars of the common law of England, from its origins in the theocracy established by Almighty God[5] on through the Magna Carta. They understood the principle of the equality of mankind which was exemplified in God's Theocracy, which did not have a monarch or other form of executive, but only judges to adjudicate infractions of the Divine Law. They understood that there was no need for a legislature in God's Theocracy, for His Divine Law is perfect and complete.

The result of God's Theocracy was total freedom for the individual, and just like today, this freedom brought prosperity, and prosperity brought complacency and apathy. Like all other prosperous people down through history, the children of Israel no longer wanted the responsibility of their freedom; this is recorded in the Book of I Samuel, Chapter 8, beginning at Verse 3:

> *Then all the elders walked not in his ways, but turned aside after lucre [money], and took bribes, and*

perverted judgment.

4. Then all the elders of Israel gathered themselves together, and came to Samuel unto Ramah,

5. And said unto him, Behold, thou art old, and thy sons walk not in thy ways: now make us a king to judge us like all the nations.

6. But the thing displeased Samuel, when they said, Give us a king to judge us. And Samuel prayed unto the Lord.

7. And the Lord said unto Samuel, Hearken unto the voice of the people in all that they say unto thee: for they have not rejected thee, but they have rejected me, that I should not reign over them.

8. According to all the works which they have done since the day that I brought them up out of Egypt even unto this day, wherewith they have forsaken me, and served other gods, so do they also unto thee.

9. Now therefore hearken unto their voice: howbeit yet protest solemnly unto them, and shew them the manner of the king that shall reign over them.

10. And Samuel told all the words of the Lord unto the people that asked of him a king.

11. And he said, This will be the manner of the king that shall reign over you; He will take your sons, and appoint them for himself, for his chariots, and to be his horsemen; and some shall run before his chariots.

12. And he shall appoint him captains over thousands, and captains over fifties; and will set them to ear the ground, and to reap his harvest, and to make his instruments of war, and instruments of his chariots.

13. And he will take your daughters to be confectionaries, and to be cooks, and to be bakers.

14. And he will take your fields, and your vineyards, and your oliveyards, even the best of them, and give them to his servants.

15. And he will take the tenth of your seed, and your vineyards, and give to his officers, and to his servants.

16. And he will take your menservants, and your maidservants, and your goodliest young men, and your asses, and put them to his work.

17. He will take the tenth of your sheep: and ye shall be his servants.

18. And ye shall cry out in that day because of your king which ye shall have chosen you; and the Lord will not hear you in that day.

19. Nevertheless the people refused to obey the voice of Samuel: and they said, Nay; but we will have a king over us;

20. That we also may be like all the nations; and that our king may judge us, and go out before us, and fight our battles.

Those who do not learn from history are condemned to repeat it—and repeat it. For instance, Thomas Jefferson outlined monarchical abuses in the Declaration of Independence, the founding document that initiated the separation of the American colonies from England:

The history of the present King of Great Britain is a history of repeated injuries and usurpations, all having in direct object the establishment of an absolute Tyranny over these States. To prove this, let Facts be submitted to a candid world.

He has refused his Assent to Laws, the most wholesome and necessary for the public good.

He has forbidden his Governors to pass Laws of immediate and pressing importance, unless suspended in their operation till his Assent should be obtained; and when so suspended, he has utterly neglected to attend to them.

He has refused to pass other Laws for the accommodation of large districts of people, unless those people would relinquish the right of Representation in the Legislature, a right inestimable to them and formidable to

6

tyrants only.

He has called together legislative bodies at places unusual, uncomfortable, and distant from the depository of their public Records, for the sole purpose of fatiguing them into compliance with his measures.

He has dissolved Representative Houses repeatedly, for opposing with manly firmness his invasions on the rights of the people.

He has refused for a long time, after such dissolutions, to cause others to be elected; whereby the Legislative powers, incapable of Annihilation, have returned to the People at large for their exercise; the State remaining in the mean time exposed to all the dangers of invasion from without, and convulsions within.

He has endeavored to prevent the population of these States; for that purpose obstructing the Laws for Naturalization of Foreigners; refusing to pass others to encourage their migration hither, and raising the conditions of new Appropriations of Lands.

He has obstructed the Administration of Justice, by refusing his Assent to Laws for establishing Judiciary powers.

He has made Judges dependent on his Will alone, for the tenure of their offices, and the amount and payment of their salaries.

He has erected a multitude of New Offices, and sent hither swarms of Officers to harass our people, and eat out their substance.

He has kept among us, in times of peace, Standing Armies, without the Consent of our legislatures.

He has affected to render the Military independent of and superior to the Civil power.

He has combined with others to subject us to a jurisdiction foreign to our constitution, and unacknowledged by our laws; giving his Assent to their Acts of pretended Legislation:

For quartering large bodies of armed troops among

us:

For protecting them, by a mock Trial, from Punishment for any Murders which they should commit on the Inhabitants of these States:

For cutting off our Trade with all parts of the world:

For imposing Taxes on us without our Consent:

For depriving us in many cases, of the benefits of Trial by Jury:

For transporting us beyond Seas to be tried for pretended offenses:

For abolishing the free System of English Laws in a neighboring Province, establishing therein an Arbitrary government, and enlarging its Boundaries so as to render it at once an example and fit instrument for introducing the same absolute rule into these Colonies:

For taking away our Charters, abolishing our most valuable Laws, and altering fundamentally the Forms of our Governments:

For suspending our own Legislatures, and declaring themselves invested with power to legislate for us in all cases whatsoever.

He has abdicated Government here, by declaring us out of his Protection and waging War against us.

He has plundered our seas, ravaged our Coasts, burnt our towns, and destroyed the lives of our people.

He is at this time transporting large Armies of foreign Mercenaries to compleat the works of death, desolation and tyranny, already begun with circumstances of Cruelty & perfidy scarcely paralleled in the most barbarous ages, and totally unworthy the Head of a civilized nation.

He has constrained our fellow Citizens taken Captive on the high Seas to bear Arms against their Country, to become the executioners of their friends and Brethren, or to fall themselves by their Hands.

He has excited domestic insurrections amongst us, and has endeavored to bring on the inhabitants of our frontiers, the merciless Indian Savages, whose known rule of warfare, is an undistinguished destruction of all ages, sexes and conditions.

As you have probably recognized, many of these abuses Jefferson outlined we are now suffering today. It is evident that our forefathers bore the abuse until it was no longer bearable, and then made the appropriate correction. Do Americans today have their courage to do what is needed? That, hopefully, remains to be seen.

God's political plan for mankind is verified by Jefferson in the second paragraph of the Declaration:

We hold these truths to be self-evident, that all men are created equal, that they are endowed by their Creator with certain unalienable Rights, that among these are Life, Liberty and the pursuit of Happiness. That to secure these rights, Governments are instituted among Men, deriving their just powers from the consent of the governed. (Emphasis added.)

Absent a divine theocracy, a free society demands that man-made government regulate minimally, only having the authority to protect Life, Liberty and Property, which will guarantee man's pursuit of Happiness. Anything beyond that would be an infringement on these certain unalienable Rights to which Jefferson referred. This principle of government is within our federal Constitution, and that government took effect in April of 1789 with the inauguration of George Washington of Virginia, who became the first president of our Constitutional Republic. The first government was a Confederacy of the States, the compact as such was ratified by the several States on March 1, 1781.

Probably the most explicit statement of these unalienable Rights is found among the writings of the individual considered to be the Father of the American Revolution, Samuel Adams, who declared:

9

If men, through fear, fraud, or mistake, should in terms renounce or give up any natural right, the eternal law of reason and the grand end of society would absolutely vacate such renunciation. The right to freedom being the gift of God, it is not in the power of man to alienate this gift and voluntarily become a slave.

Sam, as he was called by his fellow Patriots, was caught up at a very early age in the philosophy of *Individual Liberty*, adhering to the writings of the English philosopher John Locke. Locke contended that government should only be instituted for the protection of life and property.

Sam's father was a very wealthy Massachusetts businessman, who owned a brewery in Boston and was involved in other business enterprises. He left his wealth to Sam who put the entire fortune to use agitating for the separation of the colonies from the English parliamentary monarchy. He organized the Committees of Correspondence, which was the first political link between the thirteen colonies. The Royal Governor of Massachusetts Colony, Thomas Hutchinson, gave Sam the nickname "The Grand Incendiary," which he truly earned. The word of Sam's revolutionary activities reached England and caused King George enough concern to write the Governor of Massachusetts Colony and inquire of him any knowledge he may have of Sam's effectiveness. Hutchinson replied to the king not to pay Sam any mind; in the colonies Sam was considered to be nothing more than a court jester. But when the Royal Marine Garrison fled Boston, and Hutchinson narrowly escaped with his life from the burning Governor's mansion to safety aboard a British Man O' War battleship in Boston harbor, he penned a letter to King George explaining that he had erred. He wrote, *Adams is not a court jester, he is a Grand Incendiary, he has the colonies aflame.*

After being elected to the first Continental Congress, held in Philadelphia, Pennsylvania in 1774, Sam was in such poor financial condition that he could not even afford to buy a suit of clothes to wear for the occasion. His cousin John Adams, and friend John Hancock purchased a suit of clothes for him—the only suit that he wore during his tenure in that political body.

Eleven years after the beginning of the Constitutional Republic, on February 26, 1800, Thomas Jefferson wrote to Samuel Adams the following tribute:

A letter from you, my respectable friend, after three and twenty years of separation, has given me a pleasure I cannot express. It recalls to my mind the anxious days we then passed in struggling for the cause of mankind. Your principles have been tested in the crucible of time, and have come out pure. You have proved that it was monarchy, and not merely British monarchy, you opposed.

Here Jefferson verifies my theory that the *Founders* and *Framers* understood and instituted God's governmental plan for mankind. It must be realized that a representative government without the guiding hand of a monarch and aristocracy was unheard of at that time.

In this same letter, written one year before Jefferson became the third president of the Constitutional Republic, he reveals that the *Founders* fully understood the workings of those powerful greedy financial interests that have plagued the world since Babylon. By the date of his letter these powerful greedy financial interests had already started their work to destroy God's governmental plan established in North America, for which the *Founders* had struggled so hard and paid such a great price to establish:

A government by representatives, elected by the people at short periods, was our object; and our maxim at that day was, "where annual election ends, tyranny begins;" nor have our departures from it been sanctioned by the happiness of their effects. A debt of an hundred millions growing by usurious interest, and an artificial paper phalanx overruling the agricultural mass of our country, with other et ceteras, have a portentous aspect.

He continued on to disclose that at least he and Samuel Adams had aspirations that the revolution of God's governmental plan would spread throughout the world. He confers to Sam his fears that this same greed is threatening their dream:

I fear our friends on the other side of the water, laboring in the same cause, have yet a great deal of crime and misery to wade through. My confidence has been placed in the head, not the heart of Bonaparte. I hope he would calculate truly the difference between the fame of a Washington and a Cromwell. Whatever his views may be, he has at least transferred the destinies of the republic from the civil to the military arm. Some will use this as a lesson against the practicability of republican government. I read it as a lesson against the danger of standing armies.

As you can see, these *Founders* understood that greed depends on total government, at the expense of the *Cause of Liberty*. Jefferson closed this letter dispelling the claims of those who now say that he was an agnostic:

Adieu, my ever respected and venerable friend. May that kind overruling providence which has so long spared you to our country, still foster your remaining years with whatever may make them comfortable to yourself and soothing to your friends. Accept the cordial salutations of your affectionate friend.

Chapter 2

THE BIBLICAL TAX PLAN

The Lord Jesus Christ established the *Tax Plan* that was instituted by the Framers of the United States Constitution. This *Tax Plan* is found in the New Testament in the Book of Matthew, 17th Chapter, Verses 24 through 27, and states as follows:

> *24 And when they came to Capernaum, they that received tribute money came to Peter, and said, "Doth not your master pay tribute?"*
> *25 He saith, "Yes." And when he was come into the house, Jesus prevented him, saying, "What thinkest thou Simon? of whom do the kings of the earth take custom or tribute? of their own children, or of strangers?"*
> *26 Peter saith unto him, "Of strangers." Jesus saith unto him, "Then are the children free."*
> *27 Notwithstanding, lest we should offend them, go thou to the sea, and cast an hook, and take up the fish that first cometh up; and when thou hast opened his mouth, thou shalt find a piece of money: that take, and give unto them for me and thee.*

Notice that in verses 24 through 26, Jesus and Peter are in agreement that the *children* (citizens) are not the subject of internal taxation, just *strangers* (aliens). Not being within the Divine Plan for Christ to confront the Romans, Peter is instructed in verse 27 to use a coin taken from the mouth of a fish. I believe that this gesture has a very profound significant hidden meaning. For in those days there was a pagan god named Dagon. This god was half man and half fish, and was also known as the devil. Understanding this, it is obviously clear that Christ's message is that taxes, such as tribute are not within the Will of God, but most assuredly are Satanic in nature. For, as shown in Chapter I, God's governmental plan for mankind is a theocracy based on his law as given to Moses, and the only taxes found therein are to support the priests and judges, Leviticus, at Chapter 27, Verse 30:

> *And all the tithe of the land, whether of the seed of the land, or of the fruit of the tree, is the Lord's: it is holy unto the Lord.*

The circumstances were certainly different for the *Founding Fathers* than they were for the children of Israel. The *Founding Fathers* were of many faiths, and the children of Israel but one. The theocracy was instituted by the Divine Hand of God, and the Founders were but mere mortals. Even though the *Founders* and the *Framers* were mere mortals, it is evident that they were inspired by God, for, as will be shown in subsequent chapters, they set the *citizens* (children) free from internal taxation and other direct control of the national civil government.

I have attended many churches in my lifetime, and have never heard any clergy expound logically on the substance of Matthew 17:24-27. To the contrary, those who have attempted to explain it away contend it to be the temple tax without ever providing any logical examination and explanation of why the "children" should be free of the temple tax. It is amazing that they are not conscientious enough to want to properly inform their flock of the Truth of God's Word. Instead they seem to be content in blindly following the misinformation disseminated by the news and entertainment media, and from the Internal Revenue Service itself, preaching that to their flock. You hear declared from their pulpits: *Render therefore to all their dues: tribute to whom tribute is due; custom to whom custom is due;*[1] and the most famous of all, *Render therefore unto Caesar the things which are Caesar's; and unto God the things that are God's*,[2]   without understanding what tributes or customs are, or to whom they are due, what custom is; or being able to distinguish for their flock, Caesar from an impostor.

If our efforts to force the federal and state governments to honor and obey the federal and state Constitutions are in vain, and our liberties are totally lost, much of the blame will, and should, fall on these clergymen who are positively derelict in their duty to study and preach the Word of God as written; and apply it correctly to the civil law itself. Certainly they have a responsibility to know all about the text of what they are preaching, before they preach it, and preach it in its most common terms so that it can be understood by all. Instead, as I have heard some express because of their fear of government, they're more concerned with the loss of their pensions and the discomfort it will possibly bring. Unlike their predecessors of the Reformation who preached against the tyrannical acts of government, and who would rather burn at the stake than to take the government civil license to preach, these modern-day apostates are willing to take government licenses to preach, seek from government the privilege of the government's charter to incorporate; and adhere to government dictates that are not within the confines of the civil law or God's Law, and to finance such things as the murder of innocent babies. They will surely have to stand before God and answer as to why they kept their uninformed flock ignorant and submitted to conditions that are contrary to His Word.

Their predecessors came to the English colonies and established freedom of religion from British government control: they nurtured that freedom for a century and a half, setting the stage for the revolution against England that evolved into this great Constitutional Republic, affording *Liberty* for all. By and large, the Christian Church today has reverted into government bondage, with the state-licensed preachers muzzled for fear of losing a federal tax-exempt status that is not required or needed in the first place. This must be stopped. And hopefully, once enlightened, today's clergy will depend on the Lord for their strength and exonerate themselves by standing in resistance to unlawful government control.

It is my intent, by this book, to show through a very careful examination of historical facts, the federal taxing powers found within the *Constitution*, the subsequent *Acts of Congress* (federal laws) made in pursuance of the *Constitution*, the *Code of Federal Regulations*, the *Internal Revenue Manual* and various other government documents, that the *Framers* were not only cognizant of these Biblical principles of the equality of man and freedom from government, they made it the Law of the land. These established principles have NEVER CHANGED from what they were at the founding of this Constitutional Republic. That is, none of the Rights secured by the Constitution have been lost, and the scheme of federal taxation has never changed since the adoption of the Constitution by the States of the Union. I will also show that the only federal domestic taxes payable by citizens and resident aliens are duties, imposts and excise taxes, and that they only became a permanent form of taxation in 1861, to foster the unlawful expansion of federalism; that the only taxable income of CITIZENS AND RESIDENT ALIENS is from FOREIGN INVESTMENTS or their WORKING ABROAD in foreign countries having tax treaties with the United States; and that only nonresident aliens and foreign corporations having domestic income are subject to an income tax on that domestic income. For unlike other countries, within the United States, the *children* are truly FREE!

THE FORM and STRUCTURE
of OUR GOVERNMENT

Because of the widespread ignorance of the rules governing citizenship, we must first start at an elementary level. This demands an answer to: What form of government is the United States of America?

In 1991, the *Save-A-Patriot Fellowship* surveyed over a thousand individuals at three locations—Baltimore's Harbor Place, the Annapolis City Dock, and on the Mall at the Washington Monument in the District of Columbia—to determine the average citizen's knowledge of the type of our national government. Out of 1,800 surveyed, only a scant three individuals knew the correct answer, a *Constitutional Republic*. Most replied a *Democracy*, some confessed that they did not know, and believe it or not, one said it was *Presbyterian*.

What exactly is a *Constitutional Republic*? Republics do not necessarily have to have a constitution, and constitutions can be part of other forms of governments. So it is obvious that we have to first understand the meaning of these terms individually, and then combine their meaning to reach the proper conclusion.

According to *Noah Webster's 1828 American Dictionary of the English Language*, which reflects the common understanding of the legal terms for the period in question, a *Republic* is:

A commonwealth; a state in which the exercise of the sovereign power is lodged in representatives elected by the people. In modern usage, it differs from a democracy or democratic state, in which the people exercise the powers of sovereignty in person.

Hence, the *Framers* created a government run by representatives elected by the people to represent their particular State and the citizens of that State respectively.

Mr. Webster describes constitutions in general, and the *United States Constitution* in particular:

The established form of government in a state, kingdom or country; a system of fundamental rules, principles and ordinances for the government of a state or nation. In free states, the constitution is paramount to the statutes or laws enacted by the legislature, limiting and controlling its power; and in the United States, the legislature is created, and its powers designated, by the constitution.

Wherefore, constitutions are *fundamental rules, principles and ordinances* that are *paramount to the statutes or laws enacted by the legislature.* In other words, the federal and state governments are confined to the enumerated powers given them within those Constitutions. In our federal and State Republics, the written Constitutions are supreme to all other law. That is why it is said that we have a government of law, and not men. It is reasonable to conclude that governments not bound by the written law are detrimental to the *Cause of Liberty.*

Some politicians today are calling for a Parliamentary form of government to replace our *Constitutional Republic.* These forms of governments, not constrained by a supreme written law such as our Constitution, are very prone to change and consequently are always responding to the winds of political correctness, and

18

probably even more often, financial pressures.

Cecil Rhodes, a wealthy owner of the gold and diamond mines of South Africa operating as DeBeers Consolidated Mines and Consolidated Gold Fields, set up a trust fund for the sole purpose of recruiting manipulative young American students to be educated under his scholarship at Oxford University in London, England. The purpose of this scholarship was to indoctrinate these students to support, among other things, the transformation of the United States Government into a Parliamentary form of government, his ultimate goal being a world socialist federation controlled by the English Empire.[1] Today, these Rhodes Scholars are holding positions of control in governments, universities, and the establishment news media, and they are not informing the American public of their educational mission. This fraternity has been promoting itself for several decades, but the *Constitutional Republic* the *Framers* gave us has thus far withstood this onslaught.

There are three independent branches of government within our *Constitutional Republic*: *Legislative*, *Executive* and *Judicial*. All the powers of the *Legislative* are found in *Article I*, the *Executive* in *Article II* and the *Judicial* in *Article III*.[2] The reason for this division is to create checks and balances to prevent concentration of excessive power in any one branch.[3] The *Framers'* built-in provisions for the prevention of an internal military takeover was to make the *Executive* the commander in chief of the Army and Navy,[4] and the *Legislature* responsible for the funding of the military personnel and needed supplies.[5]

The *Legislative Branch* is divided into two Houses, (this is known as bicameral), the *House of Representatives* and the *Senate*.[6] The *Senate* is comprised of two *Senators* from each State, and the number of members to the *House of Representatives* from any given State vary according to the population of the particular State,[7] the total being 435 members. The members of the *Lower House* are called either *Representatives* or *Congressmen*. All tax laws must originate in the *House of Representatives*.[8]

The *Constitution* is the supreme law of the land, according to *Article 6, Clause 2*:

> *This Constitution and the laws of the United States which shall be made in pursuance thereof, and all treaties made, or which shall be made, under the authority of the United States, shall be the supreme law of the land, and the judges in every state shall be bound thereby, anything in the Constitution or laws of any state to the contrary notwithstanding.*

The main problem that we face today is the general ignorance of this *Constitution*. This is the primary basis for the widespread acceptance of the usurpation of the Law, which acts, if enacted willfully, are mere evidence of sedition. If not enacted willfully, these acts are void as if they never existed.[9] Thus, the acts of those who financially promote the political resistance to some treaty or executive order that will supposedly overturn the *Constitution* are ludicrous. Nothing could be more ridiculous and politically dangerous than for it to be possible that *Acts of Congress*, *Executive Orders* and/or *Treaties* can overturn or supersede the *Constitution*. If all the money that has been collected and wasted on such nonsense had been spent on a promotion to educate individuals on the correct application of the *Constitution*, there probably would not be any internal threats to our Liberties today.

As stated in *Article 6, Clause 2*, all laws have to *be made in pursuance of the Constitution*, and *all treaties made, or which shall be made,* are *under the authority of the United States*. What is the *authority of the United States?*—nothing else but the *United States Constitution*. Nowhere can there be found within the *United States Constitution* any authority granted for *Executive Orders* having authority outside of the *Executive Branch* of government itself (government agencies). Nor can there be found any authority for the *Legislative* or *Judicial Branches* to convey such power to *Executive Orders*. The *Judicial Branch* is bound to the Law just like everyone else. In our political society there are no exceptions. Remember the Law is written, and if the *supreme written Law* does not allow it, it is not so. One of the silliest remarks I have ever heard is that the *Constitution* is dead, and I hear this mostly from so-called "experts" such as talk show hosts. I have witnessed radio and television news commentators and government officials diminish the *Constitution* insidiously by commenting on unconstitutional acts as though they were valid and lawful. Sedition and malfeasance in office cannot be called anything else but sedition and malfeasance in office. And just because there is a multitude in government committing these acts does not change the law to make the acts legal. If a multitude of people were writing bad checks, would that make the writing of bad checks legal?

The Tenth Amendment to the United States Constitution states:

> *The powers not delegated to the United States by the Constitution, nor prohibited by it to the States, are reserved to the States respectively, or to the people.*

Because of misinformation and outright ignorance, there is a general conception by citizens, news media and even elected office holders, that federal law supersedes state law, but nothing could be further from the truth. The only two domestic powers granted to the federal government within the Constitution, other than the punishment for crimes such as counterfeiting and mail fraud, are *Interstate Commerce* and *Post Office*. Wherefore, there cannot be any superiority of either federal or state law, for it is impossible when they do not overlap. What has happened is that demagogues have excited the citizenry to not only accept unlawful federal encroachments, but to actually beg for them.

> *Treason doth never prosper, what's the reason? For if it prosper, none dare call it treason.*—Sir John Harrington, 1561-1612.

Wherefore, it is the civic duty of every citizen to insist that their representatives, in all three branches of both federal and state governments, adhere strictly to the enumerated powers within the respective *Constitutions*, and that every citizen, both mentally and physically, oppose all deviations therefrom.

Chapter 4

THE FEDERAL
TAXING AUTHORITY

There are two *Classes* of federal taxation, *Direct* and *Indirect*. *Direct* taxes are authorized under *Article I, Section 2, Clause 3*; and *Article I, Section 9, Clause 4*, and *Indirect* taxes under *Article I, Section 8, Clause 1*.

Imposition of Direct Taxes

You have probably heard all your life that the Internal Revenue Service can:

- directly tax your *wages*;
- directly tax your *self-employment earnings*;
- directly tax your *capital gains*; and/or,
- directly tax your *interest* and *dividends*;

and probably, like most Americans, you have come to accept this belief without question or investigation. Why should you, when everyone says it is so? After all, if it was not so, lawyers and other law scholars would surely not be paying these taxes. If this perception is correct, then either all of the contentions that I have made about the intent of the *Framers* would have to be incorrect, or if my contentions are correct, then the *Constitution* would have to have been changed at some point in time to allow the government such *direct* taxing powers. If the *Constitution* has not been changed, and what I am saying about *Biblical* principles and their use by the *Framers* is correct, then the past eighty years of *Income Taxation* has to be the most massive, infamous, and diabolical swindle in the history of mankind. Before we go any further, I feel compelled to tell you that ever since 1982 I have offered 10,000.00 Federal Reserve Notes (FRNs, legal tender) to anyone who can prove my contentions wrong. Since then, some have tried, but none have been successful.

Article I, Section 2, Clause 3 is the only provision within the *Constitution* by which *Congress* is allowed to impose a *direct tax*:

> *Representatives and direct taxes shall be apportioned among the several States which may be included within this Union, according to their respective numbers. . .*

First, notice that all *direct taxes* are imposed on the States of the Union, rather than the individual citizens therein, and secondly, notice that *direct taxes shall be apportioned among the several States*. The required application for this *apportionment* is found in *Article I, Section 9, Clause 4*:

> *No capitation or other direct tax shall be laid, unless in proportion to the census or enumeration herein before directed to be taken.*

The *census or enumeration herein before directed to be taken* is found in *Article I, Section 2, Clause 3*:

> *The actual enumeration shall be made within three years after the first meeting of the Congress . . . and within every subsequent term of ten years . . .*

Before the so-called Health and Safety Act of 1954, the census taker only asked each household how many citizens resided therein. Since that Act, they ask you such questions as how many bathrooms the house has, is the basement finished, or how many bedrooms, etc. By just reading the above authority and requirements for the census, would you say these census takers have the authority to ask and require an answer to these questions? Obviously the *Constitution* would first have to be amended to require such answers, but this provision has never been amended.

Notice that *Article I, Section 2, Clause 3* says very clearly that only *Representatives and direct taxes shall be apportioned among the several States . . . according to their respective numbers.* The only legitimate use of the census is to establish the number of representatives each State is authorized to have, and the amount of federal debt liability to be extinguished through the form of a *direct tax* submitted to each State proportionately. Answering unrelated questions is totally voluntary.

So far, it has become perfectly clear that the imposition of *direct taxes* is on the States of the Union. Nowhere can there be found a Constitutional provision for the imposition of a *direct tax* on the real or personal property of any individual citizen within the States of the Union. Therefore, the next logical question to be asked is how do the States collect this *direct tax*? Do they impose an equal tax on every known resident within the State?

History reveals that there have been just four *direct taxes* apportioned to the States of the Union by Congress. The first was imposed on July 14, 1798 (1 Stat 597), for two million dollars to pay for the Revolutionary War; the second was on August 2, 1813 (3 Stat 53), for three million dollars to pay for the War of 1812; the third was on January 9, 1815 (3 Stat 164), for six million dollars also for the War of 1812; and the fourth was approved by Congress on August 5, 1861 (12 Stat 292), for twenty million dollars to fund the Union army during the War Between the States. (One thing is for sure, the cost of war keeps going up.) During these times, the only tax that the States imposed for the support of State government was a property tax. As reported in the case of *Wailes v. Smith*, Maryland Reports,[1] 1893, the States only collected the *direct* federal tax from the property owners within that State:

25

By an Act of Congress, approved 5th August, 1861, a direct tax . . . was levied upon real property, and this tax was apportioned as prescribed by the Federal Constitution. . . Provision was made for the assessment and collection of this tax against the individual owners of such property. . .

At that time, the law only allowed citizens that were property owners the Right to vote. The theory behind this premise was that property owners paid the tax bills, therefore, through their vote they controlled how the state revenues would be spent. The belief was if non-tax payers were allowed to vote, they would vote the tax payers right off their property. Witnessing the spending practices of those representatives in government since, by law, the non-tax payers have been given the right to vote, this principle speaks for itself.

The *Framers'* intended use of *direct taxation* was for the sole purpose of having a debt-free federal government.[2] As described hereinafter, the normal functions of government would be supported by *indirect taxation*, and all debts arising from an emergency, such as a war, would be extinguished by the *direct tax*. After the emergency event, the total cost would be apportioned to the States by Congress, and the payments received from the States would extinguish the debt. Somebody forgot to tell that to our modern-day politicians, who are continually trying to introduce legislation to initiate the process to amend the *Constitution* to require a balanced budget. When the blind lead the blind, the usual result is they fall into a big hole, in this case a black, bottomless financial hole.

Imposition of Indirect Taxes

The imposition of *indirect taxes* is found in *Article I, Section 8, Clause 1*:

The Congress shall have power to lay and collect taxes, duties, imposts, and excises, to pay the debts and provide for the common defense and general welfare of the United States; but all duties, imposts, and excises shall be uniform throughout the United States;

Notice the difference between *Article I, Section 8, Clause 1* and *Article I, Section 2, Clause 3*. In the former, Congress is given the *power to lay and collect taxes*, where in the latter, Congress could only lay the tax proportionately on the various States, which would collect it. The reason for this is the *Founders*, and subsequently the *Framers*, never wanted the federal government to have the power to tax citizens directly, as it was correctly believed that the power to tax is the power to destroy.[3] They just rid themselves of one king; they surely did not want, even though democratic, any monarchical or imperial form in his stead. If a government has unlimited taxing powers, no matter what form of government, that power can be used to dominate, the same as any king or emperor. The powers within the *Constitution* limit the federal government to only the powers that were impractical for the States, such as foreign affairs and interstate commerce. It is not feasible to have fifty different foreign policies, while trade between the States under the Confederacy was a nightmare.

Notice also, that the taxes Congress can lay and collect are *duties*, *imposts*, and *excises*, which by their nature are *indirect*. *duties* are taxes on imported goods; *imposts* are taxes on shipping of imported products; and according to the supreme Court *excises* are taxes on the *manufacture, sale and consumption of certain commodities, privileges, particular business transactions, vocations, occupations*.[4] Obviously, there can be no tax if goods are not imported; nor if ships do not carry cargo into U.S. ports of entry; nor if *commodities* are not bought; nor if *corporations* are not *chartered*, nor if *privileged occupations* are not sought.

Because there is no semicolon after taxes, some have contended that the Congressional taxing powers are expanded

27

beyond *duties, imposts, and excises*—not so. If that was the case, the word taxes would obviously appear a second time along with the descriptive pronoun forms of taxation within *Article 1, Section 8, Clause 1.* The limitation of these taxing powers to these three forms of taxation is conclusively found in writings of the *Framers.*[5]

Notice that these taxes are for the legitimate functions of the federal government: to *pay the debts and provide for the common defense and general welfare of the United States.* Of course, the phrase *general welfare* does not mean government checks and/or food stamps issued to individuals. It means the building of canals, the dredging of harbor channels, or any other such activity that is conducive to the promotion of commerce.

Finally, notice that *all duties, imposts, and excises shall be uniform throughout the United States.* If you buy an alcohol, tobacco or firearm product in California, the federal tax for that item would be the same as in Maryland or any other State.

The demagogues now running for federal offices are presently promising the public the abolishment of the Internal Revenue Service, the establishment of a clearly unconstitutional national *flat tax* and/or a *national retail sales tax.* Because of the general ignorance of the federal tax scheme and related laws, many well-meaning Patriots are subscribing to this political rhetoric, particularly the *national retail sales tax.* Notwithstanding the difference between the educational levels of our modern society with that of 200 years ago, talk of abolition of the IRS is absolutely ridiculous. That is, unless there will be no internal taxes for a government agency to collect. Considering the socialist candidates running for office, if you believe that, I have a bridge in Brooklyn, New York that I would like to sell you.

The *national retail sales tax* as proposed is clearly unconstitutional, and it obviously defeats the restrictive intent of the *Framers* in *Article I, Section 8, Clause 1.*[6] The taxing provisions created by them were to serve more purposes than just

28

taxation. The *direct tax,* due to the nature of its imposition, was for the purpose of maintaining a balanced budget. This historical fact has somehow eluded those holding office and prospective office holders. *Excise taxes* on commodities within the States of the Union were to be used only to supplement *Duties* and *Imposts.*[7] As the only available ongoing tax, *Excises* have a built-in check on the growth of government and in that way differ from the *national retail sales tax.* Notice the supreme Court definition of the *Excise Tax* above, states that the tax is imposed on *certain commodities,* not *all commodities.* In comparison, according to Congressman John Linder of the 11th District of Georgia, the *national retail sales taxes* are imposed on all *commodities.* Wherefore, the *Excise* taxes inposed by *Article I, Section 8, Clause 1* restricts the size of government, and the proposed national retail sales taxes expands it. For example, if government needs revenue to grow, the excise tax on *certain commodities* would have to be increased, if the cost of a commodity becomes more than the market can bear, sales and revenues will dwindle. On the other hand, because the *national retail sales tax* is proposed to be on all commodities, the marketplace will be forced to bear the cost, and thus encourage the growth of government. This simple understanding of taxation must be conveyed to the general public expeditiously before it is too late.

The Constitutional Amendment That Changed It All — Or Did It?

We have been told by our parents, friends, clergy, employers, brokers, bankers, accountants, C.P.A.s, financial planners, lawyers, electronic and print news media, entertainment media, elementary and high school teachers, college professors, state and federal taxing agencies, and others, that the *16th Amendment* changed the *Constitution*[8] to allow for a *direct tax* on property without *apportionment.* Surely all of these people cannot be wrong; after all, a goodly number of these informed individuals are professionals, some of whom specialize in tax law for their livelihood.

From the time I was old enough to file a 1040 U.S. Individual Income Tax Return, I can remember questioning the logic of how this could be required in a free society. How could we be forced to file a tax return under penalties of perjury, and if we failed to do so or made a mistake therein, that meant jail time?

The *16th Amendment* provides that:

> *Congress shall have power to lay and collect taxes on incomes, from whatever source derived, without apportionment among the several states, and without regard to any census or enumeration.*

The significant features are:
- Congress can lay and collect an income tax;
- from whatever source derived;
- without apportionment among the states; and,
- therefore there is no need for any census to be taken.

Hitherto, the Congress could only *lay* and *collect duties, imposts and excises.* Has this been changed by the *16th Amendment*?

"Professionals" tell us that because of this *Amendment* the *Constitution* is now changed to allow Congress to *lay* and *collect* a *direct tax* on citizen's income within the States of the union *without apportionment*. If this was the case, *Article 1, Section 2, Clause 3* and *Article 1, Section 9, Clause 4* would have to be either *amended* or *repealed*. A search of the *16th Amendment* cannot find any mention of either condition within its language, nor can it be found anywhere else within the *Constitution*. If the professionals are correct, the *Constitution* would conflict with itself, a condition that cannot lawfully be, for if it were, it would be void for vagueness. To prevent this condition, the Congress would have to create a new class of taxation, one that would allow *direct* taxation without apportionment. This could only be accomplished with an Amendment to the *Constitution* in addition to the *16th Amendment*.

30

HOWARD

There is ~~no record~~ of such an Amendment, or even an attempt to make such a change.

Laws are exact, they cannot conflict. As explained before, we have a government based on written law. Any law that is written so that it cannot be understood by the average individual obviously cannot be obeyed. You have probably heard that *ignorance of the law is no excuse.* For such circumstances, there is a rule of law called *Void For Vagueness*.[9] In order to recognize legal absurdities, (which "professionals" are asking us to believe), these legal rules have to be understood and applied.

When taking into account the imposition of the *16th Amendment*, there are three basic questions that must be answered to arrive at the proper legal conclusion:

- **What is the class of taxation?**
- **Did this Amendment actually change the Constitution?**
- **Does it apply to everyone within a State of the union?**

The United States Supreme Court case that decided the *16th Amendment* was *Brushaber v. Union Pacific Railroad Company*, 240 U.S. 1, decided January 24, 1916. The first time I read this case was 1977, and it changed my previous understanding about the imposition of the federal *Income Tax*. Of course the news about the discovery of this case spread throughout the Patriot community and caused an intense letter writing campaign to all federal office holders asking very pointed questions about *Income Taxation* and the *16th Amendment*. In 1979 Howard Zaritsky, Legislative Attorney, American Law Division, Congressional Research Service, Library of Congress, prepared Report No. 79-131 A, entitled *SOME CONSTITUTIONAL QUESTIONS REGARDING THE FEDERAL INCOME TAX LAWS*, to answer these pointed questions.

The Congressional Research Service employs lawyers to research and answer questions that the Legislative and Executive

31

branches of government may have. Obviously the flood of questions about the *16th Amendment* must have caused a stir in Congress.

On page 3 of his report, Mr. Zaritsky writes:

> *In Brushaber v. Union Pacific R.R. Co., 240 U.S. 1 (1916), the Supreme Court held that the income tax, including a tax on dealings in property, was an indirect tax, rather than a direct tax, and that the . . .*

At this point Mr. Zaritsky quotes part of the following sentence from the *Brushaber* case. The words of the opinion utilized by him in his report are italicized:

> "Second, that the contention that the Amendment treats a tax on income as a direct tax although it is relieved from apportionment and is necessarily therefore not subject to the rule of uniformity as such rule only applies to taxes which are not direct, thus destroying the two great classifications which have been recognized and enforced from the beginning, is also wholly without foundation since *the command of the amendment that all income taxes shall not be subject to the rule of apportionment by a consideration of the source from which the taxed income may be derived forbids the application to such taxes of the rule applied in the Pollock case by which alone such taxes were removed from the great class of excises, duties, and imposts subject to the rule of uniformity and were placed under the other or direct class.*"

In the *Pollock* case, the supreme Court decided the constitutionality of an earlier Income Tax Act of Congress. This Act imposed a direct income tax on the profit of individuals from real property investments. The taxpayer in the *Pollock* case would have been the investment company, the *Farmers' Loan & Trust Company*, which would have acted as the withholding agent for the

32

payment of the *Income Tax*. The suit was brought to enjoin (prohibit) the withholding agent from withholding the tax and paying it to the Commissioner of Internal Revenue. The Court held:

> . . . *a suit in equity brought by Charles Pollock against the Farmers' Loan & Trust Company et al. to procure a decree that the provisions as to the income tax in the Act of Congress of August 15, 1894, are unconstitutional and void; and that the defendants be restrained from voluntarily complying with the provisions of said Act in the making of returns and in the payment of a tax thereunder, and for general relief.*

So, as exhibited here, the *Brushaber* Court stated the *16th Amendment* calls for an *Income Tax* that is not apportioned, and therefore, for that reason it is in the *indirect* tax class. The Court further stated that this forbids the tax from falling into the *direct class* like the tax tried in the *Pollock* case, which was struck down as unconstitutional.

This is beginning to look like the "professionals" in our society, the individuals we all count on for legal advice and services, possibly might not know exactly what they are talking about when it comes to federal taxation.

Zaritsky continued in his report:

> *This same view was reiterated by the Court in Stanton v. Baltic Mining Co., in which the Court stated that the:*
>
> > *Sixteenth Amendment conferred no new power of taxation but simply prohibited the previous complete and plenary power of income taxation possessed by Congress from the beginning from being taken out of the category of indirect taxation to which it inherently belonged.*
> >
> > *240 U.S. at 112 (1916).*

Here, Zaritsky's report points out that the Court is revealing two startling facts that fly in the face of our common understanding and belief about the federal *income tax* laws, an erroneous understanding that has been disseminated by various "professionals" for some eighty years. First, according to the report, the Court reveals that the *16th Amendment conferred no new power of taxation.* Therefore, obviously, if citizens were not subject to an *income tax* on their property, as stated by the Court in the *Pollock* case, and the *16th Amendment conferred no new power of taxation*, it is elementary to conclude that citizens are still not subject to an *income tax* on their property. Secondly, the Court reveals that the *plenary* [full and complete] *power of income taxation has been possessed by Congress from the beginning.* According to the Court, the first Congress after the ratification of the *United States Constitution* had the authority to impose an *income tax.* The common belief today is that the first *Constitutional income tax* was imposed by Congress in 1913, and before that, the power did not exist.

According to the *Statutes at Large* (the system of recording the *Acts of Congress* by the date of enactment), the first *income tax act* passed by Congress in the history of the Republic was an Act entitled **INCOME DUTY**, enacted on August 5th, 1861. It was, according to its language:

> *An act to provide increased revenue from imports to pay interest on the public debt, and for other purposes.*

The most logical question that can be asked here is: How, by any stretch of one's imagination, can an *income tax* be imposed on imports? The only way this can make any intelligent sense whatsoever, is with our contention that the federal income tax scheme imposes a tax on the income of *citizens abroad* and *foreigners within the States of the Union.* Just as we have been contending, that was the intent of the *Framers.* The Internal Revenue Service agrees with this being the intent of the Framers,

34

and states so within the Internal Revenue Manual in Chapter 1100, which states in pertinent part:

> *§ 1111.31 (7-6-83)*
> *Internal Taxation*
> *Madison's Notes on the Constitutional Convention reveal clearly that the framers of the Constitution believed for some time that the principal, if not sole, support of the new Federal Government would be derived from customs, duties and taxes connected with shipping and importations. Internal taxation would not be resorted to except infrequently, and for special reasons.*

The only problem with this IRS admission is that they put their deceptive political spin on it. Notice that they contend that the *Framers* of the Constitution believed *for some time* in this method of taxation, as if the *Framers* had changed their mind after a period of time. Believe me, this is not the case.

The delegates to the Constitutional Convention of 1787 were sent there by their respective States to make better the Confederacy that existed as of March 1, 1781. Instead of acting as instructed by their State governments, they proceeded immediately to establish the Constitutional Republic that we now have. Not wanting this to be public knowledge within their lifetime, they swore one another to secrecy until the death of the last delegate. This occurred on June 28, 1836, with the death of James Madison, who made and kept the minutes of that Convention, popularly known as *Madison's Notes on the Constitutional Convention of 1787*.

Chapter 1100 of the Internal Revenue Manual also records the date in which permanent internal taxation began in § 1111.2, as follows:

> *Organic Act*
> *(1) The Office of the Commissioner of Internal Revenue was established by an act of Congress (12 Stat.*

432) on July 1, 1862, and the first Commissioner of Internal Revenue took office on July 17, 1862.

(2) The act of July 1 provided:

". . . That, for the purpose of superintending the collection of internal duties, stamp duties, licenses, or taxes imposed by this Act, or which may be hereafter imposed, and of assessing the same, an office is hereby created in the Treasury Department to be called the Office of the Commissioner of the Internal Revenue; . . .

Wherefore, permanent internal taxation began in 1861, and the last *Framer* died in 1836—without changing his mind, I am happy to say, about the freedom from taxation for American citizens.

If any foreigner wants to invest and profit in our marketplace, he must first buy a ticket to participate. For instance, a citizen of England purchases stock and/or bonds from a broker in a State of the Union. He receives interest or dividends on his investment. Before the stockbroker pays him the interest or dividend on his capital investment, the broker must first withhold the *income tax* from that *source* and pay it to the Internal Revenue Service. This can be the only logical interpretation of the legal term *Income Duty*. You say this is far-fetched and a self-serving molding of facts to fit my theory. Well, let's continue on and see.

As stated before, the *Brushaber* case was decided January 24, 1916. On March 21, 1916 the Commissioner of Internal Revenue issued Treasury Decision 2313, which stated in part:

To collectors of internal revenue:

Under the decision of the Supreme Court of the United States in the case of Brushaber v. Union Pacific Railway Co., decided January 24, 1916, it is hereby held that income accruing to nonresident aliens in the form of interest from the bonds and dividends on the stock of domestic corporations is subject to the income tax

36

imposed by the act of October 3, 1913.

It stated further in part:

> *The responsible heads, agents, or representatives of nonresident aliens, who are in charge of the property owned or business carried on within the United States, shall make a full and complete return of the income therefrom on Form 1040, revised, and shall pay any and all tax, normal and additional, assessed upon the income received by them in behalf of their nonresident alien principal.*

From what we have examined it appears that ***what the Framers intended*** for federal taxation is that ***the children are free.*** You say you're still not convinced. Then don't stop here—there is more to examine. We still have the Internal Revenue Code, the Internal Revenue Regulations, the Internal Revenue Manual and other related documents. Surely these documents will prove the "professionals" to be correct and me to be some sort of conspiracy nut. After all, everyone knows that ***we all have to pay our fair share!!!***

Part II

THE MONEY SYSTEM ESTABLISHED by the FRAMERS

Chapter 5

WHAT is MONEY?

The Origin of Money

It states in the thirteenth chapter of Genesis at verse two:

And Abram was very rich in cattle, in silver, and in gold.

From the beginning of time wealth has been measured in the necessary products that sustained life, and silver and gold. Paper currencies have come and gone, while silver and gold remain the measure of money for the world. Since the invention of money, silver and gold have transcended every civilization known to history, and deviations therefrom have been relatively short and disastrous.

The first money system was barter. When man inhabited cities and artisans started trading their wares, it became impractical to barter. In other words, a cow cannot be an equitable trade for a pair of shoes. Therefore, a medium of exchange other than barter had to be utilized, and silver and gold fit the bill. This is because value is measured by labor, and there is considerable labor connected with the production of silver and gold. In addition, neither gold nor silver can be reduced in quantity nor their properties altered by pounding, rolling, heating or freezing. These two metals are among the most constant known to man.

Through the centuries, these metals were fixed as the medium

41

of exchange, and the fair market value was established (the buyer is willing to pay and the seller willing to accept), by the weight measurement of the silver and gold. Laws were passed to set the standards of weights and measures, and governments molded these metals into a coin form and struck an official image thereon, certifying its weight to be true and correct.

The first banks were warehouses serving those who had a need for a safe place to store their gold and silver. Originally, this service was provided by the gold and silver smiths, already having constructed a safe place to keep these precious metals used in their trade.

The first primitive form of fractional reserve banking was established in Babylon, where the smiths would give clay tablets as receipts for precious metals on deposit. It became a common practice to trade the clay tablets rather than retrieve the metals for trading. Noticing that there was only a limited demand for these precious metals in storage, the smiths began spending clay tablet receipts that had no silver or gold backing. This is an immoral and illegal trick that could make one very rich and did, and still does; only now what is spent is in paper and electronic form.

A few centuries ago in Europe, warehousemen were not only spending additional unbacked paper receipts, they loaned these fraudulent documents to others and charged usurious interest, making these warehousemen wealthy beyond their dreams, literally creating money out of nothing. Of course, it did not take long for the corrupt ruling monarchies of that day to get into the act. After all, it is well established by history that governments are corrupt, so obviously, total governments are totally corrupt. In 1694, King William of England signed into law an act of the House of Parliament that legalized this fraudulent practice of the warehousemen, by permitting the privately owned Bank of England to legally counterfeit England's paper currency. [1]

Solving The Money Problem

In colonial America, scrip[2] was used as a medium of exchange due to the lack of coins in public circulation. The Continental Congress was formed in 1774 to resist tyrannical claims from England, and upon the failure of its efforts to resolve the differences between the colonies and the mother country, in 1776, by a declaration of that Congress, the delegates voted for total independence from England. The wealth of the newborn States was agriculture, and they were lacking in hard currency. Therefore, the Congress was forced to operate on what are called *bills of credit,* commonly known as *Continentals. Bills of credit* are described by Noah Webster as:

> *The notes or bills which are issued by the public or by corporations or individuals, which circulate on the confidence of men in the ability and disposition in those who issue them, to redeem them.*[3]

The big difference between paper money and precious metal coins is that, unless it is a valid redeemable certificate, paper money is nothing more than a promise to pay. Precious metal coins have an intrinsic value that passes from one to another. Additionally, precious metal coins are very hard to counterfeit. On the other hand, when *bills of credit* and certificates pass from one individual to another, only the promise to pay passes.

The *Spanish Milled Dollar* was considered the standard for money in the world at the time of the American Revolution. This silver coin was unique in that it had a serrated edge that prevented what was called *coin clipping,* the practice of some unethical individuals who shaved off a small portion of the edge of a gold or silver coin before passing it on. One could be assured of the true weight of the *Spanish Milled Dollar* by merely looking at or feeling the edge of the coin. This coin became the namesake of our

Constitutional money units of account.

Governments that print money always fall into the same trap. If something is needed or desired, they just print some more *bills of credit*, and that is exactly what happened in the revolutionary and post-revolutionary Congresses. The financial watchword of that day was *It's Not Worth A Continental*. In fact, depreciation of the *Continental* against the *Spanish Milled Dollar* in January of 1779 was eight to one. In January of 1781, they were redeemable at one hundred to one, and in May of that same year, they ceased to pass as money, and were bought and sold as articles of speculation anywhere from as much as five hundred to one thousand to one.[4]

This misuse of *bills of credit*, coupled with problems of *interstate commerce* (States charging tariffs on commodities crossing the state line), is what forced the call for the Convention of the States held in Philadelphia, Pennsylvania, for which the first delegates arrived on May 14th, 1787.[5] The convention was called:

> . . . *for the sole and express purpose of revising the Articles of Confederation, and reporting to Congress, and to the several Legislatures, such alterations and provisions therein, as shall, when agreed to in Congress, and confirmed by the several states, render the federal Constitution adequate to the exigencies of Government, and the preservation of the Union.*[6]

On Friday, May 25th, George Washington was elected the President of the Convention and Major William Jackson was elected Secretary; on Monday, May 28th, the rules for conducting the convention were adopted; and on Tuesday, May 29th, Mr. Edmund Randolph presented a prepared draft of the framework of a national government having three branches: Legislative, Executive and Judiciary, and the Constitutional Republic was on its way.

The original draft of the Constitution, at what is now *Article*

1, Section 8, Clause 2 stated: *and emit bills on the credit of the United States.* According to Madison's Notes, this Clause was addressed by the Convention on Thursday, August 16th:

Mr. Govr. Morris moved to strike out "and emit bills on the credit of the U. States"—If the United States had credit, such bills would be unnecessary: if they had not, unjust & useless.

Mr. Butler, 2d the motion.

Mr. Madison, will it not be sufficient to prohibit the making [of] them a tender? This will remove the temptation to emit them with unjust views. And promissory notes in that shape may in some emergencies be best.

Mr. Govr. Morris, striking out the words will leave room still for notes of a responsible minister which will do all the good without the mischief. The Monied interest will oppose the plan of government, if paper emissions be not prohibited.

Mr. Gorham was for striking out, without inserting any prohibition, if the words stand they may suggest and lead to the measure.

Col. Mason had doubts on the subject. Cong. he thought would not have the power unless it were expressed. Though he had a mortal hatred to paper money, yet as he could not foresee all emergencies, he was unwilling to tie the hands of the legislature. He observed that the late war could not have been carried on, had such a prohibition existed.

Mr. Gorham. The power as far as it will be necessary or safe, is involved in that of borrowing.

Mr. Mercer was a friend of paper money, though in the present state & temper of America, he should neither propose nor approve of such a measure. He was consequently opposed to a prohibition of it altogether. It will stamp suspicion on the Government to deny it a discretion on this point. It was impolitic also to excite the opposition of all those who were friends to paper money. The people of property would be sure to be on the side of the plan, and it was impolitic to purchase their further attachment with the loss of the opposite class of citizens.

Mr. Elsworth thought this a favorable moment to shut and bar the door against paper money. The mischiefs of the various experiments which had been made, were now fresh in the public mind and had excited the disgust of all the respectable part of America. By withholding the power from the new Governt. more friends of influence would be gained to it than by almost any thing else. Paper money can in no case be necessary. Give the Government credit, and other resources will offer. The power may do harm, never good.

Mr. Randolph, notwithstanding his antipathy to paper money, could not agree to strike out the words, as he could not foresee all the occasions which might arise.

Mr. Wilson. It will have a most salutary influence on the credit of the U. States to remove the possibility of paper money. This expedient can never succeed whilst its mischiefs are remembered, and as long as it can be resorted to, it will be a bar to other resources.

Mr. Butler. Remarked that paper was a legal tender in no Country in Europe. He was urgent for disarming the Government of such power.

*Mr. Mason was still averse to tying the hands of the Legislature **altogether**.[7] If there was no example in Europe as just remarked, it might be observed on the other side, that there was none in which the Government was restrained on this head.*

Mr. Read, thought the words, if not struck out, would be as alarming as the mark of the Beast in Revelations.

Mr. Langdon had rather reject the whole plan than retain the three words "(and emit bills").[8]

The vote was taken and the following was reported by Mr. Madison:

On the motion for striking out
N.H. ay. Mas. ay. Ct. ay. N.J. no. Pa. ay. Del. ay.
Md. no. Va. ay* N.C. ay. S.C. ay. Geo. ay.
The clause for borrowing money, agreed nem. con.
Adj.[9]

The asterisk after Virginia's vote, (Va. ay.*), denotes the following footnote:

The vote in the affirmative [by Virg.] was occasioned by the acquiescence of Mr. Madison who became satisfied that striking out the words would not disable the Govt. from the use of public notes as far as they could be safe & proper; & would only cut off the pretext for a paper currency, and particularly for making the bills a tender either for public or private debts.[10]

Twelve days later, Tuesday, August 28th, in Convention, Mr. James Wilson, of Pennsylvania, and Mr. Roger Sherman, of Connecticut, proposed the following amendment to Article XII of the draft, which became Article 1, Section 10, Clause 1 of the adopted Constitution:

Art: XII. being taken up.
Mr. Wilson & Mr. Sherman moved to insert after the words "coin money" the words "nor emit bills of credit, nor make any thing but gold & silver coin a tender in payment of debts" making these prohibitions absolute, instead of making the measures allowable (as in the XIII art:) ["]with the consent of the Legislature of the U.S.["]
Mr. Gorham thought the purpose would be as well secured by the provision of art: XIII which makes the consent of the Genl. Legislature necessary, and that in that mode, no opposition would be excited; whereas an absolute prohibition of paper money would rouse the most desperate opposition from its partisans.

Mr. Sherman thought this a favorable crisis for crushing paper money. If the consent of the Legislature could authorize emissions of it, the friends of paper money would make every exertion to get into the Legislature in order to license it.

The question being divided; on the 1st part—"nor emit bills of credit"

N.H. ay. Mas. ay. Ct. ay. Pa. ay. Del. ay. Md. divd. Va. no. N.C. ay. S.C. ay. Geo. ay.

The remaining part of Mr. Wilson's & Mr. Sherman's motion was agreed to nem: con:[11]

Because of their experience with the consequence of inflationary Continental currency, the *Framers* only gave the Congress the power to *coin money*, **not to issue it**. Not taking any chances, realizing that the Usurers would probably influence the State governments to issue paper money, Mr. Sherman and Mr. Wilson lawfully barred the door with *Article 1, Section 10, Clause 1*, which was ratified by the States thusly:

No state shall enter into any treaty, alliance, or confederation; grant letters of marque and reprisal; coin money; emit bills of credit; make any thing but gold and silver coin a tender in payment of debts; pass any bill of attainder, ex post facto law, or law impairing the obligation of contracts, or grant any title of nobility.

Madison summed up the prohibition against paper money thusly:

The extension of the prohibition to bills of credit must give pleasure to every citizen in proportion to his love of justice and his knowledge of the true springs of public prosperity.[12]

Chapter 6

WHY DO WE USE
PAPER MONEY TODAY?

On April 2, 1792, Congress passed the first *Coinage Act* and established the *Decimal System*. The Dollar was declared to be the *Money of Account of the United States*. This unit was expressed at par value to be 15 parts silver to 1 part gold. The *Gold Dollar* contained 24.75 grains of fine gold, and the *Silver Dollar* contained 371.25 grains of fine silver.[1]

The Decimal System is codified in Title 31 of the United States Code, *Money and Finance*. At present, it is § 5101 of that title, enacted September 13, 1982; before that it was § 371. Comparing the difference between these two code sections gives us a clue to the treachery that has taken place:

§ 371. Decimal system established
The money of account of the United States shall be expressed in dollars or units, dimes or tenths, cents or hundredths, and mills or thousandths, a dime being the tenth part of a dollar, a cent the hundredth part of a dollar, a mill the thousandth part of a dollar; and all accounts in the public offices and all proceedings in the courts shall be kept and had in conformity to this regulation.

§ 5101. Decimal system
United States money is expressed in dollars, dimes or tenths, cents or hundredths, and mills or thousandths. A

*dime is a tenth of a dollar, a cent is a hundredth of a dollar,
and a mill is a thousandth of a dollar.
(Sept. 13, 1982, P. L. 97-258, §1, 96 Stat. 980.)*

The following is the history attached to § 5101, explaining
the emasculation of the original Decimal System law:

*HISTORY; ANCILLARY LAWS AND DIRECTIVES
Prior law and revision:*

Revised Section	Source (USCS)	Source (Statutes at Large)
5101	31:371	R.S. Sec. 3563.

*The word "money" is substituted for "money of
account" to eliminate unnecessary words. As far as can be
determined, the phrase "money of account" has not been
interpreted by any court or Government agency. The
phrase was used by Alexander Hamilton in his "Report on
the Establishment of the Mint" (1791). In that Report,
Hamilton propounded 6 questions, including:*

*["]1st. What ought to be the nature of the money unit
of the United States?["]*

*Thereafter, Hamilton uses the phrases "money unit
of the United States" and "money of account"
interchangeably and in the sense that the phrases are used
to denote the monetary system for keeping financial
accounts. In short, the phrases simply indicate that
financial accounts are to be based on a decimal money
system:*

*["]. . ., and it is certain that nothing can be more
simple and convenient than the decimal subdivisions.
There is every reason to expect that the method will*

speedily grow into general use, when it shall be seconded by corresponding coins. On this plan the unit in the money of account will continue to be, as established by that resolution [of August 8, 1786], a dollar, and its multiples, dimes, cents, and mills, or tenths, hundredths, and thousandths. ["]

Thus, the phrase "money of account" did not mean, by itself, that dollars or fractions of dollars must be equal to something having intrinsic or "substantive" value. This concept is supported by earlier writings of Thomas Jefferson in his "Notes on the Establishment of a Money Unit, and of a Coinage for the United States" (1784), and the 1782 report to the President of the Continental Congress on the coinage of the United States by the Superintendent of Finances, Robert Morris, which was apparently prepared by the Assistant Superintendent, Gouverneur Morris. See Paul L. Ford, The Writings of Thomas Jefferson, vol. III (G.P. Putnam's Sons, 1894) pp. 446-457; William G. Sumner, The Financier and the Finances of the American Revolution, vol. II (Burt Franklin, 1891, reprinted 1970) pp. 36-47; and George T. Curtis, History of the Constitution, vol. I (Harper and Brothers, 1859) p. 443, n2. The words "or units" and "and all accounts in the public offices and all proceedings in the courts shall be kept and had in conformity to this regulation" are omitted as surplus.

The reviser's explanation regarding **money units** and *money of account* might seem harmless in itself, but when you remove the conformity of the public offices and the courts, it is downright treacherous. Notice how the connection between the two is severed and explained individually. Also, notice that the Hamiltonian example is rather weak, and therefore, supported by the Jeffersonian explanation that is pre-Constitutional Convention, before the abolishment of paper money. Surely the conformity of the public offices and the courts would be surplus if the States and

Congress were both issuing *bills of credit* and both foreign and domestic coins were in circulation. But when the law only permits the tender of gold and silver coins, then, and in that case, the conformity of the public offices and the courts is a very meaningful provision.

The Coinage Acts of April 2nd, 1792 and February 28th, 1878 were codified in Title 31 at § 316 (a) through (d). This code section was repealed by an Act of Congress on June 4th, 1963, when silver coinage was removed from circulation and replaced by the worthless clad or sandwich coins. The current edition of Title 31 contains no evidence that the Coinage Acts ever existed.

How did this Come About?
Who was responsible for This Blatant Violation of the Constitution?

Actually, the problem started in the very first administration of the Constitutional Republic. President George Washington appointed Alexander Hamilton as the first secretary of the treasury. It was well-known that Hamilton was a monarchist, and that his close ties to corrupt bankers developed into a scandal for the first administration. In collaboration with these bankers, he instigated the establishment of the first private *Bank of the United States*, corrupting members of both the Senate and the House of Representatives with the promise of personal gain. Jefferson gives the following account of Hamilton's financial and banking activities in his *Anas*, (notes kept by him, from his second year as the secretary of state until his last year as president, 1791 to 1809):[2]

> But a division, not very unequal, had already taken place in the honest part of that body [the legislature], between the parties styled republican and federal. The latter being monarchists in principle, adhered to Hamilton of course, as their leader in that principle, and this mercenary phalanx added to them, insured him always a majority in both Houses; so that the whole action of

legislature was now under the direction of the Treasury. Still the machine was not complete. The effect of the funding system, and of the Assumption, would be temporary; it would be lost with the loss of the individual members whom it has enriched, and some engine of influence more permanent must be contrived, while these myrmidons were yet in place to carry it through all opposition. This engine was the Bank of the United States. All that history is known, so I shall say nothing about it. While the government remained at Philadelphia, a selection of members of both Houses were constantly kept as directors who, on every question interesting to that institution, or to the views of the federal head, voted at the will of that head; and, together with the stock-holding members, could always make the federal vote that of the majority. By this combination, legislative expositions were given to the constitution and all the administrative laws were shaped on the model of England, and so passed. And from this influence we were not relieved, until the removal from the precincts of the bank, to Washington.

Here then was the real ground of the opposition which was made to the course of administration. Its object was to preserve the legislature pure and independent of the executive, to restrain the administration to republican forms and principles, and not permit the constitution to be construed into a monarchy, and to be warped, in practice, into all the principles and pollutions of their favorite English model. Nor was this an opposition to General Washington. He was true to the republican charge confided to him; and has solemnly and repeatedly protested to me, in our conversations, that he would lose the last drop of his blood in support of it; and he did this the oftener and with the more earnestness, because he knew my suspicions of Hamilton's designs against it, and wished to quiet them. For he was not aware of the drift, or of the effect of

Hamilton's schemes. Unversed in financial projects and calculations and budgets, his approbation of them was bottomed on his confidence in the man.

But Hamilton was not only a monarchist, but for a monarchy bottomed on corruption. In proof of this . . . for the truth of which I attest the God who made me.

Jefferson did everything within his power to destroy the privileged private *Bank of the United States*. Through his efforts, republicanism advanced and the federalists lost ground. Because of his efforts and the federalist loss of political power, the bank's charter was refused renewal in 1811.

The bank was rechartered by an Act of Congress in 1816, and branches of the bank were opened in the several States. The legislature and the governor of the State of Maryland enacted a law taxing *all Banks, or branches thereof, in the State of Maryland, not chartered by the legislature*. James McCulloch, the cashier of the Baltimore branch, refused to pay the tax, was sued in the State courts, and lost. An appeal was taken to the United States Supreme Court and the opinion was handed down by Chief Justice John Marshall. This unanimous decision set the stage for what has now become rampant judicial legislation and flagrant perversion and/or disregard of the Constitution by judges in both the State and federal courts. It was the fork in the road, and the distance between the law and the sophistical practice of the courts is now hundreds of miles apart. The following demonstrates that the powers-that-be at Harvard have a different opinion than the one I just expressed:[3]

John Marshall (1755-1835), third Chief Justice of the Supreme Court of the United States, and the greatest of American judges, laid down in the following opinion certain principles which have come to be accepted as fundamental in all questions touching the respective powers of the Federal government and the State legislatures. Chief Justice Marshall, in writing the opinion of the court, is regarded as having established certain principles on which depend "the stability of our peculiar dual system of national and local governments."

Jefferson and I have a different opinion.

The questions and findings of the Marshall court must be studied in depth for us to understand the Marshall Doctrine that has been followed by the courts since the McCulloch decision. Jefferson considered Marshall to be a monarchist like Hamilton, and I believe the following analysis will prove his allegation to be correct.

Constitutionally, the issues before the McCulloch court were very simple and straightforward. But as Mr. Elbridge Gerry, a delegate to the Constitutional Convention of 1787, from Massachusetts, warned during that convention, the *sophistry* of the courts is the weak link in the Constitution.[4] Those issues were:

- does Congress have powers that are not enumerated?;
- does Congress have the authority to enact laws with respect to property?; and,
- are the laws of Congress superior to the laws of the States of the union?

Before we examine these issues, we must first look at the following principle of law called the *vagueness doctrine*. Black's Law Dictionary, 5th Edition, explains this doctrine thusly:

Vagueness doctrine. Under this principle, a law which does not fairly inform a person of what is commanded or prohibited is unconstitutional as violative of due process.

In other words, if the law is not explicitly written so that it leaves no doubt as to its *command* or *prohibition*, it is *void for vagueness*. That is not hard to understand, is it?

We must also be aware of the fact that Madison's Notes on the Constitutional Convention of 1787 were not published, in accordance with an agreement made by the delegates in attendance, until after the death of all the participants. They were published by Madison's wife after his death in 1836. The McCulloch opinion was handed down in 1819. But the Federalist Papers were published before the ratification of the Constitution by the States of the Union. In fact, when it suits his purpose, Marshall quotes from them within his opinion in the McCulloch case.

Hamilton admits in Federalist No. 32:

> The necessity of a concurrent jurisdiction in certain cases results from the division of the sovereign power; and the rule that all authorities, of which the States are not explicitly divested in favor of the Union, remain with them in full vigor, is not a theoretical consequence of that division, but is clearly admitted by the whole tenor of the instrument which contains the articles of the proposed Constitution. We there find that, notwithstanding the affirmative grants of general authorities, there has been the most pointed care in those cases where it was deemed improper that the like authorities should reside in the States, to insert negative clauses prohibiting the exercise of them by the States. The tenth section of the first article consists altogether of such provisions. This circumstance is a clear indication of the sense of the convention, and furnishes a rule of interpretation out of the body of the act, which justifies the position I have advanced and refutes every hypothesis to the contrary.

In outlining the division of jurisdiction between the States and the federal government, notice that Hamilton states that the Framers *explicitly* named the powers that the federal government was given and that the States retain all other powers *in full vigor*. He also stated that extreme care was taken that <u>like powers</u> would not reside in both State and federal governments, and that to prevent such an occurrence, the *Framers* prohibited to the States, within the *tenth section of the first article*, such powers that would be unreasonable for both governments to possess. For your convenience, the following are powers that he referred to that could be possessed by both governments, if not prohibited to the States by the *tenth section*:

> No state shall enter into any treaty, alliance, or confederation; grant letters of marque and reprisal; coin money;. . .

Now we will entertain the issues before the McCulloch Court:

The first issue according to Marshall: *The first question in the cause is, has Congress power to incorporate a bank?* He, then, declares that the first Congress incorporated the first Bank of the United States, and that it was then debated in both houses and within the Executive Cabinet and was allowed to expire without challenge to its constitutionality in the courts,[5] as if that had any legal effect. But he does admit that:

> Among the enumerated powers, we do not find that of establishing a bank or creating a corporation.

This does not bother him in the least, for he continues:

> But there is no phrase in the instrument which, like the articles of confederation, excludes incidental or implied powers; and which requires that everything granted shall be expressly and minutely described. Even the 10th amendment, which was framed for the purpose of quieting the excessive jealousies which had been excited, omits the word "expressly," and declares only that the powers "not delegated to the United States, nor prohibited to the states, are reserved to the states or to the people;"

thus leaving the question, whether the particular power which may become the subject of contest has been delegated to the one government, or prohibited to the other, to depend on a fair construction of the whole instrument. The men who drew and adopted this amendment had experienced the embarrassments resulting from the insertion of this word in the articles of confederation, and probably omitted it to avoid those embarrassments. A constitution, to contain an accurate detail of all the subdivisions of which its great powers will admit, and of all the means by which they may be carried into execution, would partake of a prolixity of a legal code, and could scarcely be embraced by the human mind. It would probably never be understood by the public.

This articulate sophistical judicial legislation flies in the face of Hamilton's explanation of powers that the *Framers* intended for both governments, as he used when selling the American public on the new Federal Constitution, published in Federalist No. 32. It seems that these aristocrats say what suits them at the moment. (It sounds like some of the like-minded politicians holding office in all three branches today.) The last sentence of the above quote, not only invokes the *vagueness doctrine*, it reveals this monarchist's contempt for the average man.

The second issue is, *does Congress have the authority to enact laws with respect to property*? Nowhere within the United States Constitution can it be found that Congress has the express authority to enact laws with respect to property. It is a well-established policy and practice that when federal agents move to seize property, the local law enforcement authorities will be notified and the property laws of that State will be observed. Additionally, the Supreme Court has ruled expressly that *there is no federal common law*, meaning no federal property law;[6] common law meaning custom and usage involving property. By its nature, a corporation would be under and subject to State property laws.

In this case, the State of Maryland argued that this

corporation, the second United States Bank, having a branch office in the State, came under State law, and as such was taxable the same as a State-chartered corporation. The constitutional question of a federal-chartered corporation did not come into question until the court action had commenced.

The third and last issue is, *are the laws of Congress superior to the laws of the States of the union?* Marshall addresses thusly:

> *That the power of taxing it by the states may be exercised so as to destroy it, is too obvious to be denied. But taxation is said to be an absolute power, which acknowledges no other limits than those expressly prescribed in the constitution, and like sovereign power of every other description, is trusted to the discretion of those who use it. But the very terms of this argument admit that the sovereignty of the state, in the article of taxation itself, is subordinate to, and may be controlled by the constitution of the United States. How far it has been controlled by that instrument must be a question of construction. In making this construction, no principle not declared can be admissible, which would defeat the legitimate operations of a supreme government. It is of the very essence of supremacy to remove all obstacles to its action within its own sphere, and so to modify every power vested in subordinate governments as to exempt its own operations from their own influence. This effect need not be stated in terms. It is so involved in the declaration of supremacy, so necessarily implied in it, that the expression of it could not make it more certain. We must, therefore, keep it in view while construing the constitution.*

In order to see how far afield of the actual law this convoluted thinking is, all we have to do is examine the actual taxing authority of the federal government which we discussed in detail in Chapter IV of this book. According to Article 1, Section 2, Clause 3 and Article 1, Section 9, Clause 4, the federal government does not have the power to tax property directly; and as clearly shown in Article 1, Section 8, Clause 1, it can only lay and <u>collect</u> duties, imposts and excise taxes. Out of the three taxes collectable by the federal government, the only one that could possibly conflict with the State would be excise taxes. And in the case of excise taxes there is no conflict—for example, the sale of gasoline has both a State and federal excise tax imposed on it. As is the practice of lawyers, it seems that Marshall just dazzled us with his brilliant sophistic expostulation of *simplex dictum*.[7] In other words, bovine fecal matter. But of course, we have the most prestigious law school in America, Harvard, as quoted above, calling him the *greatest of American judges*; now you can see why there seems to be so much contradiction in the law within this country today. The *greatest of American judges,* they say—**I say he is the father of perversion.**

Marshall is called the father of case law, which is the sophistical means of twisting and turning an act of a legislature to say what the court, or the powers behind the court, want it to say. This is attributed to the following statement from the McCulloch decision:

> *Its nature, therefore, requires, that only its great outlines should be marked, its important objects designated, and the minor ingredients which compose those objects be deduced from the nature of the objects themselves. That this idea was entertained by the framers of the American constitution, is not only to be inferred from the nature of the instrument, but from the language. Why else were some of the limitations, found in the ninth section of the 1st article, introduced? It is also, in some degree, warranted by their having omitted to use any restrictive term which might prevent its receiving a fair and just interpretation. In considering this question, then, we must never forget that it is a constitution we are expounding.*

60

I once attended a lecture on the United States Constitution given by a circuit court judge from Montgomery, Alabama. After it was over, he opened the meeting to questions. I asked him three questions which caused him to be visibly uneasy: Isn't it true that the intent of the law is the force of the law? He tried to evade the question, but finally admitted that it was. Isn't it true that if a law is written in such a way that the average man cannot understand it, that it is void for vagueness? After a feeble attempt not to answer, he answered yes. And the third, and final question: Due to the fact that the intent of the law is the force of the law, and that if an average man cannot understand a law, it is void for vagueness, then please tell me what is the purpose of case law? His immediate reaction was to lean over and say to the individual sitting alongside him, who had invited him to speak, **get me out of here.**

From this false premise, established by Marshall in 1819, the courts have grown into an out-of-control chaotic, seditious tyranny, interfering in every segment of society without any real lawful jurisdiction in most cases, usurping the lawful powers of the legislature at will. Because of this anarchical state, it does not matter who is elected to the legislature or the executive branch of government, until the courts are forced to abandon their judicial legislation through interpretation of the law.

With this in mind, the only political campaign slogan that I ever want to hear is: *I will move to impeach any office holder who violates his or her oath of office, and prosecute them for their seditious acts.*

After the McCulloch decision, the Second Bank of the United States prospered until the second presidential term of Andrew Jackson (*Old Hickory*). Jackson first took office in 1829, and during his first administration, he sought ways to abolish the bank's charter.[8] It was not until his second administration that the opportunity presented itself.

Jackson was the champion of the common man, and saw the

bank as a tool of the rich and powerful for the exploitation of the average citizen. He contended that if the bank was necessary, it should be a public bank, owned and managed by the government, not a private concern granted special privileges by Congress.[9] Frightened by Jackson's opposition to it, the bank applied to Congress for a new charter in 1832, four years before the expiration of the existing charter. Congress passed the bill for the new charter and Jackson vetoed it, and the two-thirds vote needed to override the veto could not be obtained by the bank's supporters. Jackson alleged that the bank was corrupt and unconstitutional. He ordered the secretary of the treasury, Roger B. Taney, who later became chief justice of the Supreme Court, to withdraw all of the government's deposits from the bank, which seriously hampered that bank's operations. In 1836, the bank's charter expired without renewal, and the control of banking once again returned to the States, where it lawfully belonged.

Except for some private State banks, there was not another attempt to establish the use of bills of credit or enact legislation for another national bank until the War between the States, which commenced in 1861.

The *Framers* saw standing armies as a danger to *individual Liberty*. This is reflected in Article 1, Section 8, Clause 12 and Clause 13:

> [Congress shall have the power] *To raise and support armies, but no appropriation of money to that use shall be for a longer term than two years.*
> *To provide and maintain a navy.*

As revealed in Clause 12, Congress has the power to raise an army, but can only fund it for two years. Wherein Clause 13, Congress has the power *to provide and maintain a navy*. James Madison gives the following explanation for this restriction on maintaining an army:[10]

The same causes which have rendered the Old world the theater of incessant wars, and have banished liberty from the face of it, would soon produce the same effects here. The weakness and jealousy of the small States would quickly introduce some regular military force, against sudden danger from their powerful neighbors. The example would be followed by others, and would soon become universal. In time of actual war, great discretionary powers are constantly given to the Executive magistrate. Constant apprehension of war has the same tendency to render the head too large for the body. A standing military force, with an overgrown Executive, will not long be safe companions to liberty. The means of defense against foreign danger have been always the instruments of tyranny at home. Among the Romans it was a standing maxim, to excite a war whenever a revolt was apprehended. Throughout all Europe, the armies kept up under the pretext of defending, have enslaved, the people. It is, perhaps, questionable, whether the best concerted system of absolute power in Europe, could maintain itself, in a situation where no alarms of external danger could tame the people to the domestic yoke.

Not having a standing army, Lincoln depleted the Treasury by raising and equipping one to invade the Confederate States of America. The first hostilities, as a result of this invasion, took place on July 21, 1861 at Manassas, Virginia. This battle is commonly known as the *Battle of Bull Run,* named after a creek that ran through the battlefield.

The prevailing opinion of the members of the legislative and executive branches of the United States government was that this was going to be the first and last battle of the war, and that this battle should not take more than a couple of hours. Many of them took their wives and lady friends to picnic and watch the battle on a hillside overlooking the battlefield.

The first part of the day, the Union troops carried the field. The Confederate generals had a hard time rallying their raw recruits to hold the line.

Colonel Thomas Jonathan Jackson was in command of a brigade of Confederate troops that were being held in reserve. He had them stationed behind a knoll that ran crossways to the battlefield, laying on their stomachs out of sight of the oncoming Union troops, with their bayonets fixed. His orders were that upon his command, they were to jump up, yell, and charge with their bayonets leveled at the oncoming federal troops.

General Bee was in command of the South Carolina troops that were being routed by the Union forces. He tried desperately to halt their retreat by using Colonel Jackson as an example. Jackson was a devout Calvinist Presbyterian. Having a strong belief in predestination, he did not take cover under fire. He would sit upright on his horse, Little Sorrel, to observe and command his brigade. Bee, trying to rally his troops, shouted, *rally round men, rally round, look at Jackson standing like a stone wall*. At that point, Bee was mortally wounded, and the South Carolinians ran in panic. The oncoming federal troops reached the grassy knoll and Jackson gave the command for his troops to charge. The Union army was totally caught by surprise, and fled from the field leaving their weapons behind.

Colonel Jackson, Generals Beauregard and Johnston inquired of President Jefferson Davis if they should move on to Washington, occupy the capitol and arrest Lincoln, thus ending the war. Jefferson Davis replied that the armies of the Confederate States of America would not fight a war of aggression, that his orders were to defend the borders. Jackson, now nicknamed Stonewall, resigned his commission and it took the better part of a year to talk him into accepting it again.

Lincoln was desperate, and lacked funds to re-establish and re-equip the army. It was at this point that Lincoln, in order to acquire much-needed loans, gave in to the pressure of private bankers to introduce and lobby Congress to pass *The National Bank Act*, the third try at the takeover of our Constitutional Republic.[11]

To illustrate the corruption that such activity breeds, the following is correspondence between the International Banking House of the Rothschild Brothers of London, England, and Ikleheimer, Morton and Vandergould, International Bankers in New York City:[12]

London, June 25th, 1863
Messrs. Ikleheimer, Morton and Vandergould
No. 3 Wall Street, New York, U.S.A.

Dear Sirs:

A Mr. John Sherman has written us from a town in Ohio, U.S.A., as to the profits that may be made in the National Banking business under a recent act of Congress, a copy of which act accompanied his letter. Apparently this act has been drawn upon the plan formulated here last summer by the British Bankers Association and by that Association recommended to our American friends as one that if enacted into law, would prove highly profitable to the banking fraternity throughout the world.

Mr. Sherman declares that there has never before been such an opportunity for capitalists to accumulate money, as that presented by this act and that the old plan, of state banks is so unpopular, that the new scheme will, by contrast, be most favorably regarded, notwithstanding the fact that it gives the National Banks an almost absolute control of the National finance. "The few who can understand the system," he says, "will either be so interested in its profits, or so dependent on its favors, that there will be no opposition from that class, while on the other hand, the great body of the people, mentally incapable of comprehending the tremendous advantages that capital derives from the system, will bear its burdens without complaint and perhaps without even suspecting that the system is inimical to their interests."

Please advise us fully as to this matter and also state whether or not you will be of assistance to us, if we conclude to establish a National Bank in the City of New York. If you are acquainted with Mr. Sherman (he appears to have introduced the National Bank Act) we will be glad to know something of him. If we avail ourselves of the information he furnished, we will of course make due compensation.

Awaiting your reply, we are

> *Your respectful servants,*
> *Rothschild Brothers*

Messrs. Ikleheimer, Morton and Vandergould respond:

Number 3, Wall Street
New York City, July 5, 1863
Messrs. Rothschild Brothers
London, England

Dear Sirs:

We beg to acknowledge the receipt of your letter of June 25th, in which you refer to a communication received from the Honorable John Sherman of Ohio, with reference to the advantages and profits of an American investment under the provisions of our National Bank Act.

The fact that Mr. Sherman speaks well of such an investment or of any similar one, is certainly not without weight for that gentleman possesses in a marked degree, the distinguishing characteristics of the successful modern

66

financier. His temperament is such that whatever his feelings may be they never cause him to lose sight of the main chance. He is young, shrewd and ambitious. He has fixed his eye upon the presidency of the United States and is already a member of Congress. He rightfully thinks he has everything to gain both politically and financially (he has financial ambitions too) by being friendly with men and institutions having large financial resources, and which at times, are not too particular in their methods, either of obtaining governmental aid, or protecting themselves against unfriendly legislation. We trust him here implicitly. His intellect and ambition combine to make him exceedingly valuable to us. Indeed, we predict that if his life is spared, he will prove to be the best friend the monied interests of the world have ever had in America.

As to the organization of a National Bank here, and the nature and profits of such investment, we beg leave to refer to our printed circular enclosed herein. Inquiries by European capitalists, concerning this matter, have been so numerous, that for convenience we have had our views with regard to it put into printed form.

Should you determine to organize a bank in this City, we shall be glad to aid you. We can easily find financial friends to make a satisfactory directory, and to fill official positions not taken up by the personal representatives you will send over.

Your most obedient servants,

Ikleheimer, Morton and Vandergould

Needing large sums of currency quickly, Lincoln had Secretary of the Treasury Salmon P. Chase lobbying Congress for the passage of the Legal Tender Act,[13] which was signed into law on February 25, 1862.[14] In that same year, Congress issued $150 million *United States Notes, "Lincoln Greenbacks," Bills of Credit*, totally lacking Constitutional authority. Thus the door was cracked to allow the unconstitutional foot to be stuck in.

The United States Notes were just that, debts. Black's Law Dictionary, 5th Edition, defines Notes, as:

> *Note, n. An instrument containing an express and absolute promise of signer (i.e. Maker) to pay to a specified person or order, or bearer, a definite sum of money at a specified time.*

It could be said that the birth of the Lincoln Greenback was born out of what could be called a necessity, but that is really not the case. In the time that it took for both houses of the federal legislature to pass the bill, the Lincoln administration could have borrowed on the credit of the United States as authorized by Article 1, Section 8, Clause 2:

> *Congress shall have power . . . to borrow money on the credit of the United States;*

Wherefore, there can be no other conclusion drawn, but that Congress and Lincoln conspired to open the door for the corrupt practices of the international bankers.

Now enters the third seditious conspirator, the United States Supreme Court. One of the first cases to come before the Court regarding United States Notes (Lincoln Greenbacks) was Lane *County v Oregon*, 7 Wall 81. Even though the Court ruled that Lane County had to pay the collected taxes to the Oregon state treasurer in gold and silver coin, rather than United States Notes, the decision was not based on the fact that the issuance of *bills of credit* were beyond the authorized power of Congress and therefore unconstitutional, it was based on an Oregon statute requiring the payment thusly. In fact, the Court implied within its opinion that

Congress had such power to issue these *bills of credit*, thus setting the stage for all the seditious opinion in the *legal tender* cases that followed in which the Court completely ignored the enumerated powers within the Constitution and the documented intent of the *Framers*.

Not being satisfied with the gains that they made, the bankers, led by John D. Rockefeller, wanted total control of the Republic's money. Having the ability to control the market place through their banks, they tightened the availability of credit, causing the panic of 1907 and setting the stage for the public's acceptance of the Federal Reserve Bank system.

John D. Rockefeller was furious over the breakup of the Standard Oil Company's monopoly and the accompanying twenty-nine million dollar fine by the federal court, so he conspired with other Wall Street bankers and the Rothschild banking interests in Europe to create the Federal Reserve Bank System. Using the financial panic of 1907, Rockefeller employed Professor J. Laurence Laughlin, of the University of Chicago, a Rockefeller institution, to sell the American public on the need for the Fed (the name by which it is known).[15] In conjunction with this propaganda blitz, disseminated through the Rockefeller-controlled media, Rockefeller and Rothschild factions met at the Rockefeller vacation home in Jekyll Island, Georgia, to write the legislative bills that were to be introduced in Congress. The main participants were:[16]

U.S. Senator Nelson Aldrich, John D.'s father-in-law,
    Chairman Senate Finance Committee;
Frank A. Vanderlip, President of National City Bank
    (a Rockefeller bank);
Paul Moritz Warburg, a German agent[17] and liaison between
    Rockefeller and Rothschild factions;
Henry P. Davison, senior partner of J.P. Morgan & Co.
Charles D. Norton, President of First National Bank (N.Y.)
Benjamin Strong (husband of Bessie Rockefeller).

The proposed legislation that came out of the meetings on Jekyll Island was introduced in Congress by Congressman Carter Glass, who had been maneuvered into the position of Banking Committee Chairman by the Rockefeller agent H. P. Hills.[18] With the influence of the backing of President Woodrow Wilson,[19] another known Rockefeller agent, the Federal Reserve Act was passed on December 23, 1913.

Although a private corporation, the Federal Reserve System has the appearance of being controlled by the Executive Branch of the federal government, but in fact, the presidents have continually appointed Rockefeller/Rothschild employees and associates to be Chairmen of the Board of Governors. These bankers have become so powerful that it is obvious that the Congress dare not audit the Fed as required by Article I, Section 9, Clause 7 of the United States Constitution.

Unlike the bank acts before it, the Federal Reserve Act is the framework that has given the private Federal Reserve Bank total power over our money supply. This did not happen immediately with the passage of the Act, but evolved slowly over the years that followed, until the repeal of the Coinage Act by Congress on June 4th, 1963. With that repeal, the monetary system of the United States of America went full circle, back to paper money like the pre-Constitutional bills of credit called Continentals, leaving United States Notes and Federal Reserve Notes (the private bank notes of the Federal Reserve Bank) as the only paper currency in circulation. Today, United States Notes are mainly in the hands of collectors, leaving primarily the Federal Reserve Notes in circulation, and the general public has come to call these worthless, fraudulent notes "dollars."

Nelson Aldrich Rockefeller was selected by the bankers to advise (control) the puppets placed in the White House and the Congress. Through them, he slowly guided the total take-over of our monetary system. The most effective puppet was Franklin Delano Roosevelt. The 1929 depression, caused by the bankers

70

withdrawing credit from the marketplace, assured Roosevelt's election riding the New Deal socialist steamroller. By promising every American financial security, and putting the federal government deep into debt to these bankers to deliver it, Roosevelt became god to most of the American public.[20] Anything he suggested was considered a command by the New Deal Congress.

Through Roosevelt's office, the Rockefeller family and their banking allies eradicated all the Fed's banking competition and took possession of the country's gold. Because Nelson Aldrich Rockefeller was Roosevelt's chief adviser, it can be safely alleged that he advised FDR to issue the Executive Order on March 6, 1933, and to call the special session of Congress on March 9, 1933 for the sole purpose of passing the so-called *Emergency Banking Relief Act*. With this constitutionally questionable federal law, Roosevelt was authorized to license the reopening of any bank on whatever terms the bankers chose, thus eradicating any banking competition to the Federal Reserve Bank. On April 5, 1933, Roosevelt issued an Executive Order, supposedly authorized by the very questionable law, for the surrender of all gold and gold certificates to the Federal Reserve Banks, and two weeks later, another Order that barred exporting of gold. Thus the takeover of America's monetary system by the bankers behind the Federal Reserve Bank was complete.

With the advent of World War II, in which Roosevelt played a significant part in setting the stage for the attack on Pearl Harbor by Japan,[21] he also introduced a new type of tax, one that has no Constitutional authority, when and if imposed on citizens and resident aliens—the withholding tax on wages. The rubber-stamp Congress titled this new law the *Victory Tax Act*. The main difference with this new tax and the taxes that were laid until that time is that it was not enacted and levied to collect taxes for the payment of the war effort, but rather to siphon off the excessive amount of Federal Reserve Notes being created out of thin air and circulated for payment of the war effort and other government expenses.[22] Of course, at that time, these notes were backed by silver dollars. They ceased to be redeemed by silver in 1963 with the repeal of the Coinage Act. Without payment, they do not even meet the legal requirements for a note, making them nothing other than worthless pieces of paper, whose circulation depends on the faith of the user. In this regard, they are the same as the Continental, only the *Federal Reserve Notes* are pulled out of circulation with the withholdings tax and do not accumulate in the marketplace; thus they are able to maintain the faith of the public.

To illustrate what I'm talking about, displayed here are two *Federal Reserve Notes*, one issued before the removal of the silver backing and the other after its removal:

Notice the *payment clause* in the pre-1963 note at top states: *This note is legal tender for all debts, public and private, and is redeemable in lawful money at the United States Treasury, or at any Federal Reserve Bank;* and the post-1963 note only states: *This*

72

note is legal tender for all debts, public and private. The promise to pay in *lawful money* is removed.

Black's Law Dictionary, 5th Edition, defines a lawful note as follows:

> *Note n. An instrument containing an express and absolute promise of signer (i.e., maker) to pay to a specified person or order, or bearer, a definite sum of money at a specified time. Two party instrument made by the maker and payable to payee which is negotiable if signed by the maker and contains an unconditional promise to pay sum certain in money, on demand or at a definite time, to order or bearer. U.S.C. § 3-104(1). A note not meeting these requirements may be assignable but not negotiable.*

The following is a *United States Note* that was paid into circulation by the Congress before the suspension of redemption in *lawful money* was removed from the *payment clause.* When United States Notes are paid into circulation, it interrupts the tax-and-spend scheme used by the principals of the Federal Reserve Bank:

Notice in the following certificates that the *Gold Certificate* was redeemable in gold coin, and the *Silver Certificate* in silver coin, before the repeal of the respective Coinage Acts:

Even more devastating and insidious is the use of the fractional reserve system. The following quote is found on page 83 of the Federal Reserve's 1939 publication *THE FEDERAL RESERVE SYSTEM, ITS PURPOSES AND FUNCTIONS:*

> *An increase in reserve requirements does not increase the power of the Federal Reserve Banks to lend or to hold securities. The lending and investing power of the Federal Reserve Banks is not derived from member bank reserve deposits, and larger required reserve balances do not increase that power. The lending power of the Federal Reserve Banks, is a statutory power whereby the Federal Reserve Banks may acquire promissory notes, acceptances, bonds, and other obligations and give in exchange Federal Reserve Notes or Credit to the Reserve accounts of member banks. . .*

74

Having such power, their ability to lend and to purchase securities is not limited by the volume of funds deposited with them by their member banks. . . . Federal Reserve Bank credit resembles bank credit in general, but under the law, it has a limited and special use as a source of member bank reserve funds. . . .

Federal Reserve Bank Credit, therefore, as already stated, does not consist of funds that the reserve authorities get somewhere in order to lend, but constitutes funds that they are empowered to create. The process of creation is one of giving the promise of the Federal Reserve Bank in the form of Federal Reserve Notes and deposit credits. . . . that is, Federal Reserve Bank promises or "liabilities" as they are commonly called, serve in the form of Federal Reserve Notes as the principle element of circulation medium, and serve in the form of reserve deposits as a basis for the extension of credit by member banks.

In other words, the Federal Reserve creates money out of thin air, and loans it to Congress and the public alike, with a demand for interest and principle payments. This is supposedly legal because Congress passed an Act authorizing it. Aside from the fact that Congress has no authority within the Constitution to do so, if you were to duplicate these intrinsically void pieces of paper, and get caught, the Secret Service would charge you with counterfeiting, and most likely, you would spend some time in prison.

On June 6, 1960, at a hearing on two bills before the 86th Congress, H.R. 8516 and H.R. 8627, the chairman of the Committee on Banking and Currency, Congressman Wright Patman of Texas, posed several questions to Mr. Allen, president of the Federal Reserve Bank of Chicago. The following is taken from the transcript of that Subcommittee meeting at pages 39 and 41:

Mr. Patman: *Now Mr. Allen, when the Federal Open*

Market Committee buys a million dollar bond you create that money on the credit of the nation to pay for that bond don't you?

Mr. Allen: That is correct.

Mr. Patman: And the credit of the nation is represented by Federal Reserve Notes in that case, isn't it? If the banks want the actual money, you give them Federal Reserve Notes in payment don't you?

Mr. Allen: That could be done, but nobody wants the Federal Reserve Notes.

Mr. Patman: Nobody wants them, because the banks would rather have the credit as reserves but that is the modus operandi if currency is desired.

Mr. Allen: That is right.

Mr. Patman: In other words, when the open market committee buys a million dollar bond, it doesn't take a million dollars out of anybody's account; there is no money taken from any bank or any individual; they create that money on the books of the banks, the 12 Federal Reserve Banks, to buy that bond, don't they?

Mr. Allen: That is correct.

Since 1963, having total control of the United States monetary system, the principals of the Federal Reserve Bank have, with the knowledge of Congress, as evidenced by the foregoing transcript, fraudulently put the federal government into trillions of "dollars" in debt for their own benefit. This debt cannot be paid, having a continuous escalation of interest that causes more and more of the fiat medium of exchange to be taken out of the marketplace just to pay it. Thus, under this private money system, there can be no tax relief, as the federal government must continue to find ways of either 1) justifying the raising of additional taxes, or 2) finding new ways to tax. All in all, it is a long way from the constitutional system that the Framers set up, a system that depended on taxing foreigners to support the federal government, thus making the citizens free to prosper financially.

Part III

ARE the PROVISIONS of the INTERNAL REVENUE CODE CONSTITUTIONAL?

Chapter 7

SUBTITLE A:
INCOME TAXES

As soon as the subject of law is brought up, most people's eyes glaze over, and their senses become inoperable. To prevent this from happening here, the following facts about the law are not written in legalese; they are written in such a way that it will be impossible not to understand. I promise that you should not be bored, and after you finish reading these facts about the federal tax laws, you will have more knowledge about them than most tax professionals.

The United States Code was created by Congress in 1926. The purpose of its enactment was to facilitate the use of the Acts of Congress. Before that, such Acts of Congress were recorded and published in the Statutes At Large and arranged according to the date the law was passed by Congress. The Statutes At Large co-exist with the United States Code and are kept current in the same manner as before. When the country was young with very little federal government interference in our everyday lives, the date method was sufficient. But as the federal government grew beyond its lawful function of the protection of life and property the laws became so numerous that it became very difficult to find the law by the date of its enactment, and there arose a need to make finding the law more feasible. Thus, the United States Code came into being.

The United States Code has fifty titles, all of which are topical. For example, if you wanted to find a law regarding banking, you would go to Title 12; for money, Title 31; for the federal government's agencies and employees, Title 5, and so on. The Internal Revenue Code is Title 26, and Intoxicating Liquors, Title 27. Title 26 is divided into ten Subtitles. The first five are different categories of taxation, the sixth, the procedures and administration relating to those categories, and the rest are miscellaneous. They are as follows:

Subtitle A   Income Taxes
Subtitle B   Estate and Gift Taxes
Subtitle C   Employment Taxes
Subtitle D   Miscellaneous Excise Taxes
Subtitle E   Alcohol, Tobacco, and Certain Other Excise Taxes
Subtitle F   Procedure and Administration
Subtitle G   The Joint Committee on Taxation
Subtitle H   Financing of Presidential Election Campaigns
Subtitle I   Trust Fund Code
Subtitle J   Coal Industry Health Benefits

Wherefore, if you wanted to search the laws involving income taxes, you would not go to Subtitle D or Subtitle E, you would go to Subtitle A.

For the purpose of this book, we are interested in three Subtitles—A, C, and F. Subtitle A is divided into five active chapters and one inactive, repealed chapter:

Chapter 1   Normal Taxes and Surtaxes
Chapter 2   Tax on Self-Employment Income
Chapter 3   Withholding of Tax on Nonresident Aliens and
            Foreign Corporations.
Chapter 4   Repealed [Rules Applicable to Recovery of
            Excessive Profits on Government Contracts]
Chapter 5   Tax on Transfers to Avoid Income Tax
Chapter 6   Consolidated Returns

Out of the six chapters, we will be mainly examining three,

Chapters 1, 2 and 3. Chapter 2 will be discussed in Part III, Chapter IX, when we discuss Employment taxes.

Subchapter A of Chapter 1 is the *Determination of Tax Liability.* Part 1 of the Subchapter is *Tax on Individuals*, and Section 1 is entitled *Tax Imposed*, and it states as follows:

> (a)   *Married individuals filing joint returns and surviving spouses.*
>> *There is hereby imposed on the taxable income of* —
>>> (1)   *every married individual (as defined in section 7703) who makes a single return jointly with his spouse under section 6013, and*
>>> (2)   *every surviving spouse (as defined in section 2(a)), a tax determined in accordance with the following table:*

and Section 3, *Tax Tables for Individuals*, states:

> (a)   *Imposition of tax table tax*
> (1)   *In general—In lieu of the tax imposed by section 1, there is hereby imposed for each taxable year on the taxable income of every individual —*

Notice that in both Section 1 and 3, the tax is imposed *on the taxable income of every individual.* As discussed in other chapters, with the false information coming from the news and entertainment media and the so-called tax experts, it is naturally assumed that the use of the words *every individual* would mean everyone, no matter who. Sections 7703, 6013 and 2(a), cited in § 1, deal only with the definitions involving the marital status, and for our purposes need not be examined.

The examination of the Internal Revenue Code has to be done with the thought in mind that it is written in a fashion that perpetuates the mind set of the public that everyone owes the income tax. Wherefore, it is going to take a little research outside of the Code to identify who this *individual* is. The task at hand would have been most difficult to prove conclusively to the benefit of everyone before 1980, but Congress has unquestionably solved that problem for us.

In 1980, one of those rare occasions arose when the Congress was actually trying to do good for the citizens and passed the *Paperwork Reduction Act*. The purpose of this law was to reduce the amount of material and labor in all of the government agencies by requiring those agencies to restrict all public information requests to only those authorized by law. The federal *Office of Management and Budget* (OMB) was given the authority to police all agency information requests. The procedure was for the agency to submit the proposed information request form to the OMB and cite the statute and its implementing regulation that authorized the particular request. The OMB application form for the agencies to use was designated Form SF-83, which has now been replaced by Form I-83. When the OMB completes the verification, and the information request is proved valid, the information request form and the regulation implementing the statute authorizing the request, are both assigned the same OMB Control Number as a means for the recipient to determine if the request was lawful or bogus.

In fifteen years' experience of dealing with the employees of the Internal Revenue Service, on behalf of myself and many others, I have come to the conclusion that the rank-and-file employee has but a very scant knowledge of the tax laws. But through study and use of the *Internal Revenue Regulations* and the *Internal Revenue Manual*, it has become very clear that whoever is writing these regulations for the Secretary of the Treasury and the Commissioner of the Internal Revenue Service is very knowledgeable of the Constitutional requirements of the law.

The *Paperwork Reduction Act* requires that a government agency display the issued *OMB Control Number* and the corresponding regulation within the agency's regulations. When the Internal Revenue Service complied with this provision of the law, they displayed these numbers and regulations in *Part 602 of Title 26, Code of Federal Regulations*, which is commonly called *Internal Revenue Regulations*. According to the 1988 edition of Part 602, shown below, the OMB Control Number for the tax return to be used for § 1 is 1545-0067. This is found by looking at the corresponding number for the regulation implementing § 1, which is the first one listed, § 1.1-1:

PART 602—OMB CONTROL NUMBERS UNDER THE PAPERWORK REDUCTION ACT

§ 602.101 OMB control numbers.

(a) *Purpose.* This part collects and displays the control numbers assigned to collections of information in Internal Revenue Service regulations by the Office of Management and Budget (OMB) under the Paperwork Reduction Act of 1980. The Internal Revenue Service intends that this part (together with 26 CFR 601.9000) comply with the requirements of §§ 1320.7(f), 1320.12, 1320.13, and 1320.14 of 5 CFR Part 1320 (OMB regulations implementing the Paperwork Reduction Act), for the display of control numbers assigned by OMB to collections of information in Internal Revenue Service regulations. This part does not display control numbers assigned by the Office of Management and Budget to collections of information of the Bureau of Alcohol, Tobacco, and Firearms.

(b) *Cross-reference.* For display of control numbers assigned by the Office of Management and Budget to Internal Revenue Service collections of information in the Statement of Procedural Rules (26 CFR Part 601), see 26 CFR § 601.9000.

(c) *Display*

26 CFR part or section where identified and described	Current OMB control number
§ 1.1-1	1545-0067
§ 1.25-1T	1545-0922
§ 1.25-2T	1645-0922
§ 1.25-3T	1545-0922
§ 1.25-4T	1545-0922
§ 1.25-5T	1545-0922
§ 1.25-6T	1545-0922
§ 1.25-7T	1545-0922
§ 1.25-8T	1545-0922
§ 1.31-2(a)	1545-0074
§ 1.37-1(c)	1545-0074
§ 1.37-3(b)	1545-0074
§ 1.41-4(b) and (c)	1545-0074
§ 1.42-1T	1545-0988
§ 1.42-2T	1545-1005
§ 1.43-2(b)	1545-0074
§ 1.44A	1545-0068
§ 1.44A-3(a)	1545-0074
§ 1.44B-1	1545-0219
§ 1.44C	1545-0214
§ 1.44C-5	1545-0780
§ 1.44C-6	1545-0780
§ 1.46-1(p)	1545-0123
§ 1.46-5(e)(2)	1545-0155
§ 1.46-5(h)(4)	1545-0155
§ 1.46-5(j)(6)(iv)	1545-0155
§ 1.46-5(o)(2)	1545-0155
§ 1.46-6	1545-0155
§ 1.46-11(g)	1545-0155
§ 1.47-1(b)	1545-0166
§ 1.47-1(e)(1)	1545-0166
§ 1.47-1(e)(3)	1545-0166
§ 1.47-1(h)	1545-0155
§ 1.47-3(d)	1545-0166
§ 1.47-3(f)	1545-0155
§ 1.47-3(h)	1545-0155
§ 1.47-4(a)	1545-0123
§ 1.47-5(a)	1545-0092
§ 1.47-6	1545-0099
§ 1.50A-1	1545-0189
§ 1.50A-2	1545-0189
§ 1.50A-3	1545-0189
§ 1.50A-4	1545-0189
§ 1.50A-5	1545-0189
§ 1.50A-6	1545-0189
§ 1.50A-7	1545-0189
§ 1.50B-1	1545-0189
§ 1.50B-2	1545-0189
§ 1.50B-3	1545-0189
§ 1.50B-4	1545-0189
§ 1.50B-5	1545-0189
§ 1.51-1(c)(3)	1545-0241
§ 1.51-1(d)	1545-0219
§ 1.52-1	1545-0219
§ 1.52-1(b)	1545-0219
§ 1.52-1(h)	1545-0797
§ 1.52-2	1545-0219
§ 1.52-3	1545-0219

In the Internal Revenue Regulations the number before the period is the Part of the regulation, where the section is to be found—in this case, Part 1, entitled "Income Tax." The number after the period is the corresponding number for the code section the regulation is implementing—in this case § 1. The number after the dash is the subsection of the regulation itself—§ 1 having only one subsection.

Now the question arises: Does the OMB Control Number 1545-0067 identify Form 1040, which is the form that the Internal Revenue Service mails out to individuals every year to supposedly use for income tax purposes? The so-called tax professionals also tell everyone to use the very same form. Look at the upper right-hand corner of the Form 1040 displayed below, and notice the OMB Control Number assigned to it:

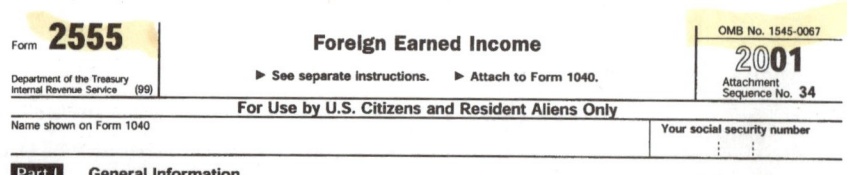

Well, evidently the tax professionals are mistaken; or the Internal Revenue Service was mistaken when it submitted Form SF-83 to the OMB; or the OMB was mistaken when it assigned the numbers, or there was a printing error credited to either the Internal Revenue Service or the Government Printing Office. No, none of the above is true. There is no mistake on anybody's part. Displayed below is the tax form the Internal Revenue Service submitted to the OMB with its SF-83 application, and the OMB Control Number displayed in its upper right hand corner is the number that the OMB assigned to it —*1545-0067*:

Form **2555**	**Foreign Earned Income**	OMB No. 1545-0067
Department of the Treasury Internal Revenue Service (99)	► See separate instructions. ► Attach to Form 1040.	2001 Attachment Sequence No. 34
	For Use by U.S. Citizens and Resident Aliens Only	
Name shown on Form 1040		Your social security number

Part I **General Information**

Well, who is the individual in § 1? If you don't already know, we will go to the implementing regulation and see who it identifies:

> *§ 1.1-1 Income tax on individuals.*
>
> *(a) General rule. (1) Section 1 of the Code imposes an income tax on the income of every individual who is a citizen or resident of the United States and, to the extent provided by section 871(b) or 877(b), on the income of a nonresident alien individual. For optional tax in the case of taxpayers with adjusted gross income of less than $10,000 (less than $5,000 for taxable years beginning before January 1, 1970) see section 3. . . .*

So we have the answer, and the Code is again proven to be Constitutional. But how is it Constitutional, you may ask, isn't the *citizen* and the *resident alien* being taxed on their income? Yes, but only on their *foreign earned income*, as Form 2555 demonstrates. If the citizen and resident alien were taxed on their domestic income, that would be a violation of Article 1, Section 2, Clause 3 of the Constitution, being a direct tax without apportionment. The reason why foreign income can be taxed is that the provisions of the Constitution do not extend beyond the geographical boundaries of the fifty States. Wherefore, any foreign earned income is fair game to be taxed.

The Save-A-Patriot Fellowship (of which I am the founder and fiduciary) made this public in 1987, and it was spread far and wide across the country by its membership. Closing the barn door after the horse had already passed through, the Internal Revenue Service removed all reference to regulation § 1.1-1 from the OMB listing in Part 602 of the regulations in 1994. At that time, I wrote the Internal Revenue Service Assistant Commissioner for Public Affairs in Washington, D.C. and asked why this regulation section was removed. They answered that it was entered in error, without any further explanation. Of course, common sense would tell you that was not so. I wrote back and asked if any event took place that would cause this change, but received no response. In 1994, the

Department of the Treasury published the change in the Federal Register thusly:

> *§ 602.101 (Corrected)*
> *Par. 2. The table under § 602.101(c) is amended by removing the entry for "1.1-1"*

In April of 1997, the following letter was received by the Fellowship:

Dear Friends:

I am writing to show you a letter I received from the IRS in response to a request for the proper OMB# to satisfy my liability under 26 CFR Sec. 1.1-1. As you can see, it does not quite fit with what you have on your web site. I was quite excited when I saw your information but once again maybe I have went down a dead end in my search to find the truth. Could you please give me your interpretation of this letter from the IRS, and an answer that I may rebut them with? Thank you so much for your fine web site and spirit of freedom. God bless you.

The Internal Revenue Service response is displayed here in its entirety, except the identification of the individual to whom it was mailed.

Internal Revenue Service Pacific-Northwest District
Problem Resolution Program 915 2nd Ave. M/S W442
1-800-829-0933 ext: 89006   Seattle, WA 98174

Person to Contact: K. Gibson
Date: April 16, 1997 PRP

Taxpayer Identification Number:
Tax Period(s) Ended: December 31, 1996
Form(s): 1040

This is in response to your inquiry of March 20, 1997, addressed to Congressman Doc Hastings. Your letter was referred to the Seattle Problem Resolution Office of the Internal Revenue Service for a response. Your inquiry concerned the correct OMB number for Form 1040, U.S. Individual Income Tax Return.

By agreement with the Office of Management and Budget (OMB), all IRS regulations that are subject to the Paperwork Reduction Act must be listed in section 602.101 of the Code of Federal Regulations (CFR), along with the OMB control numbers assigned to them. This is intended to comply with the requirement under the Act that collections of information must display OMB control numbers. Many regulations listed in section 602.101 have the same OMB number as the tax forms that are related to them. However, the listing in section 602.101 is not meant to be the legal authority for filing any tax forms represented by the OMB control numbers shown there. Some tax forms have different OMB numbers than the regulations listed in section 602.101.

Regulation section 1.1-1 is shown in the table with OMB number 1545-0067. This is an error because section 1.1-1 provides rules and cross references for the computation of income tax on individuals and does not contain any information collection or filing requirements subject to the Paperwork Reduction Act. Section 1.1-1 is mistakenly listed in section 602.101 and should not appear in the table at all. To correct this error, we removed section 1.1-1 from the table by publishing correcting amendments to 26 CFR Part 602 in the Federal Register on May 26, 1994, at page 27235 (copy enclosed).

-2-

April 16, 1997

The correct OMB number for Form 1040, is 1545-0074, which is shown on the form. OMB originally assigned 1545-0074 to Form 1040, in 1981, and the number has stayed the same since that time. I am enclosing copies of the OMB approvals for form 1040, from 1981 and 1996, which is the most recent one. Both clearly indicate that the OMB number assigned to Form 1040, is 1545-0074. Form 1040 displays the correct OMB number and is properly approved by OMB for the collection of information related to the individual income tax. Therefore, the form must be complied with by taxpayers.

If you have any questions regarding this matter, please contact me at the telephone number listed above between 8:00 am and 4:00 pm, Monday through Friday. I am closing my case at this time.

I apologize for any inconvenience.

Sincerely,

Kent Gibson

K. Gibson
Problem Resolution Caseworker

Enclosures:
  Federal Register/Vol. 59, NO. 101/page 27235
  Notice of Office of Management and Budget Actions

cc: Congressman Hastings

Notice, in the second paragraph, the Internal Revenue Service employee, K. Gibson, states:

> *Many regulations listed in section 602.101 have the same OMB number as the tax forms that are related to them. However, the listing in section 602.101 is not meant to be the legal authority for filing any tax forms represented by the OMB control numbers shown there. Some tax forms have different OMB numbers than the regulations listed in section 602.101.*

Nice try, K. Gibson. Notice that Gibson does not cite any regulations having related forms with different numbers. In all my years of studying § 602.101, I have never come across any such numbers. Internal Revenue Service employees get by with such ludicrous responses only because of the public's ignorance of the law, which was the case here. Notice how it confused the individual making the inquiry to the Fellowship. If he would have understood the intent of the Paperwork Reduction Act he would have seen right through this lame effort to cover up the truth about a citizen's requirement to file an income tax return and income tax liability. The very purpose of that act was to connect the information request form with the authorizing statute so that the individual receiving the information request could investigate its validity. If the form has a different number than the regulation, how could you do that? Also, notice that there is no reason given why Form 2555, *Foreign Earned Income*, was assigned to § 1.1-1, and consequently § 1, in the first place. When I asked that question of the Assistant Commissioner of Public Affairs, there was no answer. Obviously, anything they could possibly do or say would only make it worse for them.

Coincidentally, § 6012 of Subtitle F, *Persons required to make returns of income*, and its implementing regulation, § 1.6012-0 has the same OMB Control Number as § 1.1-1, and it has also has been removed from § 602.101, leaving § 1.6012-1 through 6. The difference with this listing is that there is more than one subsection to the regulation, listing other OMB Control Numbers. Of course, § 1.6012-0 was the main corresponding subsection to § 6012. There are just too many holes in the dike and the IRS does not seem to have enough fingers.

Another way to settle the question of who is liable to pay a tax on their income, and under what circumstances, is to research the requirements for the person required to withhold the tax—the *withholding agent*.

The Index of the Internal Revenue Code states that the definition of a *withholding agent* is found in § 7701 (a)(16). This section is in Chapter 79 of Subtitle F, and lists the general definitions of legal terms for the Internal Revenue Code.

Before we go to Chapter 79, let's examine the need for legal terms to be defined. If the laws are written in English, and mean exactly what they say, then why do legal terms need to be defined? After all, if they can't be understood by the average individual, said law is void for vagueness. The answer is, the language is constantly changing, caused mainly by the use of slang. The Constitution was written two hundred and fourteen years ago. Look at the change in the language since then. Look at the change in the language since the beginning of the last century. In addition to this, a legislature can make a legal term mean what it wants it to mean other than its true and commonly accepted meaning, such as is found in § 7701(a)(1), defining *persons*:

(1) Person. The term "person" shall be construed to mean and include an individual, a trust, estate, partnership, association, company or corporation.

Wherefore, when reading any statute, you cannot draw any conclusions as to its intent or force until all the legal terms therein are defined. One such legal term is "United States," which will be discussed more fully in another chapter.

Now, let us look at the definition of the *individual, trust, estate, partnership, association, company or corporation* that is required to *deduct and withhold the income tax*:

91

(16) Withholding agent. The term "withholding agent" means any person required to deduct and withhold any tax under the provisions of sections 1441, 1442, 1443, or 1461.

These code sections are found in Chapter 3 of Subtitle A, Income Taxes, and require withholding of the *income tax* as follows:

26 USCA	*1441*	*Withholding of tax on nonresident aliens*
26 USCA	*1442*	*Withholding of tax on foreign corporations*
26 USCA	*1443*	*Foreign tax-exempt organizations*
26 USCA	*1444*	*Withholding on Virgin Islands source income*
26 USCA	*1445*	*Withholding of tax on dispositions of United States real property interests*
26 USCA	*1446*	*Withholding tax on foreign partners' share of effectively connected income*
26 USCA	*1461*	*Liability for withheld tax*

These are the only laws requiring the withholding of *income taxes* that can be found within the Internal Revenue Code. Notice that in every one of these code sections, the activity or payee is foreign in nature.

Section 1461 also tells us some very important facts about the liability for the *income tax*:

Sec. 1461. Liability for withholding tax.

    Every person required to deduct and withhold any tax under this chapter is hereby made liable for such tax and is hereby indemnified against the claims and demands of any person for the amount of any payments made in accordance with the provisions of this chapter.

First, it tells us that Chapter 3 contains the only provisions for the withholding of the *income tax*; second, it tells us the withholding agent is not a *tax collector* but rather the *taxpayer* (a

92

law making a tax collector of someone not on the government payroll would be a violation of the 13th Amendment, the abolition of slavery); third, it tells us that this prevents anyone from suing the withholding agent for the deduction and payment of the tax to the Internal Revenue Service.

Reproduced below to further prove my point is Internal Revenue Publication 515 (Rev. Nov. 88) entitled *Withholding of Tax on Nonresident Aliens and Foreign Corporations*. For your convenience, I enlarged the pertinent parts of this Publication.

10<u>4</u>
**Department of the Treasury
Internal Revenue Service**

Publication 515
(Rev. Nov. 88)

Withholding of Tax on Nonresident Aliens and Foreign Corporations

Introduction

If you control, or are responsible for, the receipt, disposal, custody, or payment of the items of income discussed in this publication, you must withhold income tax on them. If you are required to withhold the tax, you become the taxpayer liable for its payment, especially if the alien who receives the income fails to satisfy the U.S. tax liability. You may be a tenant, manager, broker, agent, fiduciary, or spouse, but if you meet the withholding requirements, you are a withholding agent liable for the tax discussed here.

If you need information on a subject not covered in this publication, check our other free publications or write to: Internal Revenue Service, Assistant Commissioner (International), Attention:

Introduction

If you control, or are responsible for, the receipt, disposal, custody, or payment of the items of income discussed in this publication, you must withhold income tax on them. If you are required to withhold the tax, you become the taxpayer liable for its payment, especially if the alien who receives the income fails to satisfy the U.S. tax liability. You may be a tenant, manager, broker, agent, fiduciary, or spouse, but if you meet the withholding requirements, you are a withholding agent liable for the tax discussed here.

be making payments on the agent's own behalf as a lessee or mortgagor of property, or other obligor, or an agent may be paying on behalf of another fiduciary, etc. If the withholding agent appoints a duly authorized agent to act on its behalf, the withholding agent is required to file a notice of the appointment with the Internal Revenue Service, Assistant Commissioner (International), 950 L'Enfant Plaza South, S.W., Washington, DC 20024. The notice must be filed before the first payment with respect to which the authorized agent is to act. If the duly authorized agent becomes insolvent or fails to deposit the withheld tax, the withholding agent is still liable.

For example, the local U.S. promoter of an entertainment event featuring a nonresident alien performer is usually the withholding agent. How-

...interest, that is *not effectively connected* with the conduct of a trade or business in the United States is subject to a 30% tax rate, or lower treaty rate, whether or not the taxpayer also engages in a trade or business in the United States.

For example, you must withhold at 30%, or lower treaty rate, on payment of rents, dividends, interest, and other fixed or determinable annual or periodic income from sources within the United States. If this income is effectively connected with the conduct of a trade or business in the United States, the person entitled to the income may claim exemption from withholding by filing a statement to that effect with you. See *Form 4224*, discussed later.

Different withholding rules apply to a partnership's payments of effectively connected income to foreign partners, and to dispositions of U.S. real property interests by foreign persons. See *Partnership Withholding on Effectively Connected Income*, and *U.S. Real Property Interest*, later.

Withholding Agent

Any person required to withhold the tax is a withholding agent. A withholding agent may be an individual, a trust, estate, partnership, corporation, government agency, association, or tax-exempt foundation, whether domestic or foreign. Withhold-

Foreign nominees and fiduciaries. Under certain tax treaties, a foreign nominee or fiduciary in a treaty country may have to withhold additional U.S. tax from U.S. source dividends, interest, and other income.

For example, a Swiss nominee is required under Swiss law to withhold 30% of the gross dividend minus the 15% that has been withheld by the withholding agent in the United States.

Except for Canada, foreign nominees and fiduciaries must send the additional U.S. tax withheld to their own tax authorities, accompanied by whatever form may be prescribed by their national tax agencies. In turn, treaty tax authorities send the additional tax to the Internal Revenue Service Center, Philadelphia, PA 19255.

Canadian nominees and fiduciaries send the additional U.S. tax withheld, in U.S. currency, directly to the Internal Revenue Service Center in Philadelphia, accompanied by an annual Form 1042, *Annual Withholding Tax Return for U.S. Source Income of Foreign Persons*. The U.S. deposit rules, discussed later, do not apply to these foreign withholding agents.

For specific details on the procedures and types of U.S. source income on which additional withholding is required, foreign nominees and fiducia-

Notice that the *Introduction* section of this publication verifies that the withholding agent is the taxpayer, and the *Withholding Exemptions and Reductions* section verifies that

93

citizens and resident aliens are not subject to withholding tax on their income, and that it also mentions a written statement declaring their status.

Withholding Exemptions and Reductions

You should withhold any required tax if facts indicate that the individual, or the fiduciary, to whom you are to pay the income is a nonresident alien. If you fail to withhold tax, you are still liable for payment of the tax, especially if the alien fails to satisfy the U.S. tax liability. However, the alien may be allowed an exemption from withholding or a reduced rate of withholding as explained here.

Evidence of residence. If an individual gives you a written statement, in duplicate, stating that he or she is a citizen or resident of the United States, and you do not know otherwise, you may accept this statement and are relieved from the duty of withholding the tax. Or, an alien may claim U.S. residence by filing with you, in duplicate, Form 1078, *Certificate of Alien Claiming Residence in the United States.* Holders of visas that do *not* permit permanent residence in the United States should write to the Internal Revenue Service, Assistant Commissioner (International), Attention: IN:C:TPS, 950 L'Enfant Plaza South, S.W., Washington, DC 20024, for advice about filing a Form 1078 and, if filing Form 1078 is proper, about the need to make estimated tax payments.

The authority for this written statement could be found in the Internal Revenue Regulations before 1998, as follows:

Title 26 Code of Federal Regulations, § 1.1441-5
  Claiming to be a person not subject to withholding.
    (a) Individuals. For purposes of chapter 3 of the Code, an individual's written statement that he or she is a citizen or resident of the United States may be relied upon by the payer of the income as proof that such individual is a citizen or resident of the United States. This statement shall be furnished to the withholding agent in duplicate.

94

An alien may claim residence in the United States by filing Form 1078 with the withholding agent in duplicate in lieu of the above statement.

This regulation also covers the fact that there is no withholding on the income tax of U.S. business entities:

> *(b) Partnerships and corporations. For purposes of chapter 3 of the Code a written statement from a partnership or corporation claiming that it is not a foreign partnership or foreign corporation may be relied upon by the withholding agent as proof that such partnership or corporation is domestic. This statement shall be furnished to the withholding agent in duplicate. It shall contain the address of the taxpayer's office or place of business in the United States and shall be signed by a member of the partnership or by an officer of the corporation. The official title of the corporate officer shall also be given.*

And finally, it told the withholding agent how and where to send it:

> *(c) Disposition of statement and form. The duplicate copy of each statement and form filed pursuant to this section shall be forwarded with a letter of transmittal to Internal Revenue Service Center, Philadelphia, PA 19255. The original statement shall be retained by the withholding agent.*

The reason it was to be sent to the Philadelphia Service Center was because that particular service center was designated as the *International Service Center.* You could live in California or Florida and it still would be forwarded to the Philadelphia Service Center.

In 1998, all mention of any statement of citizenship and Form 1078 was removed from the regulations. In 1999, it was reinserted, and in 2000, it was taken out again. Personally, I never understood why it was there in the first place, as Chapter 3 of the Code clearly states by omission that there is no withholding of tax on the domestic income of citizens or resident aliens. Members of the Fellowship took advantage of its presence within the regulation and still do, knowing that the Internal Revenue Service will never dispute the use of the *statement of citizenship*. Additionally, it is a great learning tool for withholding agents and employers.

The so-called income tax withheld from wages will be covered when we examine Subtitle C, *Employment Taxes* in Chapter VIII.

In Chapter IV of this book, we exhibited that the first Income Tax Act of Congress was called the *Income Duty,* and the stated purpose was:

> *An act to provide increased revenue from imports to pay interest on the public debt, and for other purposes.*

It was also demonstrated in Chapter IV that *direct taxes* were imposed on property and *indirect taxes* were imposed on an activity. Additionally, we exhibited that the Supreme Court of the United States, in its ruling on the 16th Amendment, held that the income tax was an *indirect tax.* Wherefore, as exhibited in Chapter 3 of Subtitle A (the only statutes authorizing the withholding of income taxes), citizens and resident aliens[1] are conspicuous by their absence from the list of entities having income taxes withheld from their domestic income. For if they were listed, the tax would be a *direct tax* on their property, and it would be clearly unconstitutional. Applying the taxing provisions of the Constitution makes it abundantly clear that the activity taxed is the nonresident alien's and foreign corporation's privilege of investing in the American marketplace, doing business, or working within the States of the Union, just as declared in the 1861 *Income Duty* cited above.

Does this mean that citizens and resident aliens are not subject to income taxes? No, it does not. As demonstrated earlier in this Chapter, § 1 imposes the income tax on the income of every individual, and the forms that these individuals are required to use is Form 2555, *Foreign Earned Income*. This form could only be used by citizens and resident aliens; the laws of the United States would have no jurisdiction over nonresident aliens and foreign corporations in foreign countries. Chapter 1 and Chapter 3 of Subtitle A demonstrate very clearly that the *foreign earned income* of citizens, United States corporations, and resident aliens is subject to the income tax, and the domestic income of nonresident aliens and foreign corporations is subject to the income tax. Section 1444 proves this fact beyond any shadow of a doubt, as follows:

> *§ 1444, Withholding of Virgin Island source income.*
> For purposes of determining the withholding tax liability incurred in the Virgin Islands pursuant to this title (as made applicable to the Virgin Islands) with respect to amounts received from sources within the Virgin Islands by <u>citizens and resident alien individuals of the United States</u>, and <u>corporations organized in the United States</u>, the rate of withholding tax under sections 1441 and 1442 on income subject to tax under section 871(a)(1) or 881 shall not exceed the rate of tax on such income under section 871(a)(1) or 881, as the case may be. (Emphasis added.)

The possessions and territories of the United States are considered as foreign countries for legal purposes, and those who reside there, if not citizens of one of the several States, are legally known as *nationals*. Wherefore, Chapter 3 screams out the fact that the domestic income of *citizens* and *resident aliens* is not subject to the income tax.

Just about all of the federal courts, except for the Supreme Court, have held that wages are income for tax purposes. The Supreme Court defined income thusly:

Income may be defined as the gain derived from capital, from labor, or from both combined . . .[2]

The Supreme Court's definition is substantiated in Chapter 1 of Subtitle A, in § 61, *Gross income defined.* Not only is the Supreme Court's definition of income substantiated, but through this code section I will expose one of the major frauds of all time committed by Roosevelt's New Deal Congress, and perpetrated by some individuals knowingly, and by others unknowingly, holding office within the Internal Revenue Service, the Department of Justice, and the federal courts.

§ 61. Gross income defined.
(a) General definition.—Except as otherwise provided in this subtitle, gross income means all income from whatever source derived, including (but not limited to) the following items:
(1) Compensation for services, including fees, commissions, fringe benefits, and similar items;
(2) Gross income derived from business;
(3) Gains derived from dealings in property;
(4) Interest;
(5) Rents;
(6) Royalties;
(7) Dividends;
(8) Alimony and separate maintenance payments;
(9) Annuities;
(10) Income from life insurance and endowment contracts;
(11) Pensions;
(12) Income from discharge of indebtedness;
(13) Distributive share of partnership gross income;
(14) Income in respect of a decedent; and
(15) Income from an interest in an estate or trust.
Source : Sec. 22(a), 1939 Code, substantially unchanged.

Notice the only item even close to being considered "wages"is item (1), Compensation for services. But is that wages? A footnote, referring to § 22 (a), of the Internal Revenue Code of 1939, appeared in the 1982 version of the Internal Revenue Code of 1954. Since then, that footnote has been removed. Why? For a very good reason. It reveals evidence of one of the biggest frauds in history.

Notice this code section states: *gross income means all income from whatever source derived, including (but not limited to) the following items.* Earlier in this book, we covered the *void for vagueness rule.* Remember that statutes have to have their legal terms defined, and have to be all-inclusive in content. In other words, you cannot be bound to obey any part of a statute that is either ambiguous or refers to something not contained therein— such as (*but not limited to*). If not limited to those items listed, then how could you determine the limits of the term? This would make § 61 *void for vagueness* except for the following.

Noticing that the footnote source was removed in the later editions of the Internal Revenue Code causes the need to investigate that source to prove § 61 either *void for vagueness* or enforceable as law. Section 22 of the 1939 Code states:

Sec. 22. GROSS INCOME.

(a)   General Definition—"Gross income" includes gains, profits, and income <u>derived from salaries, wages,</u> or compensation for personal services (including personal service as an officer or employee of a State, or any political subdivision thereof, or any agency or instrumentality of any one or more of the foregoing), of whatever kind and in whatever form paid, or from professions, vocations, trades, businesses, commerce, or sales, or dealings in property, whether real or personal, growing out of the ownership or use of or interest in such property; also from interest, rent, dividends, securities, or the transaction of any business carried on for gain or

profit, or gains or profits and income derived from any source whatsoever. . . (Emphasis added.)

Notice that in § 61 there were two items missing that appear in § 22 (a), *salaries and wages*. Notice also, that the footnote in §61 states: *Source: Sec. 22(a), 1939 Code, <u>substantially unchanged</u>*. Which actually means that § 22 (a) of the 1939 Code is still the law, and the only thing that has been changed is the numerical identification and the form; the substance remains the same. In fact, in the index of the United States Code Annotated there is what is called the *Parallel Table of Authorities and Rules*. The purpose of this *Table of Authorities* is, according to the Code Index:

> *The following table lists rulemaking authority (except 5 USC 301)[3] for regulations codified in the Code of Federal Regulations. Also included are statutory citations which are noted as being interpreted or applied by those regulations.*

The Title 26 portion of these tables starts out with all the code sections of the 1939 Code that were brought forward into the 1954 and 1986 Codes, which are still the law unchanged. The first one listed is § 22, listing the implementing regulations as: 26 Part 519. Coincidentally, Part 519, of the Internal Revenue Regulations, pertains to tax treaties, which continues the very strong evidence of the foreign nature of the income tax.

Back to *salaries and wages*. Notice that in both sections, 61 and 22, it states: *derived from*. If income is from something, it is not that something itself. An egg comes from a chicken, but it is not the chicken. In the case of income taxes, as the Supreme Court said: *Income may be defined as gain*—in other words, a <u>profit</u>. In 1939, there were no wage taxes, so there was no problem in stating that the income was *from* the *salary* or the *wage*. But in 1954, there was a wage tax—a tax that was initiated in 1942, during World War II, supposedly for the war effort, and carried over on a voluntary basis.[4] Wherefore, it would have been impossible to get away with trying to lead Americans to believe that their wages were the "income," and not the source of the income. The income derived *from salaries or wages*, is the profit that an employer makes on the employee's *salary* or *wages*. For instance, an employer charges his customer $20 per hour for his employee's labor, and pays the employee $15 per hour, *deriving* a $5 income from the employee's labor, the source. If the tax would be on the employee's *salary* or *wages*, it would be a *direct* tax in violation of Article 1, Section 2, Clause 3 of the Constitution.

To cement this conclusion, we will examine Subchapter N, of Chapter 1, which is entitled: *Tax based on income from sources within or without the United States.* Part I of subchapter N is entitled: *Determination of Sources of Income.* Part 1 starts at §861, *Income from sources within the United States.* The regulations for § 861 list all the items of gross income that are found in § 61 and then defines the *sources within the United States at §1.861-8*, which states in pertinent part:

> *(4) Statutory grouping of gross income and residual grouping of gross income. For purposes of this section, the term "statutory grouping of gross income" or "statutory grouping" means the gross income from a specific source or activity which must first be determined in order to arrive at "taxable income" from which specific source or activity under an operative section. (See paragraph (f)(1) of this section.)* (Emphasis added.)

Notice, that before there can be any *taxable income*, there has to be *gross income from a specific source or activity*, and that specific source or activity has to be *under an operative section*. As you can see, there are three elements to *taxable income*: *specific source, activity* and an *operative section*. All three are found in (f)(1) of regulation § 1.861-8, which states:

(f) Miscellaneous matters—

(1) Operative sections. *The operative sections of the Code which require the determination of taxable income of the taxpayer from specific sources or activities and* which give rise to statutory groupings to which this section is applicable include the sections described below.

(i) Overall limitation to the foreign tax credit . . .

(ii) [Reserved]

(iii) **DISC[5] and FSC[6] taxable income.** Sections 925 and 994 provide rules for determining the taxable income of a FSC and DISC, respectively, with respect to qualified sales and leases of export property and qualified services. . . .

(iv) **Effectively connected taxable income. Nonresident alien individuals and foreign corporations engaged in trade or business within the United States,** *under sections 871(b)(1) and 882(a)(1), on* **taxable income which is effectively connected with the conduct of a trade or business within the United States.** . . .

(v) **Foreign base company income.** . . .

(vi) Other operative sections. The rules provided in this section also apply in determining—

(A) The amount of foreign source items of tax preference under section 58(g) determined for purposes of the minimum tax;

(B) The amount of foreign mineral income under section 901(e);

(C) [Reserved]

(D) The amount of foreign oil and gas extraction income and the amount of foreign oil related income under section 907;

(E) The tax base for citizens entitled to the benefits of section 931 and the section 936[7] tax credit of a domestic corporation which has an election in effect under section 936 ;

(F) The exclusion for income from Puerto Rico for residents of Puerto Rico under section 933;

(G) The limitation under section 934 on the maximum reduction in income tax liability incurred to the Virgin Islands;

(H) The income derived from Guam by an individual who is subject to section 935;

(I) The special deduction granted to China Trade Act corporations under section 941;

(J) The amount of certain U.S. source income excluded from the subpart F income of a controlled foreign corporation under section 952(b);

(K) The amount of income from the insurance of U.S. risks under section 953(b)(5);

(L) The international boycott factor and the specifically attributable taxes and income under section 999; and

(M) The taxable income attributable to the operation of an agreement vessel under section 607 of the Merchant Marine Act of 1936, as amended, and the Capital Construction Fund Regulations thereunder (26 CFR, part 3). See 26 CFR 3.2(b)(3). (Emphasis added.)

As you can see for yourself, every one of the items found in § 1.861-8, *Income from sources within the United State*s, **ARE ALL FOREIGN**, which continues to confirm the federal tax scheme to be foreign-source income for citizens and resident aliens, and domestic-source income for nonresident aliens and foreign corporations. I will continue to show you this in the remainder of the book, for the sole purpose of washing away the mindset that is the result of being brainwashed since birth.

This scam has cost Americans trillions upon trillions of dollars, which the Congress and the Executive Branch have spent all over the world, not to mention its making the Federal Reserve Bankers the wealthiest individuals in the history of the world. Harry Dexter White, Assistant Secretary of the Treasury during the

Roosevelt Administration, was overheard at a Washington cocktail party as saying: *Tax and spend, tax and spend, the American people are too stupid to understand.*[8]

Chapter 8

SUBTITLE C:
EMPLOYMENT TAXES

Employment taxes are the price we pay for Democracy—so we have been told by Roosevelt, his New Deal socialist politicians, their fellow travelers, and dupes in the news and entertainment media. And to my dismay, that is totally correct; that is, when you're talking about the socialist state that this breed of politicians call Democracy.

In 1932, Roosevelt was swept into the presidency by promising relief for the financially deprived American public. A public, who, incidentally, was being squeezed by the Federal Reserve Board's policies. The "Fed" kept the heat up, restricting the money supply to assure Roosevelt and all the New Deal Congressional and Senatorial candidates election victories, and it worked. Because of this financial pressure, and their ignorance of its cause, Americans were willing to accept radical changes in their relationship with the federal government, believing the promise that it would bring the much needed financial relief.

The first step in this plan was the *Employment Tax*, which was given birth in 1935 with the enactment of the *Social Security Act*. It was the heart of Roosevelt's New Deal, and was necessary so that the Federal Reserve could put its operation into high gear. It is also needed for the United States to enter into a world government.

Because the only jurisdiction of the federal government within the States of the Union, besides the prosecution of certain crimes and the Post Office, is interstate commerce, the first attempt to implement the New Deal programs was to test the waters with the 1934 Railroad Retirement Act. The reason the railroad worker was selected was due to the interstate nature of the railroad business. There was no difference between this Act and the Social Security Act in substance. Both Acts, if imposed on citizens, or resident aliens, would be totally unconstitutional, as was verified by the U.S. Supreme Court:

> *Provision for free medical attendance and nursing, for clothing, for food, for housing, for the education of children, and a hundred other matters, might with equal propriety be proposed as tending to relieve the employee of mental strain and worry. Can it fairly be said that the power of Congress to regulate interstate commerce extends to the prescription of any or all of these things? Is it not apparent that they are really and essentially related solely to the social welfare of the worker, and therefore remote from any regulation of commerce as such? We think the answer is plain. These matters obviously lie outside the orbit of Congressional power. RAILROAD RETIREMENT BOARD et al., Petitioners, v ALTON RAILROAD COMPANY et al. (295 U. S. 330-392.) Argued March 13 and 14, 1935. Decided May 6, 1935.*

This was only a slight inconvenience for Roosevelt. He solved the problem by entering into treaties with other countries, and established the Social Security Administration by signing the Social Security Act into law on August 14, 1935. The way this works is if you, an American citizen, are working in a country with a corresponding treaty, you would be issued a number by that country's administration, by whatever name it may be called, and forced to participate in that country's program, and the same for that country's citizens working in the United States. The following countries have such treaties with the United States: Austria,

Belgium, Canada, Finland, France, Germany, Greece, Ireland, Italy, Luxembourg, Netherlands, Norway, Portugal, Spain, Sweden, Switzerland and the United Kingdom. Of course, this means that the Social Security Act is only imposed on nonresident aliens and foreign corporations working and operating within the United States, and to also include the nationals along with the aliens in the territories and possessions. This is verified within the Social Security Act codified in Title 42 United States Code at §405(c)(2)(B)(i)(I) and (II):

> *(B)(i) In carrying out his duties under subparagraph (A) and subparagraph (F), the Secretary shall take affirmative measures to assure that social security account numbers will, to the maximum extent practicable, be assigned to all members of appropriate groups of categories of individuals by assigning such numbers (or ascertaining that such numbers have already been assigned):*
>
> *(I) to aliens at the time of their lawful admission to the United States either for permanent residence or under other authority of law permitting them to engage in employment in the United States and to other aliens at such time as their status is so changed as to make it lawful for them to engage in such employment;*
>
> *(II) to any individual who is an applicant for or recipient of benefits under any program financed in whole or in part from Federal funds including any child on whose behalf such benefits are claimed by another person;* (Emphasis added.)

This scheme was really aimed at American employers and their employees; the foreigner was only a means to an end. This is verified on the Social Security Administration's web site as follows:

> *The Social Security Act.*
> *The monumental first task was the need to register employers and workers by January 1, 1937, when workers would begin acquiring credits toward old-age insurance*

benefits. Since the SSB [Social Security Board] did not have the resources available to accomplish this, they contracted with the U.S. Postal Service to distribute the applications, beginning in November 1936. The post offices collected the completed forms, typed the Social Security number (SSN) cards, and returned the cards to the applicants. The applications then were forwarded to the SSB's processing center located in Baltimore, Maryland, where the numbers were registered and various employment records established. Over 35 million SSN cards were issued through this procedure in 1936-37.

Without the participation of American employers and their employees, and the resulting collection and payment of social security taxes and the wage withholdings, the excessive amount of Federal Reserve Notes[1] could not be easily removed from the marketplace.[2]

The most insidious part of this whole New Deal socialist plan was to have the Internal Revenue Service, rather than the Social Security Administration, collect the social security withholdings tax. This did two very important things: first, it allowed the Internal Revenue Service to set up files on individual citizens and resident aliens; second, having these files made it possible to implement the so-called *income tax on wages*. The Internal Revenue Service did not, and still does not, have any authority to initiate and maintain files on citizens without the citizen first voluntarily making an application, on Form SS-5, for a social security number card. When that number is issued, it authorizes the Social Security Administration and the Internal Revenue Service to set up a file to record credits (social security withholdings taxes) towards benefits.

Title 5 of the United States Code is entitled *Government Organizations and Employees*, and § 101, *Executive departments*, states that one of these departments is the Department of the Treasury. Chapter 3 of Title 5 contains the powers of these governmental departments (agencies), and in § 301 of that chapter, are contained the *Departmental regulations* which states as follows:

> *Sec.301.— Departmental regulations*
> The head of an Executive department or military department may prescribe regulations for the government of his department, the conduct of its employees, the distribution and performance of its business, and the custody, use, and preservation of its records, papers, and property. This section does not authorize withholding information from the public or limiting the availability of records to the public.

As you can see, there is no authority for any *executive or military department* to initiate and maintain files and or records on citizens, nor can they keep secret from the public the records they do maintain. This includes the Federal Bureau of Investigation, which is under the jurisdiction of the Department of Justice, headed by the Attorney General of the United States, which is also listed in § 101 of Title 5. But you say that § 301 does not say that. Other than certain criminal laws, no law says what can't be done, it enumerates what can be done, and everything else is excluded. It is the same principle as the *void for vagueness* rule.

Income Tax on Wages

The World War II war effort was the excuse to establish the so-called *Income Tax on Wages*, the first withholdings tax, called the *Victory Tax Act of 1942.* The following year *The Current Tax Payment Act of 1943* was passed by Congress. *The Victory Tax Act* was the camel's nose in the tent, and with *The Current Tax Payment Act*, the camel was in the tent.

The government's (Roosevelt and Federal Reserve Bank) spokesman to sell Americans on a permanent withholdings tax was Randolph Paul, the General Counsel of the Treasury Department.

The following is his explanation of *The Current Tax Payment Act of 1943*. It is taken from the text of his speech before the American Bar Association:[3]

> *For the sake of discussion the Current Tax Payment Act of 1943 is divisible into four parts. First, there are the provisions relating to the current collection of income and victory taxes through deduction and withholding at the source on wages. Second, there is the part of the Act which deals with the permanent system of current payment of income tax liabilities not collected by the withholding process. Third, there are the provisions applicable only to this year and necessary to achieve the transition from the delayed payment to the current payment system. And fourth, the Act includes various miscellaneous provisions among which are those giving special tax treatment to members of the armed forces.*

The *Victory Tax* was supposed to be a temporary war-time tax. If you read the above quote studiously you will see the method used by the New Deal Congress and Roosevelt to make the so-called withholding tax on income at the source permanent. Paul then goes on to confirm the permanent status of the Victory Tax and explains the withholding process to the Bar Association. Read this very carefully, for the truth of the federal tax scheme, as I have stated herein, is concealed within it:

> *You are all familiar with the technique of collection of taxes by withholding to the extent that this technique has been employed and is being employed in the collection of Social Security and Victory tax liability. As you know, withholding under the Victory tax was accomplished through a set of provisions specially enacted for that purpose, as part of Chapter 1 of the Internal Revenue Code. Our meager administrative experience with that tax has indicated the desirability of a more flexible system, which will have as its ultimate goal an integration*

between income tax collection at the source and Social Security collection procedure. Convenience for both employer and the Government will be served by the eventual achievement of this goal. For that reason, therefore, it was suggested by the Treasury, and agreed to by the Congress, that the income tax withholding provisions be removed from Chapter 1 of the Internal Revenue Code and be made a new subchapter under Chapter 9 of the Code relating to employment taxes.

The duty to withhold an amount for income and victory taxes is not imposed on all persons making payments of compensation for personal services rendered. First, there must exist, as in the Social Security tax, the employer-employee relationship, as distinguished from the relationship of independent contractors. (Emphasis added.)

Did you see Paul's verification of the truth about the federal tax scheme? Due to their mindset and lack of knowledge about the tax law, this went right over the heads of the Bar members present. For if it hadn't, the tax would have been represented by the Bar Association to the American public altogether differently than it has ever since then. As we proceed, you will see very clearly what I am talking about.

As shown earlier, in Subtitle A the *withholding agent* withholds the *income* tax, and in Subtitle C, the *employer* withholds the *employment* taxes. This is a very important distinction, which will be explained as follows.

Subtitle C is divided into the following Chapters:
   Chapter 21—Federal Insurance Contributions Act.
   Chapter 22—Railroad Retirement Tax Act.
   Chapter 23—Federal Unemployment Tax Act.
   Chapter 23A—Railroad Unemployment Repayment Tax
         Act.

Chapter 24—Collection of Income Tax at Source on Wages.
Chapter 25—General Provisions Relating to Employment
Taxes.

As you can see, Chapters 21 through 23A deal with Social Security taxes, and Chapter 24 contains the converted *Victory Tax Act*, now called the *Collection of Income Tax at Source on Wages*, which was converted from a temporary to a permanent tax by *The Current Tax Payment Act of 1943*, as outlined by Randolph Paul above.

Before we get into Chapter 24, we will examine the distinction between an *employer*, a *withholding agent*, and an *independent contractor*. First, as we established in Chapters 4 and 7 of this book, a withholding agent is mainly someone managing investment funds for a nonresident alien, such as a stockbroker. Second, an independent contractor is just what that term indicates, he certainly is not an employee, but he most certainly can be an *employer*. So if he can be an *employer*, what was the distinction being made by Paul? In order to determine this, we must go to the Code of Federal Regulations (CFR), Title 20, *Employees Benefits*. This is where those unknown individuals within the Congress and the Internal Revenue Service, who write and arrange the federal tax laws, deceptively placed the definitions of the legal terms for *Employment Taxes*. It is obvious that these definitions were kept out of Title 26 of the Code and Regulations, for no other purpose than to hide the true imposition of the federal tax laws:

> *Title 20 CFR § 404.1003, defines* Employment:
> *Employment means, generally, any service covered by social security performed by an employee for his or her employer.*

> *Title 20 CFR § 404.1005, defines Employee:*
> *You must be an employee for your work to be covered as employment for social security purposes.*

Title 20 CFR § 404.1009, defines Employer:
A person is an employer if he or she employs at least one employee.

Title 20 CFR § 404.1041, defines Wages:
(a) <u>The term wages means remuneration paid to you as an employee for employment</u> unless specifically excluded. <u>Wages are counted in determining your entitlement to retirement, survivors', and disability insurance benefits</u>.
(b) If you are paid wages, <u>it is not important what they are called</u>. Salaries, fees, bonuses and commissions on sales or on insurance premiums are wages <u>if they are remuneration paid for employment</u>. (Emphasis added.)

At this point, you may think that this is not conclusive, because Paul said: *that the income tax withholding provisions be removed from Chapter I of the Internal Revenue Code and be made a new subchapter under Chapter 9.*[4] Well, first you must consider that in Chapter 7, I gave you evidence that *wages* were not *income*, and Paul is talking about a withholdings tax on *wages*, and the title to Chapter 24 is *Collection of Income Tax at Source on Wages.*

To dispel any doubts, we will examine what should have been, in my opinion, Section 1 of the Internal Revenue Code—§7806—the code section that tells how to read the Internal Revenue Code:

(a) Cross references
*   The cross references in this title to other portions of the title, or other provisions of law, where the word "see" is used, are made only for convenience, and shall be given no legal effect.*
(b) Arrangement and classification
*   No inference, implication, or presumption of legislative construction shall be drawn or made by reason of the location or grouping of any particular*

section or provision or portion of this title, nor shall any table of contents, table of cross references, or similar outline, analysis, or <u>descriptive matter relating to the contents</u> of this title <u>be given any legal effect</u>. The preceding sentence also applies to the sidenotes and ancillary tables contained in the various prints of this Act before its enactment into law. (Emphasis added.)

The code section in Chapter 24 that imposes the tax on wages is § 3402. It is entitled *Income Tax Collected at Source*, which is *descriptive matter relating to the contents* of the code section. The only problem is, nowhere within § 3402 itself can you find the words *Income Tax,* except in reference to Subtitle A in three places. As demonstrated in § 3402 (a)(1) below, the only legal term to be found is *wages*.

All code sections start right after the *descriptive matter*. For example, § 3402 begins with:

§ 3402. Income tax collected at source.

The actual code section starts with:

(a) Requirement of withholding.
    (1) In general. Except as otherwise provided in this section, every employer making payment of <u>wages</u> shall deduct and withhold upon such wages a tax determined in accordance with tables or computational procedures prescribed by the Secretary. (Emphasis added.)

The fact that *wages* are not *income*, proven earlier in this book, should be enough evidence to prove the point. But we're going to go even further to prove the point, far beyond any reasonable person's doubt.

The only way the New Dealers could codify the *Victory Tax*

and make it Constitutional was to link it with social security taxes and make it voluntary for citizens and resident aliens. It was linked to Social Security as explained by Paul with *The Current Tax Payment Act of 1943*. And it is made voluntary within § 3402 at paragraph (p)(3)(B), as follows:

> *(p) Voluntary withholding agreements.*
> *(3) Authority for other voluntary withholding. The Secretary is authorized by regulations to provide for withholding—*
> *(B) from any other type of payment with respect to which the Secretary finds that withholding would be appropriate under the provisions of this chapter, if the employer and employee, or the person making and the person receiving such other type of payment, agree to such withholding. Such agreement shall be in such form and manner as the Secretary may by regulations prescribe. For purposes of this chapter (and so much of subtitle F as relates to this chapter), remuneration or other payments with respect to which such agreement is made shall be treated as if they were wages paid by an employer to an employee to the extent that such remuneration is paid or other payments are made during the period for which the agreement is in effect. (Emphasis added.)*

The connection to the *Victory Tax*, referred to by Paul as an income tax, is set out more fully in the implementing regulation for § 3402(p) as follows:

> *26 CFR, § 31.3402(p)-1 Voluntary withholding agreements.*
> *(a) In general. An employee and his employer may enter into an agreement under section 3402(p) to provide for the withholding of income tax upon payments of amounts described in paragraph (b)(1) of § 31.3401(a)-3, made after December 31, 1970. An agreement may be entered into under this section only*

115

with respect to amounts which are includible in the gross income of the employee under section 61, and must be applicable to all such amounts paid by the employer to the employee. The amount to be withheld pursuant to an agreement under section 3402(p) shall be determined under the rules contained in section 3402 and the regulations thereunder.

What is this voluntary withholding agreement? It is identified in the same regulation, § 31.3402(p)-1 as follows:

(b) Form and duration of agreement.
(1)

(i) Except as provided in subdivision (ii) of this subparagraph, an employee who desires to enter into an agreement under section 3402(p) shall furnish his employer with Form W-4 (withholding exemption certificate) executed in accordance with the provisions of section 3402(f) and the regulations thereunder. The furnishing of such Form W-4 shall constitute a request for withholding.

(ii) In the case of an employee who desires to enter into an agreement under section 3402(p) with his employer, if the employee performs services (in addition to those to be the subject of the agreement) the remuneration for which is subject to mandatory income tax withholding by such employer, or if the employee wishes to specify that the agreement terminate on a specific date, the employee shall furnish the employer with a request for withholding which shall be signed by the employee, and shall contain—

(a) The name, address, and social security number of the employee making the request,
(b) The name and address of the employer,
(c) A statement that the employee desires withholding of Federal income tax, and if

*applicable, of qualified State individual income
tax (see paragraph (d)(3)(i) of § 301.6361-1 of
this chapter (Regulations on Procedures and
Administration)), and*

(d) *If the employee desires that the agreement
terminate on a specific date, the date of
termination of the agreement.*

That's right, the Form W-4, the form that employers ask
employees to complete and return to the employer, IS
VOLUNTARY! Anyone who questions the requirement of this
form is usually told by the employer that the completion of the W-
4 Form is required to work as an employee, and this is true, but only
for the employee defined within the Internal Revenue Regulations,
which we will cover later on in this Chapter.

Notice in this regulation the Form W-4 is called *withholding
exemption certificate*. The Form W-4 is actually entitled *Employee
Withholding Allowance Certificate*. There is a big difference
between the two. The former indicates that it is only used for
claiming exemptions, while the latter states that the employee is
voluntarily allowing the employer to withhold the tax, which is
actually the case.

Not only is the Form W-4 voluntary, but as stated in the
regulation above, it can be terminated. Not only terminated by
specifying the date, but at any time, as provided for in the same
regulation, as follows:

(2) *An agreement under section 3402 (p) shall be effective
for such period as the employer and employee
mutually agree upon. However, either the employer
or the employee may terminate the agreement prior to
the end of such period by furnishing a signed written
notice to the other. Unless the employer and employee
agree to an earlier termination date, the notice shall
be effective with respect to the first payment of an*

amount in respect of which the agreement is in effect which is made on or after the first "status determination date" (January 1, May 1, July 1, and October 1 of each year) that occurs at least 30 days after the date on which the notice is furnished. If the employee executes a new Form W-4, the request upon which an agreement under section 3402 (p) is based shall be attached to, and constitute a part of, such new Form W-4.

Employment taxes, including the wages tax in § 3402, are the only taxes that require the use of government identifying numbers: Social Security Number (SSN), Employer Identification Number (EIN), and Individual Taxpayer Identification Number (ITIN).[5] Employers need the EIN, but withholding agents do not. Withholding agents without any identifying numbers existed for a short period during the temporary enactment of the income tax in the 1860s, and again from March 21st, 1916 on, when the Office of Commissioner of Internal Revenue issued the order, *T.D. 2313*, covered in Chapter IV of this book, implementing the Income Tax Act of October 3, 1913.

Withholding agents are asked to complete an SS-4 Form, *Application for Employer Identification Number*. Directly under the title of this form, the following is found: *(For use by employers and others.)*. In fact, the SS-4 Form instructs the Withholding agent on Line 12 to enter the:

12. First day wages or annuities were paid or will be paid (Mo., Day, Year). Note: If the applicant is a withholding agent, enter date income will first be paid to nonresident alien. (Mo., Day, Year).

All Internal Revenue forms that require a government identification number, such as the following commonly used forms—W-2, W-4, W-9, and 1099—are required to be used only for Employment Taxes. Of these forms, the Form W-9 is the most graphic example to prove my contentions about its restriction to Employment Taxes, and my contentions about the federal tax scheme.

Form **W-9** (Rev. January 2002) Department of the Treasury Internal Revenue Service	**Request for Taxpayer** **Identification Number and Certification**	Give form to the requester. Do not send to the IRS.

Print or type — *See Specific Instructions on page 2.*

Name

Business name, if different from above

Check appropriate box: ☐ Individual/ Sole proprietor   ☐ Corporation   ☐ Partnership   ☐ Other ▶ ....   ☐ Exempt from backup withholding

Address (number, street, and apt. or suite no.)   Requester's name and address (optional)

City, state, and ZIP code

List account number(s) here (optional)

Part I   Taxpayer Identification Number (TIN)

Enter your TIN in the appropriate box. For individuals, this is your social security number (SSN). **However, for a resident alien, sole proprietor, or disregarded entity, see the Part I instructions on page 2.** For other entities, it is your employer identification number (EIN). If you do not have a number, see **How to get a TIN** on page 2.

Note: *If the account is in more than one name, see the chart on page 2 for guidelines on whose number to enter.*

Social security number

or

Employer identification number

Part II   Certification

Under penalties of perjury, I certify that:

1. The number shown on this form is my correct taxpayer identification number (or I am waiting for a number to be issued to me), **and**
2. I am not subject to backup withholding because: **(a)** I am exempt from backup withholding, or **(b)** I have not been notified by the Internal Revenue Service (IRS) that I am subject to backup withholding as a result of a failure to report all interest or dividends, or **(c)** the IRS has notified me that I am no longer subject to backup withholding, **and**
3. I am a U.S. person (including a U.S. resident alien).

Certification instructions. You must cross out item **2** above if you have been notified by the IRS that you are currently subject to backup withholding because you have failed to report all interest and dividends on your tax return. For real estate transactions, item 2 does not apply. For mortgage interest paid, acquisition or abandonment of secured property, cancellation of debt, contributions to an individual retirement arrangement (IRA), and generally, payments other than interest and dividends, you are not required to sign the Certification, but you must provide your correct TIN. (See the instructions on page 2.)

The first indication that this form is not required of citizens is the lack of an OMB Control Number in the upper right-hand corner. This alone is strong evidence that this form is not designed for use by a citizen of the United States. The Paperwork Reduction Act of 1980 pertains to lawful information requests required of citizens, and the lack of that number is a strong clue that this form is for aliens.

Now notice in Part II Certification, item 3: *I am a U.S. person (including a U.S. resident alien)*. It is only natural for anyone ignorant of the facts about the federal tax scheme to assume that this would include both resident aliens and citizens. But that is not the case. The use of the term *U.S. person* is just one more attempt to deceive the uninformed public. To prove my point, we

119

will examine the regulation for § 6109, which is found in Subtitle F, *Procedures and Administration*, the subtitle that implements the five categories of taxation. Our evidence is found in Title 26 CFR at § 301.6109-1(b)(2)(i), (ii), (iii) and (iv). To substantiate the evidence we will start in paragraph (c):

> (c) *Requirement to furnish another's number.*
>
> *Every person required under this title to make a return, statement, or other document must furnish such taxpayer identifying numbers of other U.S. persons and foreign persons that are described in paragraph (b)(2)(i), (ii), or (iii) of this section as required by the forms and the accompanying instructions.*

This relates directly to the Form W-9, and indirectly to all other Internal Revenue Service forms that require an identifying number, and those requesting an identifying number from those required to have such a number. Now let's go see who the Internal Revenue Service identifies as *U.S. persons*:

> *(b)*
>
> *(2) Foreign persons. The provisions of paragraph (b)(1) of this section regarding the furnishing of one's own number shall apply to the following foreign persons—*
>
> *(i) A foreign person that has income effectively connected with the conduct of a U.S. trade or business at any time during the taxable year;*
>
> *(ii) A foreign person that has a U.S. office or place of business or a U.S. fiscal or paying agent at any time during the taxable year;*
>
> *(iii) A nonresident alien treated as a resident under section 6013(g) or (h);*
>
> *(iv) A foreign person that makes a return of tax (including income, estate, and gift tax returns), an amended return, or a refund claim under this title but excluding information returns, statements, or*

documents;

As you can see for yourself, the only persons[6] that are required to have and use any government identification numbers, (ITIN, SSN, and EIN) are nonresident aliens and foreign corporation or other foreign companies and businesses.

The use of the term *U.S. person* in this instance just demonstrates the lengths that those within the Internal Revenue Service, who know the truth about the lawful imposition of federal taxes, will go to hide that truth.

Then of course, there are the ignorantly enlightened experts. Some years ago, one of the members of the *Save-A-Patriot Fellowship* came into my office and asked if I would participate in a conference call with a tax attorney who had earned many letters after his name, by enduring seventeen years of tax law in college. I replied that I would be delighted to do so, and there and then succeeded in bringing this individual on the phone. As there was great interest in this event in both offices, the conversation was on the speaker phone.

He started out by giving me his well-earned collegian pedigree. I responded by telling him that my degree was SHK. He replied, 'SHK.' "I said, Yes, School of Hard Knocks." He did not respond, but rather started right in by telling me about the imposition of the Internal Revenue Code.

After about four or five minutes, I asked him if I could ask him a question. He responded, "Yes." I then asked him if he was familiar with § 3402. He responded, "Yes." I then asked him if the Code required an individual to file a tax return in conjunction with that code section. He responded, "Yes." I then asked him if he agreed that § 6012 was the code section requiring an individual to file a tax return. He answered yes. I then asked him if he had a copy of the Code, and if so, would he read § 6012 with me. He answered, "Yes." We both got our Code books and turned to

121

§6012. I started reading it and read:

> *(a) General rule*
> *Returns with respect to income taxes under subtitle A shall be made by the following:*
> *(1) (A) Every individual having for the taxable year gross income which equals or exceeds the exemption amount, except that a return shall not be required of an individual—*

I stopped him, asking, "What subtitle does that say?" He responded, "A." I then asked, "What subtitle is § 3402 in?" He got real quiet and did not respond. I said, "Isn't § 3402 in Subtitle C?" He very quietly answered, "Yes." We went on to cover some more code sections, and he was amazed how much he did *not* learn about the Code in those seventeen years spent learning about it.

Self-Employment Tax

As promised in Chapter VII, we will now examine Chapter 2 of the Internal Revenue Code, *Self-Employment Tax*. The Social Security Internet web site tells us that *self-employment taxes* were authorized by Congress in the amendments made to the Social Security Act in 1950:

> *1950 Amendments*
> *The 1950 amendments substantially expanded the scope of the Old-Age and Survivors Insurance (OASI) program by extending coverage to about 10 million additional workers. The amendments also greatly increased benefit levels, liberalized eligibility requirements, and increased the maximum amount of covered earnings considered for both benefit and tax purposes (the "earnings base"). Major provisions:*
> *Covered regularly employed farm and domestic workers, self-employed workers (except farmers and professionals), federal civilian employees not under a*

federal civil service retirement system (e.g.,
temporary employees), Americans employed outside
the United States by American employers, and
workers in Puerto Rico and the Virgin Islands. Not-
for-profit organizations could elect coverage for their
employees (except ministers). State and local
governments could elect coverage for their employees
not under public employee retirement systems.
(Emphasis added.)

The *self-employment tax* was more difficult to present to
American businessmen than the social security tax to employees. I
was sixteen years old when its misrepresentation was being sold to
the public by the news media. I can recall the editorial comments
phrased in such a way as to make it sound like businessmen were
required to participate. The problem that the socialist planners had
was that the average businessman was not interested in applying for
a social security number card and participating in that welfare
program. Therefore, to solve this problem, it had to appear that the
businessman was required to participate. This could not be
accomplished lawfully if the law was written for Subtitle C of the
Internal Revenue Code. Wherefore, the law was written for
Subtitle A, and written in such a manner to make it sound as though
there was a lawful requirement for the self-employed businessman
to obtain and use a government identifying number as exemplified
in the following regulation on *self-employment*:

§ 1.1401-1 Tax on self-employment income.
(a) There is imposed, in addition to other taxes, a tax
upon the self-employment income of every individual at
the rates prescribed in section 1401(a) (old-age,
survivors, and disability insurance) and (b) (hospital
insurance). (See subparagraphs (1) and (2) of paragraph
(b) of this section.) This tax shall be levied, assessed, and
collected as part of the income tax imposed by subtitle A
of the Code and, except as otherwise expressly provided,
will be included with the tax imposed by section 1 or 3 in

123

computing any deficiency or overpayment and in computing the interest and additions to any deficiency, overpayment, or tax. (Emphasis added.)

In contrast to this, the regulations written for the enforcement of social security statutes, found in Title 20 of the Code of Federal Regulations, *Employee's Benefits*, are more revealing of the voluntary aspect for self-employeds' participation:

§ 404.1065 Self-employment coverage.
For an individual to have self-employment coverage under Social Security, the individual must be engaged in a trade or business and have net earnings from self-employment that can be counted as self-employment income for Social Security purposes. (Emphasis added.)

Of course, from what you have learned about employment taxes earlier in this Chapter, you know that no citizen of a State of the Union can be forced to obtain or use a government identifying number. The apparent logic of putting the self-employment tax in Subtitle A of the Internal Revenue Code and attaching its imposition to §§ 1 and 3, was that it would come under a tax treaty, and as such, pose no constitutional conflicts. This is illustrated in the following regulation found in Title 20:

§ 404.1913 Precluding dual coverage.
(a) General. Employment or self-employment or services recognized as equivalent under the Act or the social security system of the foreign country shall, on or after the effective date of the agreement, result in a period of coverage under the U.S. system or under the foreign system, but not under both. Methods shall be set forth in the agreement for determining under which system the employment, self-employment, or other service shall result in a period of coverage.

Additionally, the *self-employment tax* can be enforced and

required of the nationals lawfully within the possessions of the United States as verified by the following internal revenue regulation:

§ 1.6017-1 Self-employment tax returns.
(a) In general. (1) Every individual, other than a nonresident alien, having net earnings from self-employment, as defined in section 1402, of $400 or more for the taxable year shall make a return of such earnings. For purposes of this section, an individual who is a resident of the Virgin Islands, Puerto Rico, or (for any taxable year beginning after 1960) Guam or American Samoa is not to be considered a nonresident alien individual. See paragraph (d) of § 1.1402(b)-1. A return is required under this section if an individual has self-employment income, as defined in section 1402(b), even though he may not be required to make a return under section 6012 for purposes of the tax imposed by section 1 or 3. Provisions applicable to returns under section 6012(a) shall be applicable to returns under this section.

This is effectively used by obfuscation of the definitions of the legal terms, as I pointed out earlier with the legal term *United States*. The 1939 Internal Revenue Code regarding this is more explicit than the 1954 and 1986 Codes. In the 1939 Code, it gives the definition of the legal term *State* when used in *employment tax* statutes:

Section 1426, Definitions.
(e) State.—The term "State" includes Alaska, Hawaii, and the District of Columbia.

Wherefore, everywhere you find the word *State* within the statutes for *Employment* or *Self-Employment Taxes*, it is referring to the possessions of the United States and not the States of the Union.

Chapter 2 is comprised of three code sections: 1401, *Rate of tax*; 1402, *Definitions*; and 1403, *Miscellaneous provisions*. Section 1401, read independently with no further research, would certainly give the average individual or professional with the prevailing mindset the impression that everybody, including citizens and resident aliens, were subject by law to pay a *self-employment tax*:

> *(a) Old-age, survivors, and disability insurance.*
> *In addition to other taxes, there shall be imposed for each taxable year, on the self-employment income of every individual, a tax equal to the following percent of the amount of the self-employment income for such taxable year:*

Paragraph (b) gives the false impression that the government can be in the health insurance business, and tax you for the operation thereof:

> *(b) Hospital insurance.*
> *In addition to the tax imposed by the preceding subsection, there shall be imposed for each taxable year, on the self-employment income of every individual, a tax equal to the following percent of the amount of the self-employment income for such taxable year:*

Paragraph (c) actually discusses the truth that the social security welfare programs are, other than their imposition in the possessions, treaty-based:

> *(c) Relief from taxes in cases covered by certain international agreements.*
> *During any period in which there is in effect an agreement entered into pursuant to section 233 of the Social Security Act with any foreign country, the self-employment income of an individual shall be exempt from the taxes imposed by this section to the extent that such self-employment income is subject under such agreement*

126

*to taxes or contributions for similar purposes under the
social security system of such foreign country.*

Section 1402 is where we find the deceptive use of legal
terms, in particular, the legal term *trade or business*:

§ 1402 Definitions

*(a) Net earnings from self-employment.--The term "net
earnings from self-employment" means the gross income
derived by an individual from any <u>trade or business</u>
carried on by such individual, less the deductions allowed.
. . . (Emphasis added.)*

Paragraph (c) defines this legal term:

*(c) Trade or business.—The term "trade or business",
when used with reference to self-employment income or
net earnings from self-employment, <u>shall have the same
meaning as when used in section 162</u> (relating to trade or
business expenses), except that such term shall not
include— . . . [Emphasis added]*

This deception goes beyond the average, for when we
examine § 162 very carefully, we find that the meaning of *trade or
business* is not defined at all:

*(a) In general.
There shall be allowed as a deduction all the ordinary
and necessary expenses paid or incurred during the
taxable year in carrying on any trade or business,
including —
(1)   a reasonable allowance for salaries or other
compensation for personal services actually rendered;
(2)   traveling expenses (including amounts expended
for meals and lodging other than amounts which are
lavish or extravagant under the circumstances) while
away from home in the pursuit of a trade or business;
and*

(3) rentals or other payments required to be made as a condition to the continued use or possession, for purposes of the trade or business, of property to which the taxpayer has not taken or is not taking title or in which he has no equity.

For purposes of the preceding sentence, the place of residence of a Member of Congress (including any Delegate and Resident Commissioner) within the State, congressional district, or possession which he represents in Congress shall be considered his home, but amounts expended by such Members within each taxable year for living expenses shall not be deductible for income tax purposes in excess of $3,000. For purposes of paragraph (2), the taxpayer shall not be treated as being temporarily away from home during any period of employment if such period exceeds 1 year.

When the legal term is not defined within the particular statute, then to determine the definition you must go to Chapter 79, the general definitions, and in this case the code section would be §7701(a)(26):

§ 7701. Definitions
(a) When used in this title, where not otherwise distinctly expressed or manifestly incompatible with the intent thereof—

(26) Trade or business.—The term "trade or business" includes the performance of the functions of a public office. (Emphasis added.)

So there is a hint of truth in §162 after all, in the last paragraph. Of course, if the law is applied against members of Congress or other public offices, merely for holding of that office, the law would be clearly unconstitutional, for I cannot find any authorization within the federal Constitution for such a tax. Herewith, we have once again, in this Chapter, proven the Constitutionality of the Internal Revenue Code.

Chapter 9

SUBTITLE F:
PROCEDURE & ADMINISTRATION
ASSESSMENT AUTHORITY

Subtitle F contains the procedures for, and the administration of, the five categories of taxation, Subtitles A through E, as was outlined in Chapter 7. Here too, we find harmony with the Constitution. In this Chapter, we will cover the tax assessment authority of the IRS; in Chapter 10 the enforcement authority; and Chapter 11 the criminal provisions of the Internal Revenue Code and the enforcement thereof.

Hypothetically, let's say that you have learned enough, and that you do not have any foreign earned income and just stop filing tax returns. In that case, what usually happens, after a year or two, or three, the IRS computer generates a Taxpayer Delinquency Investigation (TDI) letter. The TDI program is a series of four computer-generated letters, identified by IRS computer codes CP 515 through CP 518.[1] These TDI notices are supposed to be sent thirty days apart, but the IRS is not consistent in always sending all four notices—a "tax protestor" designation causes "acceleration of notices" skipping the 2nd and 3rd notices.

The Privacy Act of 1974 requires that the Internal Revenue Service include a Privacy Act Notice along with the TDI notice. This Privacy Act Notice is entitled Notice 609, and is reproduced here for our edification:

Department of the Treasury
Internal Revenue Service

Notice 609
(Revised June 1999)

Privacy Act Notice

The Privacy Act of 1974 says that when we ask you for information, we must first tell you our legal right to ask for the information, why we are asking for it, and how it will be used. We must also tell you what could happen if you do not provide it and whether or not you must respond under the law.

This notice applies to tax returns and any papers filed with them. It also applies to any questions we need to ask you so we can complete, correct, or process your return; figure your tax; and collect tax, interest, or penalties.

Our legal right to ask for information is Internal Revenue Code sections 6001, 6011, and 6012(a) and their regulations. They say that you must file a return or statement with us for any tax you are liable for. Your response is mandatory under these sections.

Code section 6109 and its regulations say that you must show your social security number or individual taxpayer identification number on what you file. You must also fill in all parts of the tax form that apply to you. This is so we know who you are, and can process your return and papers. You do not have to check the boxes for the Presidential Election Campaign Fund.

We ask for tax return information to carry out the U.S. tax laws. We need it to figure and collect the right amount of tax.

We may give the information to the Department of Justice and to other Federal agencies, as provided by law. We may also give it to cities, states, the District of Columbia, and U.S. commonwealths or possessions to carry out their tax laws. And we may give it to certain foreign governments under tax treaties they have with the United States.

Cat. No. 45963A

If you do not file a return, do not give us the information we ask for, or provide fraudulent information, the law says that we may have to charge you penalties and, in certain cases, subject you to criminal prosecution. We may also have to disallow the exemptions, exclusions, credits, deductions, or adjustments shown on your tax return. This could make your tax higher or delay any refund. Interest may also be charged.

Please keep this notice with your records. You may want to refer to it if we ask you for other information. If you have questions about the rules for filing and giving information, please call or visit any Internal Revenue Service office.

Therefore the party must be foreign

Notice 609
(Rev. June 1999)

First, notice that within the first paragraph the IRS is required to:

1. Tell you their legal right to ask for the information requested;
2. Tell you the reason they want it;
3. Tell you how it is to be used;
4. Tell whether the law requires you to respond; and,
5. Tell you the consequences of not providing it.

The second paragraph is out of place, and I do not believe it is out of place accidentally, as it leads the reader to believe there is a requirement before proving so, as required by the Privacy Act.

The third paragraph should be the second paragraph, for if there is no legal right to ask, then there is no need to tell you why the information is wanted.

The fourth paragraph confirms that the notice should be sent only to nonresident aliens. This paragraph is a good example of the IRS applying the law deceptively. For if you did not have the knowledge that only nonresident alien individuals were required to have and use social security numbers, you would have presumed that they were talking to you.

The fifth paragraph is a valid statement, but deceptive depending on who received the notice.

The last sentence of the sixth paragraph tells the truth about the federal tax scheme, and the social security taxes.

The seventh paragraph is the fear paragraph, and potential evidence of the misapplication of the law, if the IRS takes further steps against a citizen or resident alien. And if the the agent that receives and acts on the case file has knowledge of the federal tax scheme, it is evidence of a seditious act.

Before we move on to examine the statutes cited as the IRS's authority, I'll point out some deceptively creative use of the King's English. Look at the first paragraph—notice it says: *The Privacy Act . . . says . . . we must tell you our legal right to ask for the information, . . .* Now look at the third paragraph—notice it says: *Our legal right to ask for information is . . . They say that you must file a return or statement with us for any tax you are liable for.* The Privacy Act requires them to tell YOU their legal right to ask YOU for the information. Yet, when they state what the authorizing statutes are, they leave YOU out of the response, stating: *Our legal right to ask for information. . . .* Then, immediately after that, when they again use the personal pronoun YOU, it is meaningless

131

because it is qualified with: . . . *for any tax you are liable for.* Nowhere are they saying that these statutes say that YOU are liable for the taxes imposed.

Now let's look at the legal right they cited to ask for information, §§6001, 6011, and 6012(a). All three of these code sections are in Chapter 61, *Information and Returns.* Internal Revenue Code § 6001 states:

> *Every person liable for any tax imposed by this title, or for the collection thereof, shall keep such records,* render *such statements, make such returns, and comply with such rules and regulations as the Secretary may from time to time prescribe. Whenever in the judgment of the Secretary it is necessary, he may require any person, by notice served upon such person or by regulations, to make such returns, render such statements, or keep such records, as the Secretary deems sufficient to show whether or not such person is liable for tax under this title. The only records which an employer shall be required to keep under this section in connection with charged tips shall be charge receipts, records necessary to comply with section 6053(c), and copies of statements furnished by employees under section 6053(a).* (Emphasis added.)

So this pertains to just those who are made liable by some other code section. Notice that the IRS neglected to cite the other code section in the Notice 609.

The second Internal Revenue Code cited, § 6011, states:

> *(a) General rule*
> *When required by regulations prescribed by the Secretary any person made liable for any tax imposed by this title, or with respect to the collection thereof, shall make a return or statement according to the forms and regulations prescribed by the Secretary.*

Every person required to make a return or statement shall include therein the information required by such forms or regulations.

(b) Identification of taxpayer

The Secretary is authorized to require such information with respect to persons subject to the taxes imposed by chapter 21 or chapter 24 as is necessary or helpful in securing proper identification of such persons.

(c) Returns, etc., of DISCS and former DISCS and FSC's and former FSC's

(1) Records and information

A DISC or former DISC or a FSC or former FSC shall for the taxable year —

(A) furnish such information to persons who were shareholders at any time during such taxable year, and to the Secretary, and

(B) keep such records, as may be required by regulations prescribed by the Secretary.

(2) Returns

A DISC shall file for the taxable year such returns as may be prescribed by the Secretary by forms or regulations.

(d) Authority to require information concerning section 912 allowances.

The Secretary may by regulations require any individual who receives allowances which are excluded from gross income under section 912 for any taxable year to include on his return of the taxes imposed by subtitle A for such taxable year such information with respect to the amount and type of such allowances as the Secretary determines to be appropriate.

(e) Regulations requiring returns on magnetic media, etc.

(1) In general

The Secretary shall prescribe regulations providing standards for determining which returns must be filed on magnetic media or in other machine-readable form. The Secretary may not require returns of any tax imposed by subtitle A on individuals, estates, and trusts to be other than on paper forms supplied by the Secretary.

(2) Requirements of regulations

In prescribing regulations under paragraph (1), the Secretary —

(A) shall not require any person to file returns on magnetic media unless such person is required to file at least 250 returns during the calendar year, and

(B) shall take into account (among other relevant factors) the ability of the taxpayer to comply at reasonable cost with the requirements of such regulations.

(f) Income, estate, and gift taxes

For requirement that returns of income, estate, and gift taxes be made whether or not there is tax liability, see subparts B and C. (Emphasis added.)

As stated in paragraph (a), the Secretary must promulgate a regulation that would identify in some way the person required to file a tax return. The regulation promulgated for § 6011(a) reads the same way—*every person liable* and *when required*—except for the identification of the nonresident alien individual and the foreign corporation. As you have read for yourself, this code section depends on other sections of the Internal Revenue Code to cause the *liability* or *requirement.*

Paragraph (b) speaks for itself. As you have learned in Chapter VIII, this paragraph is identifying a liability for nonresident aliens and foreign corporations.

Paragraph (c) also speaks for itself. As you have learned in Chapter 7, a DISC is a Domestic International Sales Corporation, and a FSC is a corporation that was created or organized under the laws of any foreign government.

Paragraph (d) authorizes the request for information involving foreign earned income.

Paragraph (e) concerns requirements for professional tax return preparers.

And finally, paragraph (f) is the requirement for the filing of tax returns for income, estate and gift taxes. Subpart B is entitled Income Tax Returns, and there is where we find the third code section cited in Notice 609, § 6012(a), which we already examined and concluded in Chapter VIII as requiring the filing of Form 2555, *Foreign Earned Income*, and not requiring any filing of tax returns for the withholding taxes within Subtitle C. **Once again it is demonstrated that citizens and resident aliens are only subject to a tax on their foreign earned income and not subject at all to the employment taxes.**

Subtitle B: Estate and Gift Taxes

Estate and *Gift Taxes* are contained in Subtitle B of the Internal Revenue Code. This Subtitle contains Chapter 11, *Estate Tax*; Chapter 12, *Gift Tax*; Chapter 13, *Tax on Generation-Skipping Transfers*; and Chapter 14, *Special Valuation Rules*.

When measuring the applicability of the *estate* and *gift tax* against the taxing provisions found in Article 1, Section 8, Clause 1, of the Constitution, they could only reasonably come under the excise tax provisions. But as we already have discovered, the Supreme Court has defined *excise taxes* thusly: *Excises are taxes on the manufacture, sale and consumption of certain commodities, privileges, particular business transactions, vocations, and occupations.*[2] Wherefore, any individual or individuals receiving through inheritance the estate of another or a gift from another is certainly not engaged in any of these activities. As was illustrated before, the only taxes Congress can lay and collect are *duties*, *imposts* and *excises*. Wherefore, *estate* and *gift taxes* cannot be *excises*, and they certainly do not have anything to do with the *importation or exportation of commodities*;[3] they would have to come under the *direct* taxing provisions found in Article 1, Section 2, Clause 3. And that being the case, they could not be imposed on *gifts* or the *estates* of citizens and resident aliens within the fifty States, for they would then be a *direct tax without apportionment*.

Subtitle B is a prime example of deceptive writing to take advantage of the public's mindset about federal taxation. In examining it, we must keep in mind that words mean what the law makers say they mean. In other words, when the legal term *States* is used in Subtitle C, it means only the island possessions of the United States.[4] (Within the *definitions* listed within §3121 of Subtitle C, the District of Columbia (D.C.) is included along with the possessions, but understanding that because the Constitution only allows the District of Columbia to be the seat of government, this is jurisdictionally impossible no matter what the law says.) On the other hand, § 4612, *Definitions and special rules*, demonstrates how the United States is defined when it means the States of the Union:

> *(a) Definitions. For the purposes of this subchapter—*
> > *(4) United States.*
> > > *(A) In general*
> > > > *The term "United States" means the 50 States, the District of Columbia, the Commonwealth of Puerto Rico, any possession of the United States, the Commonwealth of the Northern Mariana Islands, and the Trust Territory of the Pacific Islands.*

Understanding these rules of legislative construction, and the deceptive writing techniques exhibited so far, let's examine the imposition of *estate* and *gift taxes* found in Subtitle B, at § 2001, and § 2501, respectively.

§ 2001 Imposition and rate of tax.
  (a) Imposition.
    A tax is hereby imposed on the transfer of the taxable estate of every decedent who is a citizen or resident of the United States.

§ 2501 Imposition of tax.
  (a) Taxable transfers
    (1) General rule
      A tax, computed as provided in section 2502 is hereby imposed for each calendar year on the transfer of property by gift during such calendar year by any individual resident or nonresident.

On their face, these two statutes could be considered as saying that everyone (citizens, resident aliens, nonresident aliens, and nationals) within the United States (the 50 States and island possessions), under the given circumstances, owed both *estate* and *gift taxes*. Of course, we know that is not the case, for if it were, it would conflict with the Constitution, as explained above.

To show that this is not the case, we will examine the regulation that implements § 2001, which states in pertinent part:

§ 20.0-1 Introduction.
  (a) In general. (1) The regulations in this part (Part 20, Subchapter B, Chapter 1, Title 26, Code of Federal regulations) are designated "Estate Tax Regulations." These regulations pertain to (i) the Federal estate tax imposed by chapter 11 of subtitle B of the Internal Revenue Code . . .
  (b) Scope of Regulations. (1) Estates of citizen or residents. Subchapter A of chapter 11 of the Code pertains to the taxation of the estate of a person who was a citizen or resident of the United States at the time of his death. . . The term "United States" as used in the estate tax regulations, includes only the States and the District of

Columbia. *The term also includes the territories of Alaska and Hawaii prior to their admission as States.* (Emphasis added.)

As shown here, the term *United States* in Subtitle B has the same meaning as the term *States* has in Subtitle C, making the entire subtitle Constitutional, and giving evidence that the *estate* and *gift taxes* are not imposed on transferable property to citizens or resident aliens within the States of the Union, but rather on nationals within the possessions of the United States, the federal states.

Another Code section in Subtitle F that is very revealing of the federal tax scheme as outlined in this book is § 6654(e)(2), which states in pertinent part:

> *(e) Exceptions*
> > *(2) Where no tax liability for preceding taxable year*
> > *No addition to tax shall be imposed under subsection (a) for any taxable year if —*
> > > *(A) the preceding taxable year was a taxable year of 12 months,*
> > > *(B) the individual did not have any liability for tax for the preceding taxable year, and*
> > > *(C) the individual was a citizen or resident of the United States throughout the preceding taxable year.* (Emphasis added.)

It cannot be made any plainer than that.

One of the major abuses of the Internal Revenue Code by IRS employees is the audit and assessment process. It has been my personal experience that this is not always intentional. Just like most other Americans, many IRS employees are ignorant of the law. But, through personal experience, I have also found that when they are enlightened, most continue violating the law. It is always the same age-old story when government expands past its lawful function. Those benefiting by the unlawful expansion seem to always fall back on "I am only following orders."

Ten or so years ago, the Internal Revenue Service Centers in Philadelphia, Pennsylvania and Ogden, Utah both forwarded to me, unsolicited, representative numbers that would allow me to represent anyone before any Internal Revenue Service administrative hearing. The IRS regulations only allow a representative to have one number, so I returned the number forwarded by the Ogden Service Center and kept the one from Philadelphia.

With this number, I started to represent Fellowship members at IRS assessment appeals conferences. The process began when the IRS would send the member a notice of deficiency, which can only be issued in accordance with § 6212 of Subtitle F. The argument that I made on the member's behalf was very simple—the Internal Revenue Service had no statutory authority to issue a notice of a deficiency assessment to the member in the first place. Of course, when this was shown to the appeals officer, they were totally amazed, and the result in 99% of the appeals conferences was that the assessment process, for reasons known only to the appeals officer, was at a dead end.

It did not take long for this to be noticed by the hierarchy of the IRS. I received a letter from the District Director of the Baltimore IRS Office, notifying me that my representative number had been revoked. I responded by asking for the formal reason for this action, and until this day I have not received an answer to this inquiry. I made Privacy Act requests for all the documents involving the revocation of the representative number, but I have been totally stonewalled.

The argument used regarding § 6212 just bolsters the facts about the federal tax scheme that have been presented to you in this book. This code section is just one more link in the daisy chain of evidence proving my point. Section 6212 states in pertinent part:

(a) In general

If the Secretary determines that there is a deficiency in respect of any tax imposed by subtitles A or B or chapter 41, 42, 43, or 44 he is authorized to send notice of such deficiency to the taxpayer by certified mail or registered mail.

To exemplify what this statute is saying, let's consider the following hypothetical scenario. You give an employer an IRS *Form W-4, Employee's Withholding Allowance Certificate*, and work for *wages*, and at the end of the year that *employer* gives you an IRS *Form W-2, Wage and Tax Statement*. You use the information on the *Form W-2* to compute a tax liability on an IRS Form 1040. You then attach the *Form W-2* to the *Form 1040* and forward the forms to the IRS Service Center as instructed. The question arises, according to § 6212 above, can the IRS send you a *Notice of Deficiency*? The answer is abundantly clear—no, of course not. As clearly stated in the code section, a notice of a *deficiency assessment* can only be sent for the reporting of a tax liability in *subtitle A, Income Taxes, subtitle B, Estate and Gift Taxes*, and four chapters in *subtitle D, Miscellaneous Excise Taxes*. *Subtitle C, Employment Taxes*, is conspicuous by its absence. Why? Because it comes under treaty law, and cannot be imposed on citizens and resident aliens. This fact is reiterated in the IRS administrative rules, which are found in Part 601 of the Internal Revenue Regulations, at § 601.102(b)(2), which states in pertinent part:

(2) Taxes not within the jurisdiction of the U.S. Tax Court. Taxes not imposed by Chapter 1, 2, 3, or 4 of the 1939 Code or Subtitle A or Chapter 11 or 12 of the 1954 Code are within this class, such as:

(i)   Employment taxes,
(ii)   Various sales taxes collected by return,
(iii) Miscellaneous excise taxes collected by return, and
(iv) Miscellaneous excise taxes collected by sale of

140

revenue stamps. (Emphasis added.)

All deficiency assessments are appealable to an administrative board entitled The United States Tax Court. Before the change to its current deceptive name, it was entitled Board of Tax Appeals. This is not a court described in Article 3 of the United States Constitution. Wherefore, this "court" cannot try matters of law, it can only try the facts of the matter in accordance with the law. This is found in its jurisdictional statement on its Internet web page:

> *The U.S. Tax Court is a Federal court of record established by Congress under Article I of the Constitution of the United States. Congress created the Tax Court to provide a judicial forum in which affected persons could dispute tax deficiencies determined by the Commissioner of Internal Revenue prior to payment of the disputed amounts. <u>The jurisdiction of the Tax Court includes the authority to hear tax disputes concerning notices of deficiency, notices of transferee liability, certain types of declaratory judgment, readjustment and adjustment of partnership items, review of the failure to abate interest, administrative costs, worker classification, relief from joint and several liability on a joint return, and review of certain collection actions.</u>* (Emphasis added.)

One of the most egregious violations of the law and individual civil rights is the IRS use of the *notice of deficiency* assessment procedures against individuals who have not filed any tax return. What is even worse than this IRS behavior is that the federal courts allow this to continue with their cooperation. The definition of a *deficiency* is found in § 6211, which states:

(a) In general
For purposes of this title[5] in the case of income, estate, and gift taxes imposed by subtitles A and B and excise taxes imposed by chapters 41, 42, 43, and 44 the term

"deficiency" means the amount by which the tax imposed by subtitle A or B, or chapter 41, 42, 43, or 44 exceeds the excess of—

> *(1) the sum of*
>> *(A) the amount shown as the tax by the taxpayer upon his return, if a return was made by the taxpayer and an amount was shown as the tax by the taxpayer thereon, plus*
>> *(B) the amounts previously assessed (or collected without assessment) as a deficiency, over— . . . the amount and rebates . . . made.* (Emphasis added.)

A deficiency is a shortage. In other words, there is more tax due than what the taxpayer has entered as due on the return filed with the IRS. How can there be a deficiency when a return was not filed? The IRS's authority to assess taxes is not § 6212; it is § 6201, which will be covered further on in this Chapter. The proper process given the IRS by Congress for someone that has a requirement to file a return and fails to do so, is not to forward them a notice of deficiency, but rather, the Secretary is authorized by code section § 6020 (b) to file a tax return for them.

Before examining these requirements set forth by Congress, let's examine paragraph (a) of § 6020, which depends on the cooperation of those with a requirement to file a tax return:

> *(a) Preparation of return by Secretary*
> *If any person shall fail to make a return required by this title or by regulations prescribed thereunder, but shall consent to disclose all information necessary for the preparation thereof, then, and in that case, the Secretary may prepare such return, which, being signed by such person, may be received by the Secretary as the return of such person.* (Emphasis added.)

Notice the law first requires the consent of the person required, and secondly, the person must voluntarily sign the return.

We know that the signing of the return by the person is voluntary, because as stated within the statute, he must first give his *consent*. In the United States, no individual can be forced to sign any document that is made under penalty of perjury, no matter what the capacity is of the individual making the request. To force such a subscription would be a crime in itself—the crime of subornation to perjury.

Paragraph (b) of § 6020 gives the Secretary of the Treasury, or his delegate (so designated by a delegation order from the Secretary), the power to make the required return without any consent from the person, nor that person's signature:

> (b) *Execution of return by Secretary*
> (1) *Authority of Secretary to execute return If any person fails to make any return required by any internal revenue law or regulation made thereunder at the time prescribed therefor, or makes, willfully or otherwise, a false or fraudulent return, the Secretary shall make such return from his own knowledge and from such information as he can obtain through testimony or otherwise.*
> (2) *Status of returns. Any return so made and subscribed by the Secretary shall be prima facie good and sufficient for all legal purposes.* (Emphasis added.)

The *returns required under the internal revenue law* will be covered within this Chapter. The real question to be answered is: how does the Secretary have knowledge of your personal affairs needed for his completion of a tax return? The answer is very plain and simple—he doesn't. He does not need such information. Why? For the very same reason we have been showing you throughout this book—through the Constitution the Founders made you free, which will be revealed again and again as we proceed.

The regulation, promulgated by the Secretary, implementing

this paragraph, § 301.6020-1(b), transfers the requirement to make and sign the tax return, given to the Secretary by Congress, to the *district director or other authorized internal revenue service officer or employee.* There are two key phrases in this mandatory requirement on the IRS: first the IRS must determine that the return is actually required of that person; and secondly, the return made by the IRS must be signed by an authorized IRS employee.

The Fellowship has investigated thousands of what the IRS calls *substitute for return* on behalf of its members. The *substitute return* made pursuant to § 6020(b) above is slightly different than a *substitute for return.* *Substitute for returns* are made by the IRS when the return filed has either been mistakenly destroyed or lost. In every instance where the IRS created a *substitute for return* for our members, the returns were not signed. Even though that is the case, the IRS continually tries to contend that these *substitute for returns* were made pursuant to the authority given them in §6020(b).

The procedure to be followed by IRS employees under these circumstances is found in the Internal Revenue Manual in Chapter 5200, *Delinquent Return Procedures.* In § 5221 of that Manual Chapter, it gives the general application of the *delinquent return procedures*:

> General
>
> *(1)   This provides guidelines to assist in developing returns compliance programs and outlines methods by which staffing can be effectively utilized. However, some of the techniques can be used only in connection with a full-scale program due to the nature of the tax situation and the need to avoid unnecessary taxpayer reaction. An example would be income tax returns compliance efforts aimed at the nonbusiness taxpayer.* (Emphasis added.)

The natural question arises: Why would the IRS be warning its agents to step lightly when it comes to the *nonbusiness taxpayer,*

144

the individual? When we go back and review the taxing authority given to Congress by the Constitution, the only taxes that can be laid and collected are found in Article 1, Section 8, Clause 1: *duties*, *imposts* and *excises*. That's right, all business activities.

This is further verified in Section 5290 of this IR Manual chapter, which outlines the *Refusal to File-IRC 6020(b) Assessment Procedure*, and subsequently in § 5291, which names the tax forms that come under the auspices of the Secretary's statutory and Constitutional authority:

> *Scope*
> *(1) The procedure applies to employment, excise and partnership tax returns. Generally, the following returns will be involved.* all Business)
> > *(a) Form 940, Employer's Annual Federal Unemployment Tax Return;*
> > *(b) Form 941, Employer's Quarterly Tax Return;*
> > *(c) Form 942, Employer's Quarterly Tax Return for Household Employees;*
> > *(d) Form 943, Employer's Annual Tax Return for Agricultural Employees;*
> > *(e) Form 11-B, Special Tax Return-Gaming Devices . . .;*
> > *(f) Form 720, Quarterly Federal Excise Tax Return;*
> > *(g) Form 2290, Federal Use Tax Return on Highway Motor Vehicles;*
> > *(h) Form CT-1, Employer's Annual Railroad Retirement Tax Return;*
> > *(j) Form 1065, U.S. Partnership Return of Income.*

Take notice that the famous IRS Form 1040, *U.S. Individual Income Tax Return*, is conspicuous by its absence. Of course, not being a business return, it could not Constitutionally come under the authority of § 6020(b).

Section 5293.3 gives the manner in which the tax return is required to be executed:

Signing Tax Returns
The following statement shall be typed or printed at the bottom of the return. "This return was prepared and signed under the authority of Section 6020(b) of the Internal Revenue Code. Do not assess failure to pay."

Inserted here for your review is a *substitute for return* which an IRS employee prepared for me for the tax year 1975, a year in which I did not file any tax return:

146

Notice that the IRS very clearly identified this Form 1040 as a *Substitute For Return,* and that it was *Prepared By Audit* [in the] *Balto.* (Baltimore District office of the IRS). Also notice that it does not contain any exemptions or any amount of money on any of the appropriate lines of entry. And of course, the most blatant omission of all, there is no signature or statement as required by the section shown above. One of the most interesting things about this fraudulent effort is that it verifies that it is a fraud. Take notice that it states very clearly at the bottom *FOR STATUTE REV.* and then *NO STATUTE DETERMINATION.* A determination being a finding of fact, translates these statements to mean there is no statutory or lawful authority for the actions taken. Of course, at that time, these IRS employees must have felt fairly safe, for it was a few years later when these documents were begrudgingly given up by the IRS through Privacy Act requests. The many lies told by the IRS disclosure officers, in their concerted effort to cover this fraud up, are covered in detail in the *Save-A-Patriot Fellowship's* video series entitled *Just The Facts,* which is available to the public. (Inquiries can be made at the Fellowship's offices, located at 12 Carroll Street, Westminster, Maryland 21157, or by telephone at 410-857-4441.)

Based on the above *substitute for return,* and another one identical to it for the tax year 1976, the IRS sent to me in the U.S. Mail a *notice of deficiency* assessment in an amount in excess of four hundred sixty-one thousand dollars. This was later reduced to three thousand four hundred twenty-eight dollars and eleven cents. Of course, no one within the IRS was ever investigated and charged with mail fraud. Believe it or not, just a cursory investigation into our practicing American justice system reveals that some individuals are above the law. That's from Presidents Nixon and Clinton on down throughout the federal government.

Further on in Chapter 5200, the *substitute for return* procedure is explained thusly:

52(10)5.1
General

> On October 1, 1986 Collection was delegated the authority to assess IMF [Individual Master File] tax and the Service Center Collection Branch started Substitute for Return (SFR) processing. Essentially, <u>an SFR assessment is a audit process</u> where the initial action by SCCB is to file a "<u>dummy</u>" return for the taxpayer for -0- amount and then assess the tax with a TC 290. (Emphasis added.)

As stated, *an SFR assessment* is not an assessment, but an *audit process* by the Service Center Collection Branch, (Service Centers receive and audit tax returns), auditing a *dummy* return for zero amount. This exemplifies, in the IRS's own words, that this procedure does not meet the Constitutional requirements outlined in the *substitute return* procedures within this manual chapter, implemented in pursuance of § 6020(b) of the Internal Revenue Code.

The substitute for return procedures turned out to be nothing more than the IRS's heavy-handed attempt to whip all of those out-of-line Patriots, who dare to insist on the proper application of the tax laws, back into line. What tyrants never seem to learn is that unjust force just brings more righteous resistance. We will talk about this in more detail when we discuss the apparent conspiracy between some of the individuals within the Internal Revenue Service, the Department of Justice and the Federal Courts.

As stated earlier in this Chapter, § 6201(a) is the *Assessment Authority* given by Congress to the Secretary of the Treasury, and it states as follows:

(a) Authority of Secretary

The Secretary is authorized and required to make the inquiries, determinations, and assessments of all taxes (including interest, additional amounts, additions to the tax, and assessable penalties) imposed by this title, or accruing under any former internal revenue law, which have not been duly paid by stamp at the time and in the manner provided by law. <u>Such authority shall extend to and include the following</u>: (Emphasis added.)

(1) <u>Taxes shown on return.</u> The Secretary shall assess all taxes determined by the taxpayer or by the Secretary as to which returns or lists are made under this title. (Emphasis added.)

(2) <u>Unpaid taxes payable by stamp</u>. (Emphasis added.)

(A) Omitted stamps. Whenever any article upon which a tax is required to be paid by means of a stamp is sold or removed for sale or use by the manufacturer thereof or whenever any transaction or act upon which a tax is required to be paid by means of a stamp occurs without the use of the proper stamp, it shall be the duty of the Secretary, upon such information as he can obtain, to estimate the amount of tax which has been omitted to be paid and to make assessment therefor upon the person or persons the Secretary determines to be liable for such tax.

(B) Check or money order not duly paid. In any case in which a check or money order received under authority of section 6311 as payment for stamps is not duly paid, the unpaid amount may be immediately assessed as if it were a tax imposed by this title, due at the time of such receipt, from the person who tendered such check or money order.

(3) Erroneous income tax prepayment credits. If on any return or claim for refund of income taxes under subtitle A there is an overstatement of the credit for income tax withheld at the source, or of the amount paid as estimated income tax, the amount so overstated

which is allowed against the tax shown on the return or which is allowed as a credit or refund may be assessed by the Secretary in the same manner as in the case of a mathematical or clerical error appearing upon the return, except that the provisions of section 6213(b)(2) (relating to abatement of mathematical or clerical error assessments) shall not apply with regard to any assessment under this paragraph.

As shown within the IRS's assessment authority, tax assessments can only be made in two ways: on a required and properly executed tax return, as shown in our review of Sections 6012, and 6020(b); and by the purchase of tax stamps by the manufacturer of the specific products subject to the excise tax. Wherefore, when a person files a tax return, that individual assesses himself, and if the IRS auditor disagrees, a notice of deficiency can be issued to the person. That is, except for when an individual files a Form 1040 reporting wage taxes withheld by an employer as displayed on a Form W-2. Because of the voluntary nature of the *employment tax* for citizens and resident aliens, the tax posted on the return cannot be added to by an IRS auditor. This was covered in our review of § 6212, earlier in this Chapter, and is referred to in Paragraph (d) of this section. Paragraph (b) and (c) tells what is not to be assessed by the IRS:

(b) Amount not to be assessed
(1) Estimated income tax.   No unpaid amount of estimated income tax required to be paid under section 6654 or 6655 shall be assessed.
(2) Federal unemployment tax.   No unpaid amount of Federal unemployment tax for any calendar quarter or other period of a calendar year, computed as provided in section 6157, shall be assessed.
(c) Compensation of child.
Any income tax under chapter 1 assessed against a child, to the extent attributable to amounts includible in the gross income of the child, and not of the parent,

solely by reason of section 73(a), shall, if not paid by the child, for all purposes be considered as having also been properly assessed against the parent.

(d) Deficiency proceedings.

For special rules applicable to deficiencies of income, estate, gift, and certain excise taxes, see subchapter B.

Everywhere we look within the Internal Revenue Code, we cannot find any provision that is unconstitutional, except for one code section which will be covered later.

Chapter 10

SUBTITLE F:
PROCEDURE & ADMINISTRATION
ENFORCEMENT of TITLE

Chapter 78 encompasses *Discovery of Liability and Enforcement of the Title*. It is divided into four subchapters:

A. Examination and inspection;
B. General powers and duties;
C. Supervision of operations of certain manufacturers; and,
D. Possessions [of the United States].

The only subchapter that we will examine is subchapter A, which consists of the following code sections:

§ 7601   Canvass of districts for taxable persons and objects.
§ 7602   Examination of books and witnesses.
§ 7603   Service of summons.
§ 7604   Enforcement of summons.
§ 7605   Time and place of examination.
§ 7606   Entry of premises for examination of taxable objects.
§ 7607   Repealed.
§ 7608   Authority of internal revenue enforcement officers.
§ 7609   Special procedures for third party summonses.
§ 7610   Fees and costs for witnesses.
§ 7611   Restrictions on church tax inquiries and examinations.
§ 7612   Cross references.

There is no need to examine all of these code sections to prove our point that the only taxing liability for citizens and resident aliens within the States of the Union are those authorized by Article 1, Section 8, Clause 1 of the United States Constitution. Because the Customs Branch of the Treasury Department collects all *duties* and *imposts*, the only taxes authorized by this provision of the Constitution left to discuss are *excises*.

The first code section to examine is § 7601, which states:

(a) General rule.

The Secretary shall, to the extent he deems it practicable, cause officers or employees of the Treasury Department to proceed, from time to time, through each internal revenue district and inquire after and <u>concerning all persons therein who may be liable to pay any internal revenue tax</u>, and <u>all persons owning or having the care and management of any objects with respect to which any tax is imposed</u>. (Emphasis added.)

(b) Penalties.

For penalties applicable to forcible obstruction or hindrance of Treasury officers or employees in the performance of their duties, see section <u>7212</u>.

Has any IRS employee knocked on your door asking to look for *objects with respect to which any tax is imposed* lately? Of course not. Do you recall the movie and television show entitled *The Untouchables*? In the series, Elliot Ness and his Treasury agents tracked down Al Capone's breweries, stills and storage warehouses and destroyed all the untaxed, and at that time, illegal booze. After the repeal of the 18th Amendment to the United States Constitution and the Volstead Act, the Treasury Department turned its attention to the routine canvassing for what is commonly known as moonshiners, which includes stills producing alcoholic beverages for public consumption without purchasing federal tax stamps.

154

(a) Entry during day

The Secretary may enter, in the daytime, any building or place where any <u>articles or objects subject to tax are made, produced, or kept</u>, so far as it may be necessary for the purpose of examining said articles or objects.

(b) Entry at night

When such premises are open at night, the Secretary may enter them while so open, in the performance of his official duties.

(c) Penalties

For penalty for refusal to permit entry or examination, see section 7342. (Emphasis added.)

The last code section in this Chapter of the Code to be examined for verification goes beyond the excise tax to other forms of taxation, but even so, it proves our contention regarding the foreign nature of the federal tax scheme. Section 7608 outlines the authority of the revenue enforcement officers, thusly:

(a) <u>Enforcement of subtitle E</u> and other laws pertaining to liquor, tobacco, and firearms.

Any investigator, agent, or other internal revenue officer by whatever term designated, whom the Secretary charges with the duty of enforcing any of the criminal, seizure, or forfeiture provisions of subtitle E or of any other law of the United States pertaining to the commodities subject to tax under such subtitle for the enforcement of which the Secretary is responsible may— (Emphasis added.)

(1) carry firearms;

(2) execute and serve search warrants and arrest warrants, and serve subpoenas and summonses issued

under authority of the United States;

(3) in respect to the performance of such duty, make arrests without warrant for any offense against the United States committed in his presence, or for any felony cognizable under the laws of the United States if he has reasonable grounds to believe that the person to be arrested has committed, or is committing, such felony; and

(4) in respect to the performance of such duty, make seizures of property subject to forfeiture to the United States. (Emphasis added.)

(b) Enforcement of laws relating to internal revenue other than subtitle E.

(1) Any criminal investigator of the Intelligence Division or of the Internal Security Division of the Internal Revenue Service whom the Secretary charges with the duty of enforcing any of the criminal provisions of the internal revenue laws, any other criminal provisions of law relating to internal revenue for the enforcement of which the Secretary is responsible, or any other law for which the Secretary has delegated investigatory authority to the Internal Revenue Service, is, in the performance of his duties, authorized to perform the functions described in paragraph (2).

(2) The functions authorized under this subsection to be performed by an officer referred to in paragraph (1) are—

(A) to execute and serve search warrants and arrest warrants, and serve subpoenas and summonses issued under authority of the United States;

(B) to make arrests without warrant for any offense against the United States relating to the internal revenue laws committed in his presence, or for any felony cognizable under such laws if he has reasonable grounds to believe that the person to be arrested has committed or is committing any such

felony; and

(C) to make seizures of property subject to forfeiture under the internal revenue laws. (Emphasis added.)

Paragraph (a) authorizes revenue agents and revenue officers to perform those required functions ONLY within Subtitle E of the Internal Revenue Code, the *excise* tax on Alcohol, Tobacco and Firearms. And what is even more interesting about this code section is that it authorizes those revenue agents and revenue officers to ONLY seize *property subject to forfeiture under the internal revenue laws.*

Paragraph (b) authorizes a *criminal investigator* to perform those required functions within Subtitles A, B, C, and D of the Internal Revenue Code, and they can ONLY seize *property subject to forfeiture under the internal revenue laws.* Isn't this curious? Well, not really, when you examine it in the light of its lawful Constitutional application.

Before we investigate why the designation of *property subject to forfeiture* is so important to support the claims about the federal tax scheme made in this book, I will demonstrate the significance of the division of the subtitles. Congress has given the revenue agent and the revenue officer (revenue agent being superior in rank) authority to enforce the Constitutional domestic application of the *excise* tax within the States of the Union; and the special agents of the Criminal Investigation Division (CID), all foreign-related taxes. The proof of the latter is found in Chapter 1100 of the Internal Revenue Manual, *Organization and Staffing*, at section 1132.75 (12-21-87), which states:

Criminal Investigation Division
The Criminal Investigation Division enforces the criminal statutes applicable to income, estate, gift, employment, and excise tax laws (other than those excepted in IRM 1112.51) involving United States citizens in foreign countries and nonresident aliens subject to

Federal income tax filing requirements. . . (Emphasis added.)

As was covered extensively in Chapters IV and VIII of this book, and conclusively exhibited here, outside of paying domestic *excise* taxes on the manufacture, sale or consumption of a *certain* commodity, the only tax a citizen is liable for is on *foreign earned income*. This income can be through foreign investment, or by working or maintaining a business within a country that has a tax treaty with the United States. Of course, it only stands to reason that the nonresident alien would have to be within the confines of the United States jurisdiction in order for the *Criminal Investigation Division* to accost him or her.

Manual section 1112.51 (7-8-83) makes clear the division of the enforcement of the Internal Revenue Code as outlined in § 7608 above:

Mission
   The mission of the Office of the District Director is to administer the internal revenue laws (except those relating to alcohol, tobacco and firearms) within an internal revenue district in conformance with Service policies and programs of the National Office and Regional Offices.

Seizure of Property

Now we will take up the matter of the *seizure of property subject to forfeiture*, which, as § 7608 exhibits, is the ONLY property that can be seized without due process. That does not mean that the person from whom the property was seized is being denied due process, since that person can sue to retrieve the property that was wrongfully seized by the IRS or Bureau of Alcohol, Tobacco and Firearms (BATF). Also, the meaning of due process within the 5th Amendment to the U.S. Constitution is an impartial hearing in a court of competent jurisdiction, not an administrative hearing within a government agency. As explained earlier in this book, administrative due process was unlawfully established by Roosevelt's New Deal political wave.

The general belief that the IRS can seize your property anytime it wants, without bothering with any court proceedings, has been sold to the public by the entertainment and news media, but nothing could be further from the truth. The law does not allow such activity, for if it did, it would be clearly unconstitutional, and as we have found so far, there have been great pains taken to mislead the public, but not violate the Constitution. The code section that is misapplied and misused for that purpose by the IRS is § 6331, *Levy and distraint*. That section begins:

(a) Authority of Secretary.

If any person liable to pay any tax neglects or refuses to pay the same within 10 days after notice and demand, it shall be lawful for the Secretary to collect such tax (and such further sum as shall be sufficient to cover the expenses of the levy) by levy upon all property and rights to property (except such property as is exempt under section 6334) belonging to such person or on which there is a lien provided in this chapter for the payment of such tax. Levy may be made upon the accrued salary or wages of any officer, employee, or elected official, of the United States, the District of Columbia, or any agency or instrumentality of the United States or the District of Columbia, by serving a notice of levy on the employer (as defined in section 3401(d)) of such officer, employee, or elected official. If the Secretary makes a finding that the collection of such tax is in jeopardy, notice and demand for immediate payment of such tax may be made by the Secretary and, upon failure or refusal to pay such tax, collection thereof by levy shall be lawful without regard to the 10-day period provided in this section. (Emphasis added.)

Go back and read the underlined portion of that paragraph again, and read it carefully. That's right, ONLY the wages of government officers, employees and elected officials can be levied upon. Nowhere in this code section authorizing levy can it be found that the wages of citizens and resident aliens can be levied. There is good reason for this, other than the obvious reason that the citizen's and resident alien's wages are not subject to any type of taxation. Additionally, I am not saying that the wages of government officers, employees and elected officials are subject to taxation, within the States of the Union. The actual point being made here is that the federal government can ONLY levy what is in its possession. That's correct, only what is in its possession.

Before we get into the meat of this fact, we will take a look at paragraph (b) of § 6331:

> *(b)   Seizure and sale of property.*
> *The term "levy" as used in this title includes the power of distraint and seizure by any means. Except as otherwise provided in subsection (e), a <u>levy shall extend only to property possessed</u> and obligations existing at the time thereof. In any case in which the Secretary may levy upon property or rights to property, he may seize and sell such property or rights to property (whether real or personal, tangible or intangible).* (Emphasis added.)

There are two things that are very interesting about paragraph (b). First, when the IRS sends a *Notice of Levy*, Form 668-A, to a third party holding the target person's property, such as an employer, on the reverse side of the form, § 6331 is printed, but what is so interesting is that they begin the reproduction of the code section with paragraph (b). Obviously those powers-that-be within the IRS do not want employers to see that the wages of employees within the private marketplace are not subject to levy as shown in paragraph (a). The second thing is a bit more devious. Preying on the public's mindset, Congress wrote the statute so that it would appear that the property levied upon was in the hands of the private third party. But that is not the case at all, for as I am about to demonstrate, the words of § 6331(b), *levy shall extend only to property possessed*, are referring to the requirement that the property levied upon must be in the possession of the government itself.

Section 6335(a) shows us that seizure is before the notice of seizure:

(a) Notice of seizure.
As soon as practicable after seizure of property, notice in writing shall be given by the Secretary to the owner of the property (or, in the case of personal property, the possessor thereof), or shall be left at his usual place of abode or business if he has such within the internal revenue district where the seizure is made. If the owner cannot be readily located, or has no dwelling or place of business within such district, the notice may be mailed to his last known address. Such notice shall specify the sum demanded and shall contain, in the case of personal property, an account of the property seized and, in the case of real property, a description with reasonable certainty of the property seized. (Emphasis added.)

So, as demonstrated in paragraph (a) above, we know that the seizure of the property is before the notice of seizure, and §6502(b), *Collection after assessment*, tells us that the giving of the notice of seizure is the date of the levy:

(b) Date when levy is considered made.
The date on which a levy on property or rights to property is made shall be the date on which the notice of seizure provided in section 6335(a) is given. (Emphasis added.)

Summing up what we have established so far, first the IRS *seizes* the property to satisfy an assessment of a tax liability for which the taxpayer has been given a notice and demand for payment, which the taxpayer has not paid. Then, *as soon as practicable after seizure of property, notice in writing shall be given by the* IRS *to the owner of the property, and this notice of seizure is the date of the levy.* Wherefore, *levy* is after *seizure*, and as stated in § 7608, the only *seizure* authority for all of the internal revenue enforcement officers is on *property subject to forfeiture.* The only thing left is to identify the *property subject to forfeiture,* and for that we go to Subchapter C, *Forfeitures,* of Chapter 75 of the Internal Revenue Code. Part I of Subchapter C, *Property subject to forfeiture,* consists of four code sections:

> § 7301, *Property subject to tax.*
> § 7302, *Property used in violation of internal revenue laws.*
> § 7303, *Other property subject to forfeiture.*
> § 7304, *Penalty for fraudulently claiming drawback.*

There are only two of these code sections that need to be examined to prove our point about the internal taxing power of Congress. They are §§ 7301 and 7303. Section 7301 states:

(a) Taxable articles.

Any property on which, or for or in respect whereof, any tax is imposed by this title which shall be found in the possession or custody or within the control of any person, for the purpose of being sold or removed by him in fraud of the internal revenue laws, or with design to avoid payment of such tax, or which is removed, deposited, or concealed, with intent to defraud the United States of such tax or any part thereof, may be seized, and shall be forfeited to the United States.

(b) Raw materials.

All property found in the possession of any person intending to manufacture the same into property of a kind subject to tax for the purpose of selling such taxable property in fraud of the internal revenue laws, or with design to evade the payment of such tax, may also be seized, and shall be forfeited to the United States.

(c) Equipment.

All property whatsoever, in the place or building, or any yard or enclosure, where the property described in subsection (a) or (b) is found, or which is intended to be used in the making of property described in subsection (a), with intent to defraud the United States of tax or any part thereof, on the property described in subsection (a) may also be seized, and shall be forfeited to the United States.

(d) Packages.

All property used as a container for, or which shall have contained, property described in subsection (a) or (b) may also be seized, and shall be forfeited to the United States.

(e) Conveyances.

Any property (including aircraft, vehicles, vessels, or draft animals) used to transport or for the deposit or concealment of property described in subsection (a) or (b), or any property used to transport or for the deposit or concealment of property which is intended to be used in the making or packaging of property described in subsection (a), may also be seized, and shall be forfeited to the United States. (Emphasis added.)

Section 7303 states:

There may be seized and forfeited to the United States the following:

(1) Counterfeit stamps.

Every stamp involved in the offense described in section 7208 (relating to counterfeit, reused, cancelled, etc., stamps), and the vellum, parchment, document, paper, package, or article upon which such stamp was placed or impressed in connection with such offense.

(2) False stamping of packages.

Any container involved in the offense described in section 7271 (relating to disposal of stamped packages),

and of the contents of such container.
(3) Fraudulent bonds, permits, and entries.
   All property to which any false or fraudulent instrument involved in the offense described in section 7207 relates.

   Once again the Internal Revenue Code itself has proven that the ONLY domestic federal tax to be paid by citizens and resident aliens are those found in Article 1, Section 8, Clause 1 of the United States Constitution—duties, imposts and excises.

Tax Crimes

   We will finish up our coverage of Subtitle F, Chapter 75, Subchapter A by examining internal revenue *Crimes*, then the question of the constitutionality of a particular code section, and finally we will examine how criminal investigation agents lie to the IRS computer to conduct an investigation on a citizen. There are sixteen code sections in Subchapter A; the two most commonly prosecuted by the IRS are § 7201, *Attempt to evade or defeat tax*, and § 7203, *Willful failure to file return, supply information, or pay tax*. For the purposes of this book, it will only be necessary to examine these code sections.

   Section 7201 is a felony, and if convicted, can bring a fairly stiff sentence:

   Any person who <u>willfully attempts in any manner to evade or defeat any tax imposed by this title</u> or the payment thereof shall, in addition to other penalties provided by law, be guilty of a felony and, upon conviction thereof, shall be fined not more than $100,000 ($500,000 in the case of a corporation), or imprisoned not more than 5 years, or both, together with the costs of prosecution.
   (Emphasis added.)

   Section 7203 is a misdemeanor, and if convicted, the

sentence, like all misdemeanors, can be no more than one year. But in recent years, the fine has increased from $10,000 to $25,000 in an apparent effort to discourage the tax law awareness movement that started in the latter part of the 1960s. Section 7203 states as follows:

> Any person *required under this title* to pay any estimated tax or tax, or *required by this title* or by regulations made under authority thereof to make a return, keep any records, or supply any information, who *willfully* fails to pay such estimated tax or tax, make such return, keep such records, or supply such information, at the time or times required by law or regulations, shall, in addition to other penalties provided by law, be guilty of a misdemeanor and, upon conviction thereof, shall be fined not more than $25,000 ($100,000 in the case of a corporation), or imprisoned not more than 1 year, or both, together with the costs of prosecution. In the case of any person with respect to whom there is a failure to pay any estimated tax, this section shall not apply to such person with respect to such failure if there is no addition to tax under section 6654 or 6655 with respect to such failure. (Emphasis added.)

In 1984, § 6050I, *Returns relating to cash received in trade or business*, was enacted by Congress and the following was added to § 7203:

> In the case of a willful violation of any provision of section 6050I, the first sentence of this section shall be applied by substituting "felony" for "misdemeanor" and "5 years" for "1 year".

Section 6050I states in part:

(a) Cash receipts of more than $10,000.
   Any person—

(1) who is engaged in a <u>trade or business</u>, and

(2) who, in the course of such <u>trade or business</u>, receives more than $10,000 in cash in 1 transaction (or 2 or more related transactions),

shall make the return described in subsection (b) with respect to such transaction (or related transactions) at such time as the Secretary may by regulations prescribe. (Emphasis added.)

Before we discuss the imposition of §§ 7201 and 7203, we will take up the matter of who is the *person* that has to make such a *return* as required in § 6050I.

A search of § 6050I does not reveal any definition of any of the legal terms contained therein. In fact a search of Chapter 61, *Information and Returns*, does not reveal any general definitions for the Chapter nor any of its Parts and Subparts. Therefore, just like we had to do in the investigation of the *Self-Employment Tax* in Chapter 9 of this book, we must go back to the general *Definitions* in Chapter 79 of the Internal Revenue Code. Coincidentally, as it turns out, we are looking at the same legal terms. For as it states in § 6050I, the person required to make the return must be *engaged in a trade or business*, and as we saw in Chapter 9, according to § 7701(a)(26), that person must hold a *public office*. I am going on the record here and now that I am 100% in favor of this law, for any holder of *public office* that takes cash must be made to report it on Form 4789, *Currency Transaction Report*. What I do disagree with is the threshold amount of $10,000. It should be no more than $1, since evidence in the past has proven some of them come pretty cheap. Of course, if some politician does not report the receipt of $10,000 or more, and is later charged with accepting a bribe, it would be a violation of the 5th Amendment to charge him in accordance with the reporting requirements of § 6050I for failure to report the bribe.

The only reason that such a deception could be successful is the general ignorance of the Constitution, including law professionals. For it just stands to reason that if the American population was knowledgeable about the provisions of the Constitution, they would realize right off that the government cannot demand the reporting of or question any money transaction without having probable cause to believe that such transaction was illegal in itself, or part of an illegal act. And in the case of the federal government, only when it involves interstate commerce or mail fraud. Without a resounding demand for our educational institutions to teach the Constitution from and along with the intent of the *Framers* and philosophy of the *Founding Fathers*, this *Republic* is doomed to follow the same destructive course as the Roman Republic.

Like all criminal offenses, and as shown above, both §§ 7201 and 7203 state that the offender must *willfully* commit the crime. Black's Law Dictionary, 5th Edition, defines the *willful* commission of a crime thusly:

> *Willful. . . . An act or omission is "willfully" done, if done voluntarily and intentionally and with the specific intent to do something the law forbids, or with the specific intent to fail to do something the law requires to be done; that is to say, with bad purpose either to disobey or to disregard the law.*

So the only person that can be charged with willfully committing one of these Internal Revenue Code offenses would be the person who has the liability or requirement, but intentionally disregards that liability, or that requirement, or both.

The second element of §§ 7201 and 7203 to be addressed is that there must be some law within the *Title* (Title meaning the entire Internal Revenue Code), that is violated before these two penalty sections can be imposed. Notice that § 7201 says:

> *Any person who <u>willfully</u> attempts in any manner to evade or defeat any <u>tax imposed by this title</u>.* (Emphasis added.)

and that § 7203 says:

> *Any person <u>required under this title</u> to pay any estimated tax or tax, or <u>required by this title</u> or by regulations made under authority thereof <u>to make a return, keep any records, or supply any information,</u> . . .* (Emphasis added.)

As is evident within these sections, some code section within the Internal Revenue Code that imposes a tax on the income, wages or an activity of a person would have to be intentionally ignored and/or violated by that person to invoke the penalties within §7201. In the same manner, if some code section within the Internal Revenue Code required a person to make an information return to report a liability of a tax, and that person intentionally ignored and violated that required reporting, that violation would invoke the penalties within § 7203. Without the unnamed code section being violated, §§ 7201 and 7203 cannot be legally used to prosecute anyone. The problem is, the IRS and the Department of Justice are, and have been for years, charging and prosecuting individuals with only the allegation of one or the other, or both, of these penalty sections being violated, which is an impossibility. And an even greater problem is that the federal courts are conspiring with them to do so, even in spite of the prohibition within the Federal Rules of Criminal Procedure to do so. Rule 7(c) states:

> *(c) Nature and Contents.*
> *(1) In General. <u>The indictment or the information shall be a plain, concise and definite written statement of the essential facts constituting the offense charged</u>. It shall be signed by the attorney for the government. It need not contain a formal commencement, a formal conclusion or any other matter not necessary to such statement. Allegations made in one count may be incorporated by reference in another count. It may be alleged in a single count that the means by which the defendant committed*

the offense are unknown or that the defendant committed it by one or more specified means. *The indictment or information shall state for each count the official or customary citation of the statute, rule, regulation or other provision of law which the defendant is alleged therein to have violated.*

(2) Criminal Forfeiture. No judgment of forfeiture may be entered in a criminal proceeding unless the indictment or the information shall allege the extent of the interest or property subject to forfeiture.

(3) Harmless Error. Error in the citation or its omission shall not be ground for dismissal of the indictment or information or for reversal of a conviction if the error or omission did not mislead the defendant to the defendant's prejudice. (Emphasis added.)

The first time, to my knowledge, this fact about §§ 7201 and 7203 only being penalty sections, and that in accordance to Rule 7(c), the statute violated has to be named within the indictment or information, was in a case in the federal court in northern Illinois, argued by one of the *Save-A-Patriot Fellowship's* members at his arraignment without the assistance of an attorney. When he explained to the judge, by reading § 7203 aloud, that it was only a penalty section and that the section alleged to be violated was missing, the judge read § 7203 three times and then stated to the member, "You're right." I no longer remember if it was an indictment or an information, but the judge dismissed the criminal complaint brought by the IRS. That was the first and only time, to my knowledge, that a positive result was achieved by presenting these facts to the court. That does not mean that the courts are not informed of these facts, they just tyrannically ignore the law and go on with an illegal prosecution.

Unconstitutional Code Section

To my knowledge the Internal Revenue Code, as written, as I have demonstrated, is Constitutional—that is, except for, in my opinion, § 7421.

Section 7421, prohibiting any court of competent jurisdiction from enjoining (stopping) the collection of a federal tax assessment, states as follows:

> Section 7421, *Prohibition of suits to restrain assessment or collection*
> *(a) Tax*
> Except as provided in sections 6015(e), 6212(a) and (c), 6213(a), 6225(b), 6246(b), 6330(e)(1), 6331(i), 6672(c), 6694(c), and 7426(a) and (b)(1), 7429(b), and 7436, *no suit for the purpose of restraining the assessment or collection of any tax shall be maintained in any court by any person, whether or not such person is the person against whom such tax was assessed.*
> *(b) Liability of transferee or fiduciary*
> No suit shall be maintained in any court for the purpose of restraining the assessment or collection (pursuant to the provisions of chapter 71) of —
> (1) the amount of the liability, at law or in equity, of a transferee of property of a taxpayer in respect of any internal revenue tax, or
> (2) the amount of the liability of a fiduciary under section 3713(b) of title 31, United States Code [1] in respect of any such tax. (Emphasis added.)

Before we examine the exceptions, take note of the underlined portion above. This language prevents, what has been the case so often, the victim from stopping the theft of his or her property without *due process of law*, as guaranteed by the 5th Amendment to the United States Constitution, to wit:

> . . . *nor be deprived of life, liberty, or property, without due process of law; . . .*

Due process of law is defined by Black's Law Dictionary, 5th

170

Edition, as:

> *Due process of law. Law in its regular course of administration through courts of justice. . . . A course of legal proceedings according to those rules and principles which have been established in our systems of jurisprudence for the enforcement and protection of private rights. . . .*

Now, to prove this point, we will examine the exceptions found in § 7421(a):

Section 6015(e) has been repealed.

Section 6212(a) and (c) were covered earlier in detail, and we found they only cover the question of the amount of tax due, not whether or not there is a liability.

Section 6213(a) is nothing more than the setting of the time limit for a taxpayer, issued a Notice of Deficiency in accordance with § 6212, to petition the Tax Court for a determination of the amount due, not to settle the question of liability.

Section 6225(b) deals with assessments and collection activity carried on before the 150 day notification time afforded partnerships.

Section 6246(b) has practically the same text content as 6225(b), except the limit set is 90 days instead of 150 days.

Section 6330 was enacted by Congress in 1998 in response to numerous complaints about abusive IRS assessment collections. It is nothing more than an attempt to give an appearance of due process, but a careful examination reveals otherwise.

This code section allows for the person faced with seizure and levy collection the right to an administrative hearing to challenge the collection procedure. Paragraph (c) gives a veiled illusion that the tax liability can be challenged, but upon careful examination, we find otherwise:

(c) Matters considered at hearing

In the case of any hearing conducted under this section—

(1) Requirement of investigation

The *appeals officer shall at the hearing obtain verification from the Secretary that the requirements of any applicable law or administrative procedure have been met*.

(2) Issues at hearing

(A) In general

The person may raise at the hearing any relevant issue relating to the unpaid tax or the proposed levy, including—

(i) appropriate spousal defenses;

(ii) challenges to the appropriateness of collection actions; and

(iii) offers of collection alternatives, which may include the posting of a bond, the substitution of other assets, an installment agreement, or an offer-in-compromise.

(B) Underlying liability

The person may also raise at the hearing challenges to the existence or amount of the underlying tax liability for any tax period *if the person did not receive any statutory notice of deficiency for such tax liability or did not otherwise have an opportunity to dispute such tax liability*. (Emphasis added.)

This may sound good, but in practice it turns out to be little more than nothing. It has been the experience of the Fellowship's caseworkers, in helping its members with these 6330 hearings, that the *appeals officer shall at the hearing obtain verification from the Secretary that the requirements of any applicable law or administrative procedure have been met* turns out to be the hearing officer merely stating that they have, thus closing the door to any discussion of the matter. As for the *Underlying liability*, the IRS

172

sends *statutory notices of deficiency* to persons not having any tax liability and this precludes the liability challenge. Additionally, because there was no tax liability when the *statutory notice of deficiency* was received, there was no jurisdiction within the tax court. So instead, the member moves the IRS with a petition for abatement of the tax assessment pursuant to IR Code section 6404(a)(3), the IRS ignores the legal arguments within the petition, and then the 6330 hearing officer contends that the member had *an opportunity to dispute such tax liability*. So in essence, Congress gave the IRS the loopholes needed to continue to misapply the law.

> Section 6331(i) is a prohibition on the levy collection when the person whose property is being levied upon is in court suing for the refund of a portion of alleged taxes due that were already paid.
>
> Section 6672(c) covers a dispute between a person required to collect and pay a tax and the IRS, and allows that person the right to sue after either paying the disputed amount or posting a bond for the same.
>
> Section 6694(c) deals with the understatement of taxpayer's liability by income tax return preparer.
>
> Section 7426(a) and (b)(1) allows a person whose property has been wrongfully levied to file suit for its return.
>
> Section 7429(b) are the provisions for a determination on the validity of a jeopardy assessment seizure of property already made.
>
> Section 7436 is merely an appeal from a tax court ruling to the federal district court, where the amount of tax, rather than the liability, is tried.

As displayed above, the only attempt at affording the victim due process is the deceptive illusion in the exception for § 6330, which actually does not afford someone not liable for the tax, and therefore not required to file a tax return, due process to stop the illegal assessment. Thus, without the ability to have remedy at law, this individual is denied due process, making § 7421 clearly unconstitutional. It was never the intent of the *Founding Fathers* and the *Framers* of the Constitution for acts passed by Congress, and signed into law by the President, to act in a way that prevents truth and justice. The *Fellowship* has numerous records of IRS agents assessing exorbitant sums as the taxes due from individuals without any tax liability, who were merely earning a living wage, and then extorting such fraudulent sums through their employers by using fear tactics and unlawful levies.

The high-handed approach used in § 7421 cannot even be justified in a time of emergency, such as a war, for the *Framers* gave the power to the Executive Branch to borrow on the credit of the United States, and then assess a direct tax to pay that debt. There can be no reason known to man to allow government agents to commit such acts of theft and protect them from the victim's having his day in court, other than the establishment of raw tyranny.

Criminal Investigation of Citizens

Because, as we have shown over and over again in this book, the federal tax law, except for one code section, is Constitutional, and as also stated before, the IRS computer software systems are programmed for the application of those Constitutional laws, in order for the IRS agents to investigate a citizen or resident alien they have to lie to the computer for it to function. In order to illustrate this fact, I am reproducing part of a page of an IRS computer file regarding myself:

```
140 022186              0.00        8609 28249-052-00000-5
                                         PRC-
914 110387  ---------------         8745 52277-707-30000-7
596 111987  ---------------         8750 28214-723-50003-7
                                          COLCLOS-57
912 100688  ---------------         8842 52277-680-30005-8
425 100389  ---------------         8941 52277-276-20000-9
                                         SOURCE-65  ORG-1403  PRO
                                         PTR DO-
```

The three-digit numbers in the left column are called *transaction codes*. The six-digit number to the right of the *transaction code* is the *date of the transaction* identified by the *transaction code*. To the right of that is a four-digit number

174

representing the *posting cycle,* which is roughly the "week of the year"— i.e., *1402* would be a transaction posted in the 14th week of 2002. To the right of that is a fourteen-digit number known as the *document locator number.* By the use of the document locator number, the IRS can locate any physical document in a matter of minutes.

Internal Revenue Manual Document 6209 decodes IRS computer codes. Section 8 of that document, *Master File Codes,* contains *Transaction Codes* and describes their use thusly:

> *1 Transaction Codes*
> *Reference IRM 3(27)(68)0*
> *Transaction Codes (TC) consist of three digits. They are used to identify a transaction being processed and to maintain a history of actions posted to a taxpayer's account on the Master File. . . .*

The *transaction codes 914* and *912* on the computer file above are defined in Document 6209 as:

Section 8.   Master File Codes

1   Transaction Codes

Reference IRM 3(27)(68)0

Transaction Codes (TC) consist of three digits. They are used to identify a transaction being processed and to maintain a history of actions posted to a taxpayer's account on the Master File. Every transaction processed by ADP must contain a Transaction Code to maintain Accounting Controls of debits and credits, to cause the computer at MCC to post the transaction on the Master File, to permit compilation of reports, and to identify the transaction when a transcript is extracted from the Master File. Transaction codes that are unique to IDRS are also included.

912	I/B/A	Criminal Investigation	77	Reverses TC 914 freeze.
914	I/B/A	Active Criminal Investigation	77	Identifies a tax module assigned to the Criminal Investigation Division. Establishes modular freeze which causes all transactions except the following to be unpostable: IMF only—Corr. UPC 183; IMF/BMF—TC 428, 910, 912, 920 and 99X; BMF only—Corr. UPC 333, TC 019, 424 (SPC 049), IRAF Corrected Unpostable Code 733. BMF/IMF: Pre-

As you can see, on November 3, 1987, the Criminal Investigation Division (CID) started a criminal investigation of me, and on October 6, 1988, they ended the investigation without taking any actions to prosecute me. The question we want to ask is this: being a citizen, what violation of the Internal Revenue Code were they alleging I committed? In order to get that answer, we must examine the document locator number.

Section 4 of Document 6209 defines Document Locator Numbers:

Section 4.   Document Locator Number

1   DLN Composition

(1)   The document locator number (DLN) is a controlled number assigned to every return or document input through the ADP system. The fourteenth (last) digit is the year of processing and is assigned by the Service Center computer at the time of the original input.

(2)   The DLN is used to control, identify, and locate documents processed in the ADP system.

(3)   The DLN should not be confused with the tax account number the tax account consists of nine digits, for example:

> Social Security Number XXX-XX-XXXX (IMF, IRAF)
> Employer Identification Number XX-XXXXXXX (BMF, EPMF)

Note: A temporary SSN is sometimes assigned by the Service Center. The first three digits (900-999) indicate the number is temporary. The 4th and 5th digits are the code of the Service Center assigning the number. The last four digits are numbers assigned consecutively beginning with 0001. The printed format is TXXXXXXXXX* (The "T" Indicates a temporary SSN, and the asterisk (*) indicates the number is invalid.)

(4)   Returns and documents are blocked and filed by DLN.

(5)   The format for a DLN is as follows:

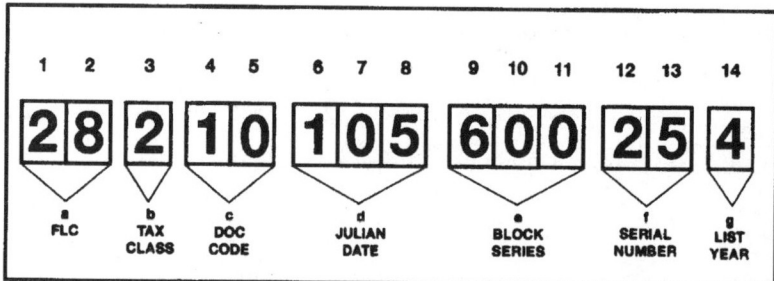

Notice the first two digits are designated FLC (File Location Code). In the case of both *transaction codes 914* and *912,* the *file location code* is 52, which identifies the IRS District Office in Baltimore, Maryland. In other words, the criminal investigation against me was started by the CID in Baltimore. The third digit identifies the *tax class* or type of tax. In this case the digit is 2 and that identifies the *tax class* as income tax. The fourth and fifth digits identify the *document code*. A review of Section 2 of the 1987 edition of Document 6209 reveals that there are sixteen documents identified with the document code 77, wherefore we will use other means to identify the document in question. The sixth, seventh and eighth digits identify what is called the *julian date*, the control date of the document. In order to keep from having two documents with the same control date, one of the documents will have a *julian date* with 400 added to it. Wherefore, in this case the *julian dates* in question are 707 and 680 respectively. The ninth, tenth and eleventh digits are called the *blocking series*. *Blocking series* indicate the nature of the adjustment to the computer file, or as another way of saying it, the activity in question. The twelfth and thirteenth digits are the *serial numbers*. The *serial numbers* are a block of 100 documents attached to an 813 Document Register form for storage purposes, numbered from 00 to 99. The fourteenth digit is the *year in question*, by the decade. Wherefore, the document locator number tells you everything involving the transaction entry to the computer file represented by the transaction code.

Now that we have determined that *transaction code 914* started the criminal investigation, and that *transaction code 912* reversed the *transaction code 914*, thus stopping the criminal investigation, we will investigate to determine what crime the CID was contending I allegedly violated. As indicated above, the *blocking series* within the *document locator number* identifies the nature of the activity associated with the *transaction code*. In the case of the *914* and *912 transaction codes* within computer transcript shown earlier, they both had the same *blocking series* code, "*300.*" This computer transcript is identified by the IRS as an *IMF (Individual Master File)*, so we will consult the *Document 6209* for the year the entry was made, 1987, to try to determine this alleged crime through researching the blocking series:

.09 *Returns Processing Adjustment Blocking Series*

Service center processing of taxpayer accounts for adjustment purposes must use the following blocking series to indicate the nature of the adjustment. The return must be associated with the subsequently generated IDRS transaction record unless the blocking series is specified as non-refile DLN.

IMF	Description
000–099	Adjustments with Original Return, unless specified below.'
100–149	Reserved.
150–198	Tax adjustments made without the original return, including penalty, interest and/or freeze releases. Non-refile DLN. When using this Blocking Series, no unpostable checks are made for prior Examination or mathematical/clerical errors because the original return has not been secured. Be careful when adjusting accounts using this Blocking Series.
199	Expired balance write-offs (TC 534/535) Non-refile DLN.
200–289	Forms 1040X processed by Returns Analysis Branch.
290–299	FORM 1040X Disaster Claims
300–399	Reserved
400–479	Form 4136 claim with Form 843. Non-refile DLN. Preassessment refund only.

BMF	Description
150–198	Tax adjustments without the original return, including penalty, interest and/or freeze release adjustments. Non-refile DLN. When using this blocking series, no unpostable checks are made for prior examination or math/clerical error because the original return has not been secured. Exercise caution when adjusting accounts using this blocking series.
199	Expired balance write-offs. (TC 534/535). Non-refile DLN.
200–299	Forms 1120X processed in Returns Analysis.
300–398	U.S.-U.K. Tax Treaty Claims. Non-refile DLN.
400–479	Form 4136 claim with Form 843. Preassessment refund only—non-refile.
480–489	Form 6249 Claim with Form 843. Non-refile DLN. Preassessment refund only.

Notice the *IMF blocking series 300—399* merely states *Reserved*. Knowing that citizens have no liability for domestic income, and theorizing that *reserved* means not in use, we will examine the *Business Master File (BMF)*.

Here we have an explanation: *300—399* has a designation of *U.S. - U.K. Tax Treaty Claims*. If the CID had to lie to the computer to initiate a criminal investigation regarding me, this would make sense. It would somehow involve some foreign earned income, or something along that line. But we can't leave anything to chance, and we have to find out if the CID was using *BMF* codes for their entries.

I wrote to the Assistant Commissioner, Public Affairs, and asked what the term "reserved" meant when used in a particular file in Document 6209, such as the IMF and the BMF. Here is the response I received:

DEPARTMENT OF THE TREASURY
INTERNAL REVENUE SERVICE
WASHINGTON, D.C. 20224

COMMISSIONER

OCT 1 9 1990

Mr. John B. Kotmair Jr.
P.O. Box 91
Westminster, MD   21157

Dear Mr. Kotmair:

Thank you for your letter of September 5, 1990, in which you asked "Whenever I encounter the term "RESERVED' in the Document 6209, does it mean that such numbers are set aside for future usage; such numbers are "RESERVED" for use in another computer file, such as IMF or the BMF?

In response to your question, the numbers that are shown in Document 6209 as "RESERVED" are not in current use and are set aside for future usage.

I hope this information is helpful.

Sincerely,

Robert Childers

Robert Childers
Chief, Field Services Staff
(Public Affairs)

Now our suspicions have been confirmed—they were using the BMF codes. The only thing left to do is identify the document that somehow alleges the crime. We find in the Internal Revenue Manual in Chapter 3, *Extracting, Sorting and Numbering*, at section 3(10)(72)7.3, a link between *blocking series 300* and Form 8288:

FORM NO.	DO/SC CODE	TAX CLASS & DOC CODE	BLOCKING SERIES	SPECIAL INSTRUCTIONS
6008	AU	868	500–599	AUSC only
6009	AU	668	000–499	AUSC only
6069/2758	C	689	500–599	CSC only
7004	D	819	000	
8027	AN	557	000–499	ANSC Only Established Master File
8271	P	562	000–999	Program 70:00
8288	P	641	300–319	
8404	D	669	600–699	
8612/2758	D	621	000–099	

In Chapter 3, *Law Enforcement Manual III*, at section 3(27)(68)4.3 it identifies the title of Form 8288 as, *Foreign Investment Real Property Tax Acct.* The title of Form 8288 even better explains its use:

Law Enforcement Manual III

Form	Title	Doc. Code	Tax Class
8271	Investors Reporting of Tax Shelter Request Number	62	5
8278	Computation and Assessment of Miscellaneous Penalties	54	2,3
8279	Election to be Treated as a FSC or Small FSC		
8288	FIRPTA—Foreign Investment Real Property Tax Acct.	88	2
8288A	Seller—Foreign Person of U.S. Real Property Interest	89	2
8300	Report of Cash Payments	64	5

By using the OMB Control Number displayed in the upper right hand corner on the Form 8288, we can discover the explanation for its use, as given to the Office of Management and Budget by the IRS when applying for the OMB Control Number:

**U.S. Withholding Tax Return for
Dispositions by Foreign Persons of
U.S. Real Property Interests**

OMB No. 1545-0902

Complete Part I or Part II. Also complete and attach Copies A and B of Form(s) 8288-A.
(Attach additional sheets if you need more space.)

Part I	To Be Completed by the Buyer or Other Transferee Required To Withhold Under Section 1445(a)

1 Name of buyer or other transferee responsible for withholding (see page 4)	Identifying number

Street address (apt. or suite no., or rural route. Do not use a P.O. box.)

By the use of the OMB *Register of Approved Forms*, listed by *OMB Control Numbers*, we find the IRS's explanation given the Office of Management and Budget for the approval of its lawful use of Form 8288:

```
         Department of the Treasury
         LIST OF ACTIVE INFORMATION COLLECTIONS
         APPROVED UNDER THE PAPERWORK REDUCTION ACT
                    AS OF 01/31/91

         Internal Revenue Service
```

OMB NUMBER	PURPOSE
REPORT TITLE	AFFECTED PUBLIC
AGENCY FORM NUMBERS	FREQUENCY

```
1545-0890                                               4
  U.S. CORPORATION SHORT-FORM INCOME TAX RETURN          3  4
                                                         7

    1120-A

1545-0892                                               4
  RETURNS RELATING TO CASH IN EXCESS OF $10,000 RECEIVED IN   3  4
  A TRADE OR BUSINESS                                    2
  IA-41-89 TEMPORARY REGULATIONS AND NPRM
    8300

1545-0894                                               5
  IRS CONSUMER FILMS - PUBLICATION 1237 (FORMERLY        1  6
  PUBLICATION 1030)                                      2
    PUBLICATION 1237

1545-0895                                               4
  GENERAL BUSINESS CREDIT                                3  4
                                                         2
    3800

1545-0901                                               4
  MORTGAGE INTEREST STATEMENT                            1  4
  LR-214-84 FINAL                                        7
    1098

1545-0902                                               4
  U.S. WITHHOLDING TAX RETURN FOR DISPOSITIONS BY FOREIGN     1  4
  PERSONS OF U.S. REAL PROPERTY INTERESTS - STATEMENT OF 2
  WITHHOLDING ON DISPOSITIONS BY FOREIGN PERSONS OF U.S. .....
    8288 8288-A

1545-0904                                               4
  T.D. 8125   FOREIGN MANAGEMENT AND FOREIGN ECONOMIC    4
  PROCESSES. REQUIREMENTS OF FOREIGN SALES CORPORATION   9
```

The following IRS instructions for Form 8288 are very explicit for Form 8288's purpose and use:

181

Form 8288 (Rev. 8-2000)

General Instructions

Section references are to the Internal Revenue Code unless otherwise noted.

Purpose of Form

A withholding obligation is generally imposed on the buyer or other transferee (withholding agent) when a U.S. real property interest is acquired from a foreign person. The withholding obligation also applies to certain partnerships, foreign and domestic corporations, and the fiduciary of certain trusts and estates. This withholding serves to collect tax that may be owed by the foreign person. Use this form to report and transmit the amount withheld.

Note: *You are not required to withhold if any of the Exceptions (which begin on this page) apply.*

Amount To Withhold

Withholding, to report and pay over the withheld amounts. **Do not** use Forms 8288 and 8288-A for these distributions. See Regulations section 1.1445-8.

When To File

A transferee must file Form 8288 and transmit the tax withheld to the IRS by the 20th day after the date of transfer.

You must withhold even if an application for a withholding certificate is or has been submitted to the IRS on the date of transfer. However, you do not have to file Form 8288 and transmit the withholding until the 20th day after the day the IRS mails you a copy of the withholding certificate or notice of denial. But if the principal purpose for filing the application for a withholding certificate was to delay paying the IRS the amount withheld, interest and penalties will apply to the period after the 20th day after

Transferor. For this means any f U.S. real propert gift, or any other

Withholding age this means the b acquires a U.S. r foreign person.

Foreign person. foreign corporati election under se domestic corpor foreign trust, or a individual is **not**

U.S. real proper than an interest

1. Real propert or the Virgin Islar

2. Certain pers

Through the use of the *document locator number*, and in particular the *blocking series* number *300*, we have discovered that the crime the IRS alleged that I committed was that I bought real property from a *foreign person* and did not withhold 31% of the payment for it, and consequently did not report the transaction on Form 8288 to the IRS. The only problem is, no such transaction ever took place to be reported. Of course, none of this fable would be in evidence at any resulting trial. The U.S. Attorney would argue that I failed to file a Form 1040, telling the jury that everyone knows that I had a requirement to do so, including me, and he or she would produce old Form 1040 tax returns, embossed with gold seals over red, white and blue ribbons to display their evidentiary importance, filed by me when I was ignorant of the law, as evidence of that knowledge. I have watched this scenario for the past thirty years.

Just like the prohibition era, the so-called war on drugs has not only caused a tremendous increase in the use of recreational drugs, it has also caused a resurgence of crime. So much so that there is an outcry for more police powers, regardless of the compromise of individual rights—a blueprint for a police state. This has fostered a public attitude that is conducive to a rush to judgment that overshadows the *innocent until proven guilty* judicial principle. Wherefore, the average jury has a preconceived belief that the accused is guilty just by being charged by the police authority. This being the case, the jury keys in on the prosecutor and the judge, and in tax cases, are most always misled. By using the mindset of well-meaning jurors, the IRS and the Department of Justice, with the intentional help of federal judges, have put numerous innocent Americans in jail. This must be stopped.

Part IV

. . . and "Justice" for All

Chapter 11

THE DEPARTMENT of JUSTICE
and
the FEDERAL COURTS

Thomas Jefferson warned American citizens *to bind men's mischief with the chains of the Constitution*. The only problem is, just like the Israelites of the Old Testament, Americans have taken what appears to be the easy road, believing that the government can and will take care of every need, leaving them free to seek their pleasures in life. What is forgotten, in this lust to be taken care of, is the historical fact that governments are naturally corrupt.

The branch of government whose job it is to protect your rights and to administer justice is the Judiciary. The only problem is, history tells us that this is very rarely the case. It is recorded in James Madison's *Notes on the Constitutional Convention* that some of the *Framers* believed a flaw to the Constitutional plan would be the sophistry of the courts. Like many of their fears, it's turning out to be true. I'm not saying that all judges are corrupt and unpatriotic. What I am saying is the *Save-A-Patriot Fellowship* has documentation that many of them are knowingly violating their oath of office, putting innocent citizens in jail, and takening citizens' property unlawfully. Whatever their reason, when they knowingly do this, that is, in my opinion, sedition. Sedition is defined in Noah Webster's 1828 American Dictionary of the English Language as:

A factious commotion of the people, or a tumultuous assembly of men rising in opposition to the law or the administration of justice, and in disturbance of the public peace. Sedition is a rising of commotion of less extent than an insurrection, and both are less than rebellion; but some kinds of sedition, in Great Britain, amount to high treason. In general, sedition is a local or limited insurrection in opposition to civil authority, as mutiny is to military. (Emphasis added.)

Article 6, Clause 3 of the U.S. Constitution states:

The Senators and Representatives before mentioned, and the members of the several state Legislatures, and all executive and judicial officers, both of the United States and of the several states, shall be bound by oath or affirmation to support this Constitution; but no religious test shall ever be required as a qualification to any office or public trust under the United States.

The oath taken is as follows:

I do solemnly swear that I will support and defend the Constitution of the United States against all enemies, foreign and domestic; that I will bear true faith and allegiance to the same.

Notice that the oath taken is not to defend the flag, the federal or State government, nor the United States, but rather the Constitution of the United States. This Constitution as written, prevents government from interfering with inalienable rights to *Life, Liberty* and the *Pursuit of Happiness* (Property). When a person within the government takes an oath to uphold and defend the Constitution, and then commits acts that are destructive to that end, he is violating that oath: that, in essence, is an act of overthrowing the intent and purposes of the Constitution, and is SEDITION. When two or more work in harmony to that end, that is a violation of Title 18 of the United States Code:

Section 2384.—Seditious conspiracy
    If two or more persons in any State or Territory, or in any place subject to the jurisdiction of the United States, conspire to overthrow, put down, or to destroy by force the Government of the United States, or to levy war against them, or to oppose by force the authority thereof, or by force to prevent, hinder, or delay the execution of any law of the United States, or by force to seize, take, or possess any property of the United States contrary to the authority thereof, they shall each be fined under this title or imprisoned not more than twenty years, or both.
    (Emphasis added.)

Of course, the *authority thereof the United States* is the Constitution; and a court order is *force*: if you try to resist it, you will find out how much force it really has. So, when a federal prosecutor and IRS employees prosecute citizens or resident aliens who are not in violation of the tax laws, and this fact has with pointed out to the presiding judge, and they all proceed acting indifference to this fact, that is a *seditious conspiracy*. Yet with this in mind, we will proceed to examine a few such instances.

In 1994, Norman Lehnhardt, a member of the *Save-A-Patriot Fellowship*, filed a civil suit in the Federal District Court in North Carolina against four Internal Revenue Service employees in their individual capacity, asking the court to order the employees to obey the law as written. The suit was brought pursuant to Title 28 United States Code, § 1361, which states in pertinent part:

The district court shall have original jurisdiction of any action in the nature of mandamus[1] to compel an officer of the United States or any agency thereof to perform a duty owed to the plaintiff.

The suit arose out of an unlawful tax assessment against

189

Norman, of which he gave notice to the IRS by the means of a petition for abatement, made pursuant to Internal Revenue Code section 6404(a)(3), which states:

(a) General rule
The Secretary is authorized to abate the unpaid portion of the assessment of any tax or any liability in respect thereof, which—
(1) is excessive in amount, or
(2) is assessed after the expiration of the period of limitation properly applicable thereto, or
(3) is erroneously or illegally assessed.

The employees named within the suit ignored the petition and proceeded with collection of the assessment, sending a Notice of Levy by certified mail to third parties holding Norman's property and to Norman.

As explained in Chapter XI, when the IRS sends a third-party a Notice of Levy, the reverse side of the form has printed on it the authority for Levy, § 6331. The only problem is, they do not print the entire section thereon. They start with paragraph (b), which describes the authority for *seizure and sale of property*, and leave out paragraph (a), which states that:

Levy may be made upon the accrued salary or wages of any officer, employee, or elected official, of the United States, the District of Columbia, or any agency or instrumentality of the United States or the District of Columbia . . .

Norman notified the third party of the lawful procedure to be followed by the IRS. In addition to this, he asked the IRS employees to reconsider his appeal, and he received notification from them that it was denied. Not having any alternative, and knowing about the unconstitutional *Anti-Injunction Act*, § 7421, he filed his action in the Federal District Court for the Middle District of North Carolina, case number 2:94CV00453, asking the court to order the IRS employees to obey the law as written, citing Title 28 USC, § 1361. From past experience, any action filed alleging wrongful assessment procedure would be responded to by the Department of Justice with a motion to dismiss, citing the Anti-Injunction Act. The courts have routinely granted such motions, summarily dismissing the suit regardless of any factual lawful argument to the contrary.

The IRS employees were sued in their individual capacity, because their actions were not in accordance with the written law. They only have immunity from suit in the lawful performance of their duties. Additionally, due to the fact that their actions were not in accordance with the written law, they could not be lawfully defended by the Department of Justice. The law never got in the way of Lawrence P. Blaskopf, the trial attorney from the Tax Division of the Department of Justice, who answered the complaint with a motion to dismiss, stating:

> The defendants, J.R. Starkey, C.R. Mobley, Richard March and Gail J. Roberson, by their undersigned counsel, hereby move to dismiss this case. The defendants are making this motion pursuant to Rule 12(b)(1) of the Fed. R. Civ. P. on the basis that this Court does not have subject matter jurisdiction over the complaint. The defendants are submitting a brief in support of this motion and a proposed Order granting the requested relief.

In his brief in support of his motion to dismiss, Blaskopf pulls the old switcheroo trick out of his hat. He admits that Norman cited § 1361 as the jurisdiction for the Court to hear his complaint, but then departs from that and goes to Norman's *accompanying memorandum* to his complaint and extracts an off-hand statement:

> ...that there has been no legal assessment of the tax against him, that the tax liens against him are defective and that a notice of intent to levy that was issued by the

I.R.S. was defective.

He then referred to a previous action filed by Norman that did not cite as its jurisdiction § 1361, and was dismissed by the same Court for want of jurisdiction because of the Anti-Injunction Act. He then institutes the old switcheroo:

> *As will be discussed, this action, although nominally against the defendants, is in reality against the United States because it seeks to frustrate administration actions taken by the United States to collect taxes. As such, it is barred by the doctrine of sovereign immunity. In fact, because the action seeks to restrain the collection of taxes, it is specifically barred by the Anti-Injunction Act. As a result, this action should be dismissed.*

Through his magical efforts, the law, § 6331(a), which clearly indicates that Norman cannot be the subject of a Notice of Levy, has somehow evaporated; and for that reason § 1361 should not come into play.

He continues to build on the switcheroo in his argument:

> *The plaintiff has sued the named defendants, employees of the Internal Revenue Service, "in their individual capacity." The plaintiff asserts the defendants were "acting outside the scope of their employment." The essential nature of the proceeding, however, is to seek to restrain the ability of the United States from collecting taxes from the plaintiff through its agents, the named defendants. Therefore, the United States is the real party in interest in this action.*

He then takes a couple of Supreme Court decisions out of context to continue to fog the issue that Norman's complaint is really about the Court ordering the IRS employees to obey the law as written. He attempts to proceed further down the sovereign immunity track which he switched to, never clearly showing any legitimate reasons why the defendant IRS employees should not be sued in their individual capacity:

> *It is well settled under the doctrine of sovereign immunity that suits cannot be brought against the United States unless it has expressly consented to be sued.*

Nowhere within Norman's complaint does it state that the United States is the defendant. Remember, all Norman is doing is asking the Court to order these IRS employees to obey a law they are subject to. But this man has no shame, for he then goes on, in effect, to rewrite Norman's complaint:

> *There is no waiver of sovereign immunity for the plaintiff's action. The plaintiff has averred that this Court has jurisdiction over this action pursuant to 28 U.S.C. Section 1361. Section 1361 grants District Courts jurisdiction over mandamus actions against officers, employees or agencies of the United States. Section 1361, however, does not constitute a waiver of sovereign immunity by the United States. . . . Therefore, since this action is in reality one against the United States and there has been no wavier of sovereign immunity for this action, it must be dismissed.*

He then reverts back to the Anti-Injunction Act, citing its provisions to the Court. He continues on justifying its use:

> *This statute embodies Congress' long-standing policy against premature interference with the <u>orderly</u> administration process by which taxes are determined, assessed and collected.* (Emphasis added.)

In his mind, it is *orderly* for IRS employees to assess the gross earnings of an individual, or even pluck an amount to assess right out of the air, and he sees no problem with that individual being required to pay this excessive tax, before shouldering the further expense of filing suit for the return of the property. The Fellowship has evidence of hundreds of thousands of Federal Reserve Notes in taxes being wrongfully assessed to working individuals without the ability to pay it, even if they had a mind to. This results in the IRS filing tax liens to encumber any property those individuals may own. But as far as this bureaucratic fat cat is concerned, that is perfectly all right. He would have made out fabulously in the employ of the Sheriff of Nottingham.

He concludes his memorandum in support of his motion to dismiss, by the following statement reverting back to the complaint as written by the plaintiff, asking the Court to overlook the IRS employees' violation of the law, so that they can continue robbing Norman without justifying their actions in the obviously wrongful assessment:

> *Here, similarly, the plaintiff seeks to have the defendants comply with the Internal Revenue Code and its regulations. The plaintiff, in essence, is seeking to restrain the conduct of the defendants in their efforts to collect tax from the plaintiff.*

In other words: *Hey Judge, if you Order these IRS employees to obey the law, they will not be able to collect the tax.* Unbelievable, that an attorney for the Department of "Justice" would make such a confession openly for the Court record. But that is not the worst of the matter. What is even more deplorable is that the judge granted his motion and dismissed Norman's complaint, thus openly conspiring with the IRS employees and the attorney from the Department of "Justice" in committing a seditious act with impunity.

I am sad to say, the record reveals that when it comes to tax cases, this case does not stand out as the exception, but the rule. This case stands out from among many others that the Fellowship has been involved in because of the attorney's bold use of the truth about the law itself.

Even though there is a right to a jury trial in civil matters, such as the case we just reviewed, it is impossible to obtain one in a tax case. Not that the law does not provide for one. The state and federal government attorneys and the state and federal judges simply will not allow it to get that far, as demonstrated in the case just discussed. In all my years as an activist in the Constitutional tax movement, I have never heard of a civil tax trial going to a jury.

The Maryland Constitution's Declaration of Rights, similar to the Bill of Rights in the United States Constitution, states in Declaration Number 23:

> *In the trial of all criminal cases, the Jury shall be the Judges of Law, as well as of fact, except that the Court may pass upon the sufficiency of the evidence to sustain a conviction.*

Though such jury powers do not appear in the federal Constitution, that does not mean that it does not exist in the federal court jurisdictions. The *Framers* probably saw no need for it to be included, for it was widely understood and accepted at the time of the framing and adoption of the Constitution by the several States. In 1794, the first jury trial was conducted in the United States Supreme Court, The case was *State of Georgia v Brailsford* (3 Dall 1), and the first Chief Justice of that Court, John Jay, presided over the trial and instructed the jury before their deliberations as follows:

> *It is presumed, that juries are the best judges of facts; it is, on the other hand, presumed that courts are the best judges of law. But still both objects are within your power of decision. You have a right to take it upon yourselves to judge of both, and to determine the law as well as the fact in controversy.*

This very principle of court procedure came into play in one of the most egregious political trials within this modern day struggle for *Individual Liberty*, the trial of my son, Edward L. Kotmair.

Assistant United States Attorney David J. Cortes stuck his neck out when a federal grand jury met and evidently did not return an indictment against Edward. On February 21, 1997, Cortes charged Edward with a three count *Information*, alleging that Edward had a requirement to file income tax returns for the years 1990, 1991 and 1992, and willfully failed to do so. Section 7203 was covered extensively earlier, in Chapter X of this book. For the reader who does not know what an *Information* is, Black's Law Dictionary, 5th Edition, defines it thusly:

> **Information.** *An accusation exhibited against a person or some criminal offense, without an indictment. An accusation in the nature of an indictment, from which it differs only in being presented by a competent public officer on his oath of office, instead of a grand jury on their oath.*

In this case, the "competent" public officer is Cortes, and he stuck his neck out when he filed criminal charges against Edward in the United States District Court for the Eastern District of North Carolina, case number 5:97-M-123, because if Edward was to be acquitted of the charges by the trial jury, he would have a perfect civil action against Cortes for false arrest; and because he spent some time in jail before the trial, false imprisonment. As you read the details of what transpired before, during, and after the trial, you will most likely come to one of the following conclusions, or all three:

> a) *there was collusion between Cortes and the Assistant Federal Public Defender, Stephen C. Gordon, to convict Edward;*
> b) *there was collusion between Cortes, Gordon and Chief*

United States District Judge Terrence W. Boyle, the
trial judge; and/or

c) *Cortes, Gordon and Boyle worked hard to prevent the*
truth about the federal tax laws from being presented to
the jury through witness testimony.

During the years in question, Edward was operating a commercial construction business out of North Carolina. His company installed cabinets and fancy moldings in the Library of Congress, the Capitol Building of the United States, the FDIC Building in Washington, D.C., Wake Forrest University, Senator Strom Thurmond's Oval Office, at Clemson University, and the V.I.P. Deck in the Baltimore Orioles ball park at Camden Yards. He managed to do all of this without the use of government identifying numbers or withholding taxes from his non-union employees.

While working on the V.I.P. Deck, a dispute broke out, and rumor had it that it was brought to the attention of then-governor of Maryland, William Donald Schaefer. The dispute concerned the fact that federal and state taxes were not being withheld from Edward's employees. Edward was told that King Willy Don (as the radio talk-show hosts in Baltimore call him) was very upset that such a contracting company was working on his pet project. It was not long after that IRS CID agents in Raleigh, North Carolina, started a criminal investigation early in 1993.

In February of 1997, Craig Jarvis, a writer for *The News & Observer* in Raleigh, North Carolina called to interview me in his preparation of an article announcing criminal charges made by the United States Attorney's Office against Edward. The article was prompted by a press release from the United States Attorney's Office that was put on the wire service and circulated all over the fifty States, announcing that the son of the founder of the *Save-A-Patriot Fellowship* was charged with tax crimes. This was just four years after the IRS's unsuccessful raid on the Fellowship.

Jarvis' article was published in *The News & Observer*, and a

Fellowship member from the Raleigh area faxed me a copy. The following is a letter I wrote Jarvis after I read the article:

Dear Mr. Jarvis:

I was faxed a copy of your article about my son Edward by one of our members. Considering the circumstances, it was fairly objective.

I am enclosing a couple of audio tapes and one video tape. If after watching and listening to these tapes you are interested in more information, we have a twelve-hour lecture on the law. This tape has an effect on the IRS, much like the cross on Dracula.

I am challenging Mr. George Muench to a public debate on the federal tax laws before Edward's trial. I have challenged other IRS officials in other parts of the United States, and as of this date not one of them has accepted, they all ran just like Dominic La Ponzina, the head of IRS Public Relations in Baltimore, did on the audio tape that I enclosed with this letter. These charlatans count on the mindset of the public to do their dirty deeds.

Thank you for the interest. I am looking forward to any comments or questions that you might have.

Semper Fidelis ad Libertas, Veritas que Justitia,
John B. Kotmair, Jr., Fiduciary

Enclosures to you and Mr. Muench:
Two audio tapes of the Zoh Hieronimus Radio Talk show: Dominic La Ponzina and myself and Linda Benson, Public Affairs for Social Security Administration and myself; and a video tape presentation entitled, "The Truth Behind The Income Tax."

I never heard any more from Jarvis or Muench. In fact, after the government's media splash, everything got real quiet.

Edward was living in Maryland at the time of the U.S. Attorney's news release announcing the three-count information for violation of *Section 7203: Willful failure to file return, supply information, or pay tax.* There was no contact from the government and the news release was the only notification Edward received. In the last week of August 1998, I announced that *Liberty Works Radio Network* would start broadcasting with talk-show programming. About two weeks later, on September 11, 1998, one year, six months, and two weeks after the U.S. Attorney's press release, Edward was arrested by IRS CID agents. On the way to the lockup in the Federal District Court in Baltimore, Michael O'Hanlon, the agent who was in charge of the raid on the Fellowship headquarters in 1993, struck up a conversation with Edward, inquiring about the capabilities of the radio network. The announcement that was made about the radio network was not public. In the time that elapsed between the news release and his arrest, Edward did not run and hide, but lived openly in Westminster, Maryland.

Due to some personal problems, Edward lost his business, and due to his lack of funds and his inability to defend himself, he accepted the assistance of the Federal Public Defender's Office. Stephen C. Gordon of that Office was appointed to defend him.

Because Edward relied on what he had learned from me, on March 18, 1999, I forwarded to one Ken Hall, an investigator for the office of the public defender, the following letter:

Dear Mr. Hall:

This is a notice of material and expert witnesses that

will testify in Edward L. Kotmair's defense during any trial that may take place regarding his instant incarceration:

> *John B. Kotmair, Jr.: Material Facts*
> *George E. Harp: Expert Witness*
> *Attorney at Law*
> *509 Marshall #219*
> *Shreveport, Louisiana 71101*
> *Mr. Jan Holland: Expert Witness*
> > *Degree in Accounting*
> > *Post Office Box 17461*
> > *Shreveport, Louisiana 71138*

If you have any questions, please call me between 9 AM and 5 PM Monday through Friday at 410-857-4441, Ext. 131.

Semper Fidelis ad Libertas, Veritas que Justitia,
John B. Kotmair, Jr.

In response to this, I received the following letter from Gordon, dated March 29, 1999:

Dear Mr. Kotmair:

Your letter to Ken Hall of March 18, 1999, has been forwarded to me. I represent your son, Edward Kotmair, and, consistent with my legal and ethical duties to him as my client, all matters involving the conduct of his case, including the conduct of any trial, I will discuss with him only.

Thank you for your understanding in this matter. I am returning your letter to you under this cover.

Sincerely,

WILLIAM W. WEBB
Federal Public Defender

STEPHEN C. GORDON
Assistant Federal Public Defender

After receiving this response, I had a suspicion that an honest defense in this trial might be wanting, and with that in mind, I answered Gordon as follows:

Dear Mr. Gordon:

I received your letter dated March 29, 1999, regarding my direct contact with you concerning my son's defense. Please be advised that I have years of experience in the federal court system and have worked with the Office of the Public Defender on behalf of members of the Fellowship. What does it matter if notification of witnesses comes to you under my signature or Edward's? You're going to get the witness list either way.

You can be assured that we're not going to lay down and let the U.S. Attorney get by with misrepresenting the federal tax laws. The truth will come out in spite of anyone's effort to prevent it.

If you have any questions, please call me between 9 AM and 5 PM Monday through Friday at 410-857-4441.

Semper Fidelis ad Libertas, Veritas que Justitia,
John B. Kotmair, Jr.

There was no response to this letter, and things became more cordial between Gordon and myself, with me still keeping a suspicious eye on him.

I received the following letter, dated August 5, 1999, from Gordon:

Dear Mr. Kotmair:

As you know from previous discussions we have had, I would like to have you and Mrs. Kotmair come to Raleigh for the purpose of meeting with me so that we can prepare for your possible testimony at the trial of my client, Edward Kotmair. The trial is now set for September 7, 1999, in Elizabeth City.

I realize it is an inconvenience for you to come to Raleigh from Maryland. If you are to testify on your son's behalf, however, it is critical that we go over what your testimony will be, and that you be sufficiently prepared to give testimony. I do not believe it is possible to do this over the telephone.

The time for preparing for this grows shorter with each passing day. Therefore, I would very much appreciate you and Mrs. Kotmair meeting with me at your very earliest possible convenience. Please call me and let me know when you are available to come to the office. I will then try to arrange for as much of the staff as has worked on this case, to be present.

Thank you for your understanding and cooperation in this matter.

Sincerely,
WILLIAM W. WEBB
Federal Public Defender

STEPHEN C. GORDON
Assistant Federal Public Defender

Nancy and I went to Raleigh within a week of receiving that letter.

Due to the fact that Gordon was basing Edward's defense on willfulness, my testimony would be my knowledge of the Internal Revenue Code that Edward relied upon. Gordon faxed the following request to me on August 17, 1999:

Dear Mr. Kotmair:

Pursuant to, and confirming, our telephone conversation today, I am writing to request that you send me, at your earliest convenience, your outline of the Tax Code and related Federal Regulations which you told me will help the jury understand that Edward Kotmair did not have a duty to file tax returns. We discussed during our conversation 26 U.S.C. §§ 1, 61; however, there are specific questions I still have, even after my viewing of your videotape, and meeting personally with you. As direct an answer as you can give me to these questions, and as quickly as you can give it, will be most helpful.

First, why is a legal duty to file income tax returns not imposed on citizens living in the 50 states of the Union, on their domestic-earned-income, under 26 U.S.C. § 1 and also under 26 U.S.C. § 6012?

Second, why is the definition of "gross income" under the curent version of 26 U.S.C. § 61 not the legal definition of "gross income"?

Third, are wages income?

Fourth, why does the definition of "person" under 26 U.S.C. § 7701(a)(1) not include all citizens living within the 50 states of the Union?

Fifth, why is the OMB control number for 1040 form different from the number on the 2555 form, and why is the 2555 form to be attached to the 1040 form, and not vice-versa?

Sixth, does the furnishing of a statement of citizenship to a withholding agent relieve the citizen of an obligation to file a tax return on the wages received from that withholding agent?

As I have stated, it is essential that we be able to present Edward Kotmair's reading of the tax code as concisely, and coherently, as we can. I am going to need to be able to walk the jury through the relevant statutes and relevant C.F.R. Sections, in a logical order, that show why the code can be read as not imposing a duty on American citizens to file tax returns. To that end, I believe it is going to be necessary for us to meet again, in person, prior to trial. It may well be necessary to meet several times, in fact. Please let me know if you are willing to return to Raleigh for any additional meetings. I appreciate that the journey is arduous for you, but my ability adequately to prepare your testimony will determine whether I think it best to call you as a witness at the trial.

Please call me if you have any questions. Finally, let me take this opportunity formally to thank you, Mrs. Kotmair, and Mr. Stein for coming to Raleigh last Friday.

Sincerely,

WILLIAM W. WEBB
Federal Public Defender

STEPHEN C. GORDON

Assistant Federal Public Defender

The following answers were faxed and mailed to him on August 25, 1999. The exhibits are not included here, since all of the facts in the exhibit documents have been covered in preceding Chapters of this book:

Dear Mr. Gordon:

Hopefully the following will answer your questions.

Question 1:

Why is a legal duty to file income tax returns not imposed on citizens living in the 50 states of the Union, on their domestic-earned-income, under 26 U.S.C. § 1 and also under 26 U.S.C. § 6012?

Answer:

Part I:

It would be in violation of Article 1, Section 2, Clause 3 and Article 1, Section 9, Clause 4 of the United States Constitution which prohibits the federal government from taxing real and personal property directly:

Representatives and direct taxes shall be apportioned among the several States...according to their respective numbers...

and,

No capitation or other direct tax shall be laid, unless in proportion to the census or enumeration herein before directed to be taken.

In 1797, in the case of Hylton vs. United States, the

205

Supreme Court held that a tax on carriages, under an Act of Congress on June 5, 1794, was not a direct tax even though it was a tax on the personal property of citizens. This egregious ruling set a precedence that continued until it was finally overturned by the Pollock decision.

When Charles Pollock prosecuted his challenge to the constitutionality of the Income Tax Act of August 15, 1894, the United States Supreme Court was missing one Justice and the decision was deadlocked. It was through the efforts of one of Mr. Pollock's attorneys, Mr. Joseph H. Choate, that the Court granted a re-hearing. When the re-hearing was heard the Court had a full complement of nine Justices. Mr. Choate's argument was so factual and compelling that he persuaded five Justices to overturn all the Court's rulings regarding income tax since the Hylton case in 1797.

Thank God that there were five honorable men sitting at that time. On the dishonorable side we have, among others, Justice Harlan who complained in his dissenting Opinion:

> And so the judgment now to be entered takes from the government the entire revenue that Congress expected to raise by the taxation of incomes.

Harlan went on to expound that the majority of the Court was wrong by reiterating the convoluted logic reached by the Supreme Court in the Hylton case. That is, only real property and slaves were property subject to direct taxation, contending that a federal tax on personal property itself was not "direct," but rather an indirect tax:

> That from the foundation of the government, until 1861, Congress following the declarations of the judges in the Hylton case, restricted direct taxation to real estate and slaves, and in 1861 to real estate exclusively, and has

never, by any statute, indicated its belief that personal property, however assessed or valued, was the subject of "direct taxes" to be apportioned among the states

Of course, as stated above, through the efforts of Mr. Pollock's attorneys, the majority of the Court saw the fallacy in this convoluted logic and unconstitutionality of the acts of Congress started in 1794, by declaring federal taxes on personal property a direct tax.

The issue of the possibility of taxes on personal property as being an indirect excise was put to rest in 1909 in the Supreme Court case of Flint v. Stone Tracy when the Court defined indirect excise taxes as:

> ...taxes laid upon the manufacture, sale, or consumption of commodities within the country, upon licenses to pursue certain occupations, and upon corporate privileges.

Part II:

The certified ratification documents on the 16th Amendment were gathered from each State of the Union and published in 1985, and the count reveals very clearly that the States did not ratify this Amendment. Beside that fact, even if we consider the Amendment ratified, the Supreme Court in 1916 stated in very clear language as follows:

Brushaber v. Union Pacific Railroad Company, 240 US 1.

> [The] command of the amendment that all income taxes shall not be subject to the rule of apportionment by a consideration of the source from which the taxed income may be derived forbids the application to such taxes of the rule in the Pollock case by which alone such taxes were removed from the great class of excises, duties, and imposts subject to the rule of uniformity and were

placed under the other or direct class.

and again in that same year;

<u>*Stanton v. Baltic Mining Company*</u>, *240 US 112:*

> Sixteenth Amendment conferred no new power of taxation but simply prohibited the previous complete and plenary power of income taxation possessed by Congress from the beginning from being taken out of the category of indirect taxation to which it inherently belonged.

The above facts are substantiated by the Internal Revenue Code itself. For instance, all the sources which the income must come from before it can be taxed are foreign sources, and the only withholding of income tax found in Chapter 3 is from nonresident aliens, foreign corporations, foreign tax exempt organizations and Virgin Island income.

Part III:

A careful reading of Section 6012 reveals that it pertains to "Every individual." But it states:

"Returns with respect to income taxes under subtitle A shall be made..."

Subtitle A contains Chapters 1 through 6. Chapter 1 being entitled "Normal Taxes and Surtaxes." Part I of Chapter 1 is entitled "Tax on Individuals," and Section 1, "Tax Imposed." Since the "individuals," whose income the tax is imposed upon, are within Section 1, their identity and the tax return they're to use is found within 26 CFR Part 602, pursuant to The Paperwork Reduction Act of 1980.

The regulation implementing Section 1, 26 CFR 1.1 *[handwritten: Stanton US. Bartec meng]* lists an OMB control number 1545-0067. OMB control number 1545-0067 identifies Internal Revenue information request Form 2555, "FOREIGN EARNED INCOME."

The 1993 edition of 26 CFR Part 602 was modified by removing 26 CFR 1.1-1 and its OMB control number listing. From then to this date the listings start at 26 CFR 1.23-5, which lists the OMB control number of 1545-0074, the number for IRS Form 1040. To explain this attempted cover-up by the IRS, I am enclosing a copy of a letter that I received in 1997, regarding this change, and my response to that letter. It is attached as Exhibit A.

Question 2:

Why is the definition of "gross income" under the current version of 26 USC § 61 not the legal definition of "gross income"?

Answer:

Part I:

It is the modified legal definition. Just is as stated in Just The Facts, if the words "(but not limited to)" were left to stand without any connection to § 22 of the 1939 IR Code, the current § 61 would be void for vagueness. Wherefore, § 22 was brought forward intact when you insert the words "wages" and "salaries" in the stead of "(but not limited to)" as modified. This conceals the fact that wages are income, but rather, as stated in § 22, income is from the "wages" and from the "salaries." The "wages" and "salaries" are items of "gross income" the same as all the rest in § 61.

Part II:

Income from the item of gross income in § 61 are taxable only when it comes from a source that is listed in Subchapter N of Chapter 1. Subchapter N starts at § 861 and ends at § 999. Attached as Exhibit B is all the index of 26 CFR starting at § 1.861-1 and ending at § 1.927(d)-2T dealing with income sources involving income received by individuals. Notice that § 1.861-8 is from sources within the United States. The content of § 1.861-8, which identifies the individuals subject to liability within the United States, is attached as Exhibit C, please notice that citizens are not among the listings.

Question 3:

Are wages income?

Answer:

This question is answered in question 2 above.

Question 4:

Why does the definition of "person" under 26 USC § 7701(a)(1) not include all citizens living within the 50 states of the Union?

Answer:

The question as it relates to § 7701(a)(1) has no legal significance. The only purpose for the definition of person within § 7701 (a)(1) is to identify that entities listed therein, could be, or would be, the person cited within a particular section of the IR Code.

Question 5:

Why is the OMB control number for the 1040 form different from the number on the 2555 form, and why is the 255[5] form to be attached to the 1040 form, and not vice-versa?

Answer:

Part I:

Each IRS form has a different OMB control number so that it can be traced to the statute that authorizes it. The purpose of the Paperwork Reduction Act was to give citizens the ability to discover whether they have a legal requirement to complete and respond on a particular government agency form that the agency is requesting the citizen to complete, sign and submit.

Part II:

Form 2555 is instructed to be attached to the front of Form 1040 because Form 2555 is the primary return and Form 1040 is not. This is shown by example of the twenty pages or so of all the returns that are required to be filed I sent your office some time ago.

Question 6:

Does the furnishing of a statement of citizenship to a withholding agent relieve the citizen of an obligation to file a tax return on the wages received from the withholding agent?

Answer:

First, as stated in the IRS regulations, the purpose of the Statement of Citizenship is to give notice to the withholding agent not to withhold income taxes, and has nothing to do with any requirement to file any IRS tax form.

Second, the withholding agent only withholds income taxes and does not withhold tax on wages; the tax on wages is an employment tax, and there is no requirement to withhold employment taxes from any citizen or resident alien.

And, there is no requirement within the IR Code to file a tax return regarding wages paid to individuals. The wage tax is § 3402 in Chapter 24 of Subtitle C, and the only requirement for an individual to file a tax return, as stated in § 6012, is in Subtitle A.

I hope that the above answers have helped to clarify what liability citizens have regarding the Internal Revenue Code. If you have any further questions please give me a call.

Semper Fidelis ad Libertas, Veritas que Justitia,
John B. Kotmair, Jr.

cc: Edward Kotmair

Five days after Gordon received my response, Cortes filed with the Court a MOTION IN LIMINE, which states in pertinent part:

The United States, by and through the United States Attorney for the Eastern District of North Carolina, hereby moves __in__ __limine__ to exclude the testimony of John Kotmair, Jr., under Rule 403 of the Federal Rules of Evidence.

Rule 403 states:

212

Rule 403. Exclusion of Relevant Evidence on Grounds of Prejudice, Confusion, or Waste of Time. Although relevant, evidence may be excluded if its probative value is substantially outweighed by the danger of unfair prejudice, confusion of the issues, or misleading the jury, or by considerations of undue delay, waste of time, or needless presentation of cumulative evidence.

Cortes went on to say within his motion:

Mr. Kotmair has a long history of participating in tax protest litigation. As the U.S. District Court of Maryland put it, he is "the corpse at every funeral, the bride at every wedding and the baby at every christening." . . . It is expected that, if allowed to testify, Mr. Kotmair will attempt to assert many of the discredited views that he . . . espoused for the past twenty years.

In his motion, Cortes concludes that:

Indeed, it will be the very aim of the elder Kotmair to persuade the jury that, contrary to settled law, wages are not income, that U.S. Citizens do not have to file returns on domestically earned income, and so on. This he should not be allowed to do. Indeed, it is no defense at all that the defendant disagrees with what he knows to be settled law.

The Government therefore requests that the court permit Edward Kotmair to present his defense, if any, through his own testimony and through a reasonable number of admissible documents, rather than through the studied confusion that John Kotmair will attempt to foist on the jury.

So Cortes' reasoning for the use of Rule 403 is that my testimony would *confuse* the jury as to the imposition of the federal tax laws. Why should he be so afraid of that? If my understanding of the written law is obviously so wrong, he should have a very easy time demonstrating this to the jury. Instead of wanting to prevent me from taking the witness stand, he should be eager to get me there to expose me for the charlatan that he claims I am. The *settled law* that he is talking about is not the written law itself, which I have been exposing in this book, but rather the perverted version thereof by some federal district and appellate court judges, which is very easy for me to expose for what it is: intentional perversion of the law. That is why he did not want to face me in that courtroom. Knowledge is strength, and he knew, from my past courtroom experiences, that I could not be intimidated by either him or the judge.

The Sixth Amendment to the United States Constitution says:

> *In all criminal prosecutions, the accused shall enjoy the right to a speedy and public trial*, by an impartial jury of the State and district wherein the crime shall have been committed, which district shall have been previously ascertained by law, and to be informed of the nature and cause of the accusation; to be confronted with the witnesses against him; *to have compulsory process for obtaining witnesses in his favor*, and to have the Assistance of Counsel for his defence. (Emphasis added.)

Notice that the Sixth Amendment does not state: *to have compulsory process for obtaining witnesses in his favor*, except that if such witnesses were thought to possibly *confuse* the jury, then, and in that case, they should not be allowed to testify.

Gordon responded with DEFENDANT'S RESPONSE IN OPPOSITION TO GOVERNMENT'S MOTION IN LIMINE and argued:

> *The defendant, Edward L. Kotmair, by and through undersigned counsel and pursuant to the Fifth and Sixth Amendments of the United States Constitution, hereby files this Response in Opposition to the government's motion in limine to exclude the testimony of John Kotmair, Jr. Mr. John Kotmair is the father of Edward Kotmair, and he has material knowledge about factual aspects of this case. The government, with no basis for believing that Edward Kotmair has any intention of doing so, baldly asserts that Edward Kotmair's purpose in calling his father as a witness is to have the latter deliver a tax seminar to the jurors, in the hopes of confusing the issues at trial. Edward Kotmair intends no such thing. John Kotmair's testimony is necessary to establishing Edward Kotmair's defense of good faith to the charges against him, and Edward Kotmair has a right to present that testimony. Accordingly, this Court should deny the government's motion.*

Every time Gordon visited Edward, he tried to convince him to plea bargain, promising that he would be released with time served if he would file tax returns. Edward related to me that at his arraignment, of which more will be covered in the next paragraph, Judge Boyle indicated to him that he would be released with time served if he would file tax returns. Edward further stated that when the U.S. marshal was taking him back to the holding cell, he was trying to convince him to take Boyle's deal, saying, "*Man, did you hear what he said? You can go home.*" This did not happen just once, the marshal would continue to urge Edward to take the judge's deal every time he would escort him during the different recess breaks in the trial.

The federal district courts in North Carolina hold the arraignment in criminal trials on the same day just before the trial in an obvious attempt to defeat the provision of the speedy trial

215

found in the 6th Amendment to the United States Constitution, codified in Title 18 USC 3161, *Speedy Trial Act*, which states in pertinent part:

> *(c) (1) In any case in which a plea of not guilty is entered, <u>the trial</u> of a defendant charged in an information or indictment with the commission of an offense <u>shall commence within seventy days from the filing date (and making public) of the information</u> or indictment, or from the date the defendant has appeared before a judicial officer of the court in which such charge is pending, <u>whichever date last occurs</u>. If a defendant consents in writing to be tried before a magistrate judge on a complaint, the trial shall commence within seventy days from the date of such consent.* (Emphasis added.)

From the date of the Information, February 21, 1997, to the date of the arraignment was 2 years, 6 months, and 14 days after the Information, and 2 years, 6 months, and 8 days after it was made public.

Over the objections of Gordon, and with the help of the paralegal department of the Fellowship, on July 30, 1999, Edward filed a *Petition for Writ Of Habeas Corpus* in the Federal District Court in North Carolina. In the Petition, he asked the Court to dismiss the Information with prejudice because of the violation of the *Speedy Trial Act*, and the fact that the Information was deficient in that it did not cite the statute that he allegedly violated. And of course, § 7203 cannot be violated, as covered in Chapter X of this book; it is merely the penalty provisions for the statute having the requirement allegedly violated, a factual argument that Gordon would not present to the Court. The respondent was Judge Boyle, whose custody he was in. At that time, since the filing of the Information, he had been locked down a total of 170 days. Nothing was heard from the government.

Nancy and I were subpoenaed by Gordon to testify at the

trial. In response to that subpoena, we traveled to Elizabeth City, North Carolina, on September 6, 1999. The next day, we were at the courthouse for the start of the trial. I fully expected to testify regarding the answers to the six questions that Gordon had faxed me. As soon as the proceedings started, Nancy and I were sequestered, being told to stay in the hallway just outside the courtroom. It was a very uncomfortable day, as there was nothing to sit on but some marble steps that led to the floor above. The Court recessed for the day without calling either one of us.

The next morning we ran into Gordon outside of the courthouse, and I asked him if, due to the uncomfortable conditions in the hallway, it were possible for Nancy and I to wait at the motel, just a few city blocks away, to be called. He told us that would be all right, that he would call us in plenty of time to get there.

We returned to the motel to wait. Around two or three o'clock in the afternoon the telephone rang and to my surprise, it was not Gordon, or any of his staff, it was my ex-daughter-in-law, who told me that the trial was over. To say that I was displeased is putting it mildly.

Nancy and I rushed back to the courtroom and got there in time to hear the final arguments and the judge's instructions to the jury. It was all I could do to sit there without correcting aloud all the lies that were being told to the jury about me by the prosecutor and the judge. They misrepresented me and my activities so much that I thought that I was the one on trial. I could hardly keep from blurting out: *If what I do and say is so wrong, why don't they charge me and try me for it?* I thought surely the jury had enough common sense to understand that. It was obvious that they did not want me on the stand telling this jury that I had not filed tax returns or withheld any taxes from my employees since 1973, and also about how the IRS failed in their raid on the Fellowship in 1993. I guess that would *confuse* the jury, as Cortes contended in his motion asking the judge to prevent me from testifying. After the final arguments, Court was recessed until the next morning.

The next morning, September 9th, the judge gave the jury his instructions, and the jury left the courtroom to deliberate, and it seemed that they hardly had enough time to discuss anything before they returned with the guilty verdict. They were politely thanked and excused by the judge. The courtroom was empty except for Gordon and Cortes and their staff who were collecting all the paperwork used during the trial. Nancy and I were in the back of the courtroom just observing what was going on. Cortes approached me saying, *Mr. Gordon did a good job for your son.* Believing at that time Cortes' motion to prevent me from testifying was granted, it was all I could do to be civil. I contained myself as best I could and blurted out: *You were afraid to face me on the witness stand.* He replied, "That's not so," as he turned and walked away. The U.S. marshal came over to me and asked me to leave the courtroom, and not seeing any advantage to being arrested, Nancy and I left.

Later, after obtaining a copy of the court docket from the clerk, it was revealed that right after the arraignment, the judge *terminated* the *motion in limine* without ruling on it. Therefore, because Edward's defense was based on my testimony, there is reason to believe that there was a conspiracy between the prosecutor and the public defender, to prevent Edward from having a chance to be acquitted by the jury. This is probably why, from the time we returned to the courthouse from the motel the day before, Gordon did not once look in the direction of Nancy and me. It is also interesting to note that in the partial trial transcript (the whole trial transcript was not obtained), I was referred to 179 times, making it obvious why they did not want me on the witness stand.

On the 14th of September, Assistant United States Attorney Robert E. Skiver filed a motion to dismiss Edward's *Habeas Corpus* action arguing that: *Indeed because he* [Edward] *did not bring a Speedy Trial motion at his arraignment, Petitioner waived this issue and it cannot be revived.* Edward's answer is as follows:

The Petitioner filed his petition for a writ of habeas

218

corpus against Judge Terrence W. Boyle, due to the fact that Mr. Kotmair was in the custody of Judge Boyle at that time. Judge Boyle was presiding over E.D.N.C. Case No. 5:97-M-123 (hereinafter, "the case"). Since then, Judge Boyle conducted a sham trial wherein Mr. Kotmair was found guilty of violating an unidentified or non-existent law that purportedly required Mr. Kotmair to file federal tax returns for tax years 1990, 1991 and 1992.

Mr. Kotmair could not enter a plea of any kind, within the 70 days afforded by the speedy trial act, through no fault of his own. It is the unorthodox practice of this district to deny defendants the right to enter timely pleas— contrary to the constitutional provision guaranteeing a speedy arraignment. Because of this, E.D.N.C. Case No. 5:97-M-123 should be overturned, as a matter of law, and Mr. Kotmair released.

Mr. Kotmair's attorney was also grossly negligent, in that he prevented the primary witness to testify on behalf of the defendant. See "Supplemental Affidavit of Edward L. Kotmair in Support of Petition for Writ of Habeas Corpus" ("supplemental affidavit"), paragraphs 4 through 14; this affidavit is incorporated herein in its entirety, by reference thereto. Mr. Kotmair was also ill-advised on the matter of entering a plea. See supplemental affidavit, paragraphs 15 through 23.

This court may take judicial notice of the fact that Judge Boyle did not recuse himself from presiding over the trial, even though he was the Respondent in this action and properly served. Judge Boyle is currently detaining Mr. Kotmair pending sentencing.

The *Petition for Writ of Habeas Corpus* was assigned to Judge Malcolm J. Howard, U.S. District Court Judge for the Eastern District of North Carolina, who issued an Order on

November 1, 1999, in response to *Boyle's Motion toDdismiss*, which states in pertinent part:

> *Because Petitioner did not raise the issue of his rights under the Speedy Trial Act at his arraignment, Respondent contends that he has waived those rights. To the contrary, however, a defendant waives the right of dismissal under the Speedy Trial Act only if he fails to move for dismissal prior to trial or entry of a plea of guilty or nolo contendere. See 18 U.S.C. §3162(a)(2). Petitioner properly filed this action, prior to his September trial, seeking habeas corpus relief because his rights under the Act were allegedly violated. Accordingly, Respondent's motion to dismiss is denied.*

The *Fellowship's* paralegal who wrote the pleading and I could not believe it; finally, an honest judge holding to the law. This was unheard-of in tax cases, particularly a judge ruling against the chief judge of his district, his superior. Of course, he did not overturn Edward's conviction, or make a mention of the merits of the *habeas corpus* action, and eventually, as you will see, the celebration was short-lived.

On the very same day Judge Howard denied Boyle's motion to dismiss, Skiver, on behalf of the United States of America (not Boyle) filed a *Motion For Extension of Time to Reply to Edward's Response* to the *Motion to Dismiss the Habeas Corpus*. This was followed up with a *Motion to Reconsider and Transfer Case for Further Proceedings*, to, of all places, Judge Boyle's Court, the very judge who is the defendant in the *habeas corpus* action, giving the following reasons:

> *In the November 1, 1999 Order, this Court held that Petitioner's original pro se § 2241 motion is now properly considered a Speedy Trial Act (STA) motion for dismissal of his criminal charges in EDNC Case 5:97-m-123. Resolution of any STA dismissal motion requires careful*

consideration of all trial court motion dates, orders, events, excludable periods, and reasons therefor. 18 U.S.C. §§ 3161-3162.

Consideration of these matters is normally undertaken by the trial court who has first-hand knowledge of all proceedings between a defendant's charging and trial dates. For this reason, it is requested that Petitioner's STA motion to dismiss, as set forth in his § 2241 action, be transferred to Judge Boyle, who has supervised Petitioner's criminal case since its commencement, and who will conduct Petitioner's sentencing hearing on December 13, 1999.

Additionally, as noted in the United States' November 1, 1999 motion for Extension, Petitioner's October 18, 1999 Response raises new issues beyond those in his original § 2241 action. Petitioner's new issues include claims of "grossly ineffective counsel," "sham trial," and "non-existent law."

These new claims are either sentencing considerations, potential appeal issues, or 28 U.S.C. § 2255 grounds, and all are normally the province of the trial court. Because Petitioner has been assigned new counsel since the trial, allowing these matters to be explored at his sentencing hearing might lead to their resolution or, at least, would serve to complete the record. For this further reason, it is requested that Petitioner's pending § 2241 action be transferred to Judge Boyle.

Wherefore, it is respectfully requested that this Court reconsider its November 1, 1999 Order and transfer Petitioner's pending § 2241 action to the Honorable Terrence W. Boyle for further proceedings. In the alternative, it is requested that this Court reconsider and withdraw its November 1, 1999 Order, allow the United

States to Reply after Petitioner's December 13, 1999 sentencing hearing, after which this Court can make its ruling.

Outrageously, in essence, this guy is saying that Boyle is the only one having a record of what has transpired since Edward's arrest (apparently, Skiver wants us to believe that there is no clerk's office containing a docket and a copy of all that has transpired in the federal court in the Eastern District of North Carolina), and that the very judge that was violating Edward's rights, who is the defendant in the *habeas corpus* action, is the only one that can render a fair and just decision. God forbid.

Then he misrepresents what was argued, in response to the government's lame reason (given in its *Motion to Dismiss the Habeas Corpus*) that the *Speedy Trial Act* was not brought up at the arraignment, by ignoring the fact that Edward was also ill advised on the matter of entering a plea by his ineffective counsel. Even if new issues of violation of rights were raised, are they grounds to move the *habeas corpus* proceedings to the court of Boyle, one of the very individuals committing such violations?

It was very obvious that the U.S. Attorney's Office did not give much consideration to the allegations in that *Habeas Corpus* which claimed that *Judge Boyle conducted a sham trial wherein Mr. Kotmair was found guilty of violating an unidentified or non-existent law that purportedly required Mr. Kotmair to file federal tax returns for tax years 1990, 1991 and 1992,* since he contended that this was a new issue, when it was one of the two charges of violation of rights in the original petition.

On November 17, 1999, Judge Howard evidently got the message about the political consequences of this trial, and dutifully issued the following infamous Order:

This matter is before the court on Respondent's motion to reconsider and transfer for further proceedings. Also,

222

before the court is Respondent's motion for an extension of time within which to reply. These matters are ripe for disposition.

Respondent's motion to dismiss this action was denied by order of this court on November 1, 1999. Petitioner, who was found guilty on September 9, 1999, is scheduled for a sentencing hearing on December 13, 1999, before the Honorable Chief United States District Judge Terrence W. Boyle.

As an initial matter, Respondent's motion for an extension of time to file a reply is moot and is therefore denied.

Moreover, it is apparent that Chief Judge Boyle is not Petitioner's custodian and therefore is not the proper respondent in this matter. For this reason, the clerk is directed to substitute the United States of America as the Respondent.

Upon careful consideration of this matter, the court concludes that it is in the interest of justice and judicial economy, that this case be reassigned to Chief Judge Boyle so that the collateral issues relating to Petitioner's criminal proceedings may be disposed of in an expeditious manner.

Accordingly, Respondent's motion for an extension in time is denied and the motion to transfer or reassign this action is granted.

Even though Howard orders the clerk to substitute the United States of America for Judge Boyle, he must surely know that the United States cannot be a respondent for *habeas corpus* purposes. The United States cannot violate rights, only individuals working for the United States can violate rights. Also, notice that Howard does not address any of the merits of whether or not Boyle violated Edward's rights, or the merits of any of the other trial abuses. He just dutifully repeats the instructions within the written orders that Boyle's messenger brought him, contained within the motion to transfer, and then has the audacity to say that in the *interest of justice . . . that this case be reassigned to Chief Judge Boyle.* I do have to admit that his decision to transfer the case does result in the interest of judicial economy, since it saves the government any expense for a fair and just hearing, or for that matter, any hearing.

Edward filed a motion to reconsider, citing all kinds of authority why the *habeas corpus* action should not be transferred, and because judges are supposed to cite the reasons they ruled as they did on the facts and the law in question, concluded with a request for the following:

> *The Petitioner prays that this court prepare a memorandum of facts and conclusions of law to fully explain how it determined that,*
> 1. *Judge Boyle "is not Petitioner's custodian and therefore not the proper respondent in this matter"; and,*
> 2. *how it is "in the interest of justice and judicial economy, that this case be reassigned to chief Judge Boyle so that collateral issues relating to Petitioner's criminal proceedings may be <u>disposed of in an expeditious manner</u>."* [Emphasis added.]

On January 12, 2000, Howard issued an Order in response to Edward's motion for reconsideration. It was, to put it mildly, not responsive to the above request:

> *Turning first to Petitioner's motion for reconsideration, Petitioner has failed to state any meritorious grounds to support his motion. Therefore, this motion is denied.*

Well, at least he did not misuse the word "frivolous" like so

224

many other federal judges do. Of course, the outcome was predictable: On April 17, 2001, Chief Judge Terrence W. Boyle issued an Order which stated:

> *Because Kotmair was found guilty by a jury and was appropriately sentenced, he is now legally in the custody of Respondent. Petitioner's habeas petition must therefore be denied as moot.*

This is not the worst of it. The sentencing transcript, beginning at page 17, reveals either gross ignorance or just raw tyranny. In either case, it's *prima facie*[2] evidence of Boyle's malfeasance in office. The dialogue is between Boyle and Cortes. Gregory Ramage, the lawyer appointed by the court to replace Gordon, was also present. The matter being discussed is regarding the length of the sentence due Edward for allegedly committing obstruction of justice. The following is verbatim from the transcript, starting with Cortes saying:

> *Mr. Cortes: . . . He gets obstruction because he committed perjury. The case was all about this. Do I, Edward Kotmair, do I believe that I really didn't have to file. He said that to the jury in so many ways, and he said it expressly - I don't have the transcript with me here—but he made that direct assertion, I believe that I did not have to.*

> *The Court: It's hard to tag him with perjury for that because he has gone to jail for that belief. He seems to be committed to the belief, whether or not objectively the government agrees with it. It's a fact that it's not a well-founded belief to the public; doesn't mean that he is in the process of committing a lie.*

> *Mr. Cortes: Your Honor, if he— the whole case, again, was about whether he believed that he didn't have to file. Any person who lives in a society would agree that—that*

it would be unreasonable to think that you don't have to file, but if the defendant had persuaded the jury that he did, in fact, believe that he didn't have to file, then he walks, so that is what the case was about and that is the reason why I, myself, as a prosecutor, fought for this right to put in evidence about what he believed.

He is entitled to do that. He is entitled to do that because that is what the case is about. Remember the jury came back three times asking for an instruction on the good faith defense, so they were well aware of that and they were prepared to walk this defendant if they found in their good conscience that he did not believe or rather that he believed that he did not have to file. They were going to acquit him if they thought—if they believed his defense.

The other side of it is when he takes the stand as he did and says I believe that I did not have to file and the jury knowing what is at issue then says you are guilty, they are telling the Court, they are telling the world through their verdict, you have committed perjury on that point. That is what this whole case is about.

The Court: No, I don't think that is right. I will disallow the obstruction.

Amazingly, the charge Edward was convicted of is *Willful failure to file return, supply information, or pay tax.* Black's Law Dictionary, 5th Edition, defines *Willful* as:

Willful: *Proceeding from a conscious motion of the will; voluntary. Intending the result which actually comes to pass; designed; intentional; not accidental or involuntary.*

An act or omission is "willfully" done, if done voluntarily and intentionally and with a specific intent to do something the law forbids, or with the specific intent to fail to do something the law requires to be done; that is to say, with bad purpose either to disobey or to disregard the law.

The word [willful] often denotes the act which is intentional, or knowing, or voluntary, as distinguished from accidental. <u>But when used in a criminal content it generally means an act done with a bad purpose; without justifiable excuse; stubbornly, obstinately, perversely.</u> The word is also employed to characterize a thing done without ground for believing it is lawful conduct marked by a careless disregard whether or not one has the right so to act. (Emphasis added.)

So we have Cortes concluding that Edward should get a longer sentence because, in essence, the jury, by its verdict, concluded Edward lied on the witness stand, thus committing perjury, and in doing so, obstructed justice. Then we have Judge Boyle responding that Edward did not commit perjury and obstruct justice, because he actually believes that he is not required to file tax returns. Then we have Cortes saying, [Hey judge, yoohoo], *the whole case . . . was about whether he believed that he didn't have to file.* Then we have Boyle ending the possibility of a longer sentence because he disagrees with the jury and Cortes, for he knows that Edward was not willful. Of course, if Edward did not *willfully fail to file returns,* then he's NOT GUILTY. Did Boyle restore Edward's liberty? Did Cortes say, well your honor, if you believe that Kotmair is not *willful,* then, and in that case, his liberty must be restored? It is the duty of the judge and the U.S. Attorney, under such circumstances, to do so, for if they do not, they have committed *malfeasance* in office. Black's Law Dictionary, 5th Edition, defines *malfeasance* in pertinent part as:

> **Malfeasance** *is a wrongful act which the actor has no legal right to do, or any wrongful conduct which affects, interrupts, or interferes with performance of official duty, or any act for which there is no authority or warrant of law or which a person ought not to do at*

all, or the unjust performance of act, which party performing it has no right, or has contracted not, to do.

Did Edward's court-appointed attorney stop the judge to remind him of his duty to follow the proper judicial practice and restore Edward's liberty? No, he did not. Instead, the transcript shows that the next thing from his mouth is just an argument for a lighter sentence than what Cortes is asking for, by merely holding to the guidelines:

The Court: Okay. Do you want to say anything about that?

Mr. Ramage: Your honor, it's what the guideline says. . .

The case involving my son is not an isolated incident in Judge Boyle's courtroom. Gross unethical behavior by him was reported by a North Carolina dentist, Steven A. Roebuck, in pertinent parts of the following petition to the United States Court of Appeals for the Fourth Circuit for a *Writ of Habeas Corpus*:

COMES NOW Steven A. Roebuck, Sui Juris, In propria persona (my natural person), filing this "Exparte Motion to Expedite The Hearing On The Petition For Writ of Habeas Corpus.

ADDITIONAL FACTS:

The facts are: I am going to be sentenced on February 13, 2002. I have been illegally incarcerated on January 29, 2002 and will continue in the future to be incarcerated. Such incarceration is illegal because petitioner was coerced by the court to enter a "guilty" plea. Petitioner was further instructed by the court to deny such coercion took place. Petitioner's counsel was instructed by the court to inform the petitioner to enter a "guilty" plea as he had no alternative as there was no defense available to him. Based upon these representations by petitioner's counsel, petitioner believes he had incompetent assistance of counsel, and had his counsel not made such representations as stated herein, petitioner would not have entered a "guilty" plea. Based on the foregoing, petitioner respectfully moves this court to expedite consideration of this petition for writ of habeas corpus.

FACTS:

After being indicted and first contacting Rob Aldrich [hereafter Rob] to be my attorney, I had asked him on several occasions, could I not file some pre-trial motions. He said he did not want to do that because it would do no good and only make it harder on me at trial by pissing off the Judge.

In the morning, on September 4, 2001, my plea of not guilty was heard in court. That afternoon the jury was picked and opening statements said. The prosecutor was heard completely, but the judge interrupted my attorney twice in a confrontational and scolding demeanor. The judge appeared to be the lead prosecutor. After the second interference into the opening statement, which caused yet another loss in train of thought by my attorney, he simply closed opening statements and did not try to proceed any further.

At approximately 3:30 PM September 5th, 2001 in the U.S. Courthouse in Elizabeth City, NC a recess was called by the Judge Terrence Boyles. I, along with my wife, Donna, and my two attorneys left the courtroom. Donna left the courthouse to call back to Raleigh and have something faxed to show perjury on the part of one of the witnesses.

I just walked up and down the hallway outside the courtroom. Everyone had gone, including the two *attorneys. No one was in sight except a U.S. Marshal (in charge of protecting the jury room) and he and I talked. In about 15 minutes I noticed that Rob appeared at the main entrance to the courtroom saying, "Judge is back, let's go." So, I hurried back into the courtroom realizing that Donna, my wife, was not back yet which made me a little unsettled; she had been there for all the trial up to this point. My eyes scanned the jury box which should be full of jurors if the Judge is in the courtroom. The jury box was empty. As I turned to enter the area where the Prosecutor and Special Agent were as well as my two attorneys, I saw the Judge standing behind the bench. Confusion was clouding my mind as I realized that something was very wrong. I noticed as I approached my seat that the doors beside the Judge's bench now had someone, possibly a U.S. Marshal, standing in front of each, as well as the two doors at the rear of the courtroom. As reality sank in, I realized that there were now U.S. Marshals standing at every entrance as if strategically placed. I looked at my attorneys, wondering what was going on, but they both were acting as if these were normal procedures that took place in the middle of a trial. All doors were closed and the agents of the government and my two attorneys and I were there. Donna was not back yet.*

*At the moment that I sat down the Judge began to speak in a very stern, forceful, threatening manner. He was aiming his vehement dislike for me through his mannerisms and tone of voice in a verbally assaulting diatribe. He started by saying, to the best of my recollection, the following speech: **"Unless your attorneys can give me good cause or reason for not throwing you in jail, I am throwing you in there tonight. You scare me. You frighten me.** I'm afraid to have you walking the streets of the town. You must be mentally imbalanced in thinking that you had not been breaking the*

230

law. You have been posturing yourself at me and the court all day long. You have been playing eye games with me and because of this I am scared of you and see you as a threat to society."

*By this time my heart was racing. I was shaking all over. The fear caused tears to well up in my eyes. My emotions were running in all directions, but fear for my well-being and my family was foremost. In my mind I was trying to think, why and what was this Judge doing? What had I done to cause the wrath of this Judge to fall on me; throughout the trial I had been respectful to the court and the Judge, even when outrageous lies and accusations were said to my injury by the witnesses and the Prosecutor. On several occasions, the Judge even interjected his own nefariously biased opinion to the jury. I had simply wanted my day in court and my chance to convey my reasons and beliefs to the jury and now this man was going to take that away from me. How was it possible that this was happening in America in our court systems? I could understand it in other countries but not here. I found myself unable to even speak. I was waiting for my attorneys to object, to speak up, or to at least do something, but Sam was just sitting there and when Rob finally stood up to speak saying, "Your honor," the Judge turned to him and said, **"Sit down Mr. Aldrich (very firmly), I know who you are. You are one of those movement attorneys. I know what you are all about. You come in here from Oklahoma making this man think he has a case against the government. You'd be better off representing drug dealers and murderers."** All Rob said was, "But your honor." Then the Judge started back on Rob again. **"I'm thinking about starting disbarment proceedings against you. With what has gone on here today, you'd better just sit down and be quiet."** Rob then turned to me, shrugged his shoulders, his mouth fell about half open and that was that.*

231

There sat my lead attorney, the one that had worked on my defense case for what he said was hundreds of hours. The man who had been through dozens of cases as a paralegal for over 12 years, the guy who had come across in his presentation as being both knowledgeable of the law and ready for anything, the person who I had come to believe in as the one who could help me to prove my innocence, had within a few seconds been silenced and turned into a whipped puppy. No longer was Rob confident, boisterous or ready for a fight. He looked incapable now of doing anything. He had tucked his tail between his legs and just sat there.

With Rob now out of the picture and Sam, up to this time not saying or doing anything, it was my turn again for the Judge to throw his threats upon. Looking back at me again, he, the Judge, continued. "Mr. Roebuck, you must be a member of some White Supremacist Group. Which one? The Klan? The Montana Freemen? The Miller Group? You must be a member of some sort of anti-government group, which one? Who has been feeding you all of this information? Who is helping and sponsoring you? Who is it?!!" With tears running down my face and a huge lump in my throat, I was able to finally swallow and whimper out, "No one. I have done my own research and studies."

At this time, Sam had now stood up and had motioned for me to do likewise. Rob remained seated. I was terrified totally by now. I was scared to death. My heart pounding and tears flowing down my cheeks, I tried to speak and answer his questions, but I couldn't. His verbal vituperations were unrelenting. Disbelief of what was happening was overpowering. I was frozen. All I could think of was, let me out of here, but there was no escape. I turned and looked. My wife, Donna, still wasn't there. Questions were flying through my head. Where was she?

Had she been arrested downstairs and not allowed to come back? What was going on? The attorneys that I had counted on were doing nothing. When would this stop? When would someone do something about what this Judge was doing? My mind was simply screaming, STOP! STOP!! STOP!!!, but it wasn't stopping. I was in a nightmare but I wasn't dreaming. I couldn't just wake up and it all be over. This was real and it seemed nothing and no one was going to stop it.

I felt a sense of shock coming over me more and more. I felt fear like I had never felt before. In my mind I knew full well that I did not deserve to go to jail. The Judge was ABSOLUTELY threatening my life. I FEARED FOR MY LIFE! He was going to have me arrested and thrown into jail downstairs. Into a jail with at least three other prisoners who had plead guilty the day before for federal drug violations. I felt that he was letting me know that I would be thrown downstairs with those guys. I cannot say it enough, that the Judge let me know by the way he spoke and looked at me that he was not going to allow me to have my day in court and my trial to continue. The fear that had been placed in me by the Judge told me that if I went downstairs into that jail that night I would probably not see the sunrise the next morning. He also set up the fear by mentioning that I must be mentally imbalanced, that I was a threat to society. I knew that somehow the story that would be told the next day would be either I would be found hung to death or that I threw such a fit in the night that the jail officials would have had to sedate me and place me into restraints and transport me to a federal institution for a mental evaluation that could continue for years or the rest of my life.

There was no way that Judge Terrence Boyles was going to allow me to refute the case of the Prosecutor and the Government. He himself, on several occasions during

233

the trial, had interjected his own questions to the witnesses or he had made derogatory statements about me to the jury. Where was the impartiality that he had spoken of at the first day of the trial? At one point and time he announced to the jury that "I don't know where all this evidence is leading, the counts are two counts of 7203 Willful Failure to File Forms for the years 1994 and 1995. He willfully did not do this and that's what this trial is about." The Prosecution had not and could not prove willfulness; therefore, this Judge, I felt, did not want to allow the jury and my constitutional process to continue.

Back to September 5th, this Judge was threatening to throw me into jail once again. The Judge looked at the local counsel, Sam, ex-federal prosecutor appointed by President Reagan at the same time that Judge Boyles was appointed, and said, "I can understand you, Mr. Currin, because your door for your business is here and that if someone walks in you take the case because you live here and need to make a living." He said, "However, I do not understand Mr. Aldrich coming in from Oklahoma except that I do know who he is, he's one of those movement attorneys." The Judge said, "You give hope to these people, Mr. Aldrich, who think they have a tax case and you know full well he doesn't even have a defense case." You need to be defending drug dealers and murderers and not people protesting taxes."

At this time Sam asked the Judge if we could have another recess so that they could talk with their client. I proceeded to get up and walk out of the court with Sam and Rob. We go out into the hallway and both attorneys walk over to me and say, "Are you going to be okay Steve?" "We need to go and talk to the Prosecutor." And not knowing what to do and relying upon their knowledge, I told them "Yeah, sure, I'll just be waiting here for you, I'm waiting for Donna to come back." The attorneys *simply walked off and went upstairs to speak to the Prosecutor. Many times I looked out the windows hoping to see Donna coming back, but I didn't see her. Thoughts of being thrown in jail frightened me and in a matter of moments the trial Judge had taken my entire case from me. I was feeling very depressed and very despondent. What did I have to do to get out of this situation and for justice to be served? I had not prepared my children for the possibilities of being thrown into jail and their not seeing me again, nor had either of my attorneys told me that this was a possibility. This was in no way, shape or form what the attorneys had prepared me for. I couldn't just leave the building. This was real and something had to change or I was not leaving that building that day if I stood my ground of innocence. I was willing to do anything to get back to my home, wife and kids Finally Donna came back. When she saw me she knew that something was terribly wrong. She ran up to me and said, "Steve, what in the world is wrong?" I told her that the Judge was going to put me in jail that night and Rob and Sam had gone to talk to the prosecutor to try and work something out. She was totally shocked and could not believe what I was saying to her. It was now a little past 4:00 PM.*

Sam and Rob came down the stairs and called me over away from Donna. Rob, my lead attorney, placed his arms around me and said quietly in my ear, "I'm sorry". (Looking back at this, I feel that I had been sold for a bag of silver just as Jesus was betrayed.—just using symbolism.) Next, Sam says, "Now listen Steve, I'll say it this way. You don't want to go down into that jail and there is no way you're going to get out of this courthouse tonight unless you change your plea to guilty." I knew that I was not guilty of either one of these charges, so I asked Sam and Rob, "Why would I plead guilty when I'm not guilty?" Sam kept saying that I was not going to get out of this unless you do. [sic] Sam said, "If you don't start

235

cooperating, this is going to get bad. You will spend the night in jail." I asked them, "How could this be happening?" They said, "The Judge can do whatever he wants. It's his courtroom and he makes up the rules." I was still so frightened and all my thoughts at this time were centered on getting myself and my wife out of that federal building back to Raleigh to our family. To keep from going to jail and from what I felt, certain death, I was willing to do whatever it took, so I told Sam and Rob to do what was necessary to get me out of here today. [sic] It now seemed that my lead attorney was Sam because Rob had backed off.

We then entered the courtroom. This time Donna was there. I was told to sit down and Sam and the Prosecutor approached the bench and spoke with the Judge. After a few minutes they returned to their seats and, now in a much more subdued speech, [the Judge] *said that he had been advised that I was wishing to make a change of plea. He asked me if I understood the charges against me. Was I mentally competent to understand the charges? Had I been coerced into changing my plea? To that question, I did not immediately answer. Sam leaned over to me and said to say no. I said, "No." I was not thinking of the word coerced. I was thinking of extorted, forced, being under duress, fraud, conspiracy, fear for my life and lots of other things were running through my mind. Had I been forced to change my plea? Absolutely! With what had happened over the last 30 to 45 minutes, I was being forced to recant everything that I had researched and studied for the past nine years. The Judge then turned to me and said, "How do you wish to plea?" I hesitated, and Sam, once again, leaned over and said quietly, **"You'd better say, guilty."** So, I very reluctantly told the Judge, "Guilty." I felt betrayed by my own mouth, saying these words. How could I forgive myself for saying that. My only justification was that I wanted to get back to my home and* *family.*

The Judge went down a list of instructions to me and my attorneys and said, I'm going to release you under the same pre-trial bond that you have been on. You are free to go back to Raleigh but you must stay in touch with your pre-trial person and a probation officer that will be assigned to your case. No sentencing date was given at that time. He then brought the jury back in. (During the whole time that the Judge was attacking me earlier he was a wild man. In my studies of medicine and dentistry, his behavior was almost as that of a manic depressive or an inherently evil person or a sociopath. He had possibly gone manic while the jury was out. Now since they had returned he was just as calm, cordial, and friendly as he could be. He had overwhelmed someone and now was preparing to punish them.) He smiled and proceeded to tell the jury that there had been a change in the trial. The defendant had changed his plea to guilty. The Judge thanked them for their time and service and release them. He then adjourned court. We left and came back to Raleigh.

Sam seemed so protective of the events that had just occurred in the courtroom. Sam was concerned that some mention of the trial could possibly cause Judge Boyles a problem with his possible upcoming appointment by President Bush to the 4th Circuit Court of Appeals. Because of this Sam said it would be best if we did not ask for a transcript of the trial; Rob concurred. They both said this might piss off the Judge and make it worse for me at sentencing.

Sam said that this judge would be more lenient at sentencing than another judge because he knew that he had forced me into changing my plea and that if I did everything the court asked me to do; i.e., admit that I was wrong and accept responsibility for my actions of not filing and paying taxes and also seeing a psychiatrist for evaluation to see if I had been under so much stress that I had become irrational about my responsibilities. Sam said I would get at least a two point downward departure as well as we would try for a Koon's departure. He explained that this was a special departure that came from the Rodney King trial in California.

I asked both Rob and Sam after the trial the following week about getting a transcript of what happened at the trial. Both said it would do me no good and also cost a lot of money. Rob said once again that it would piss off the Judge.

The only thing that Sam would say that day was that he was totally amazed at what had gone on there. He told me, "Steve, at least you get to go home to your children and we'll be getting back together. Give me a call next week and let me know how you're doing and everything. We'll be setting up a time when we can go and see the probation officer." Rob didn't say much. Sam and Rob stayed in Elizabeth City that night. Rob came by the office the next day. He was flying back to Oklahoma that afternoon. He was still upset and scared about some sort of reprisal from the Judge. Rob said that he sure hoped that the Judge didn't file anything against him because he would have no choice but to fight it with every part of him.

Neither Donna nor I heard anything from either attorney. On the following Tuesday I called Rob and asked him to write me a affidavit as to [what] happened in the courtroom on September 5th. He said, "Steve, that wouldn't do you a bit of good. Above all, that might piss off the Judge and get him mad and you don't want to do that. I'm also scared of having charges brought up on disbarment against me."

238

I then called up Sam and asked him if he could tell me what happened in court last week? How could I have been forced to change my plea? How could he throw me in jail? Sam said, "I just don't remember him saying anything like that. That was a week ago. He said there was a chance that you may have been thrown in jail but he didn't hear a threat." Sam had told both Rob and me before the court date not to be surprised at anything the Judge did, that he was unpredictable.

I was totally taken back that all of a sudden neither of my attorneys would, on the record, be able to remember what happened in Elizabeth City. Everyone in that courtroom that afternoon were officers of the court, or government agents, except me. Donna was not there to back me up and to hear what went on.

[signed]
Steven A. Roebuck
6817 Chasewick Circle
Raleigh, NC 27615

AFFIRMATION

I, Steven A. Roebuck, do hereby affirm that the foregoing "Petition for Hearing a Writ of Habeas Corpus Under my Unalienable Right to Petition the Government For Redress of Grievances; and, Petition for the Impaneling of a Grand Jury for Presentment for Indictment Against Respondents" is true, accurate and correct to the best of my knowledge, information and belief.

Don't get the idea from the two examples above that this is just happening in North Carolina. In 1980, I had a challenge in the Maryland courts to the imposition of the Maryland income tax. A month or so after arguing to the Court, I received some telephone calls from various friends asking me if I had read that day's Baltimore Sun newspaper. Not subscribing to this pro-socialist paper, I bought the May 1, 1980 edition, and therein was the judge in my case being quoted as saying: *If we had ruled for Kotmair, we would have destroyed the taxing structure of the State of Maryland.* A short time later, I happened to meet the judge in the courthouse cafeteria, and engaged him in conversation about the decision and the quote in the Sun newspaper. He stated to me that he knew I was right, but the system we have has been in place a long time, and to change things now would be very destructive to our society. Of course I argued without success that the very opposite is true.

This was not the only time I was told that by a judge. In 1977, I had an action in the Federal District Court of Maryland, in Baltimore, intervening in the enforcement of an IRS third-party summons for business records pertaining to me held by the A & J Electric Company of Baltimore. In the pre-trial briefing, I asked Judge James Miller for an extension of time to file a memorandum of law regarding my position. He gave me until the day of the hearing.

The memorandum contained, among other things, the Supreme Court cases on the 16th Amendment discussed earlier in this book. Before the hearing started, I gave the memorandum to the judge's clerk, who took it to the judge's chambers. The judge was a few hours late coming out to start the hearing. When he did come out, he did not even bother to sit down. He leaned on the bench, and stated in a very loud voice: *Kotmair, it has been a long time ago since those court cases; there has been a lot of water under the bridge; we have been doing it this way all these years, and we're not going to change now.* I burst out laughing, and my electrical contractor turned to me and said: *What are you laughing at? He is ruling against you.* I told him in a very loud voice: *Don't you understand? He is saying that I am right. It is only a matter of time now.*

240

Four years later, this very same judge conducted a criminal trial in which I was the defendant having been charged with two counts of *Willful failure to file return, supply information, or pay tax* for the years 1975 and 1976. Having very little knowledge about the Internal Revenue Code, or even the Supreme Court cases on the 16th Amendment, I filed what was called 5th Amendment tax returns for those two years.

The story of the trial, which lasted one month, is a book in itself, wherefore, for our purposes here, I will only discuss the sentencing. The judge asked the U.S. Attorney, Steve Allen, if he had anything to say before he sentenced me. Allen responded that it was reported in the Philadelphia Magazine that I spoke at a tax protest rally in Boston at the same time this trial was being conducted, and that I should be given the maximum sentence. The judge then asked me if I had anything to say. I answered yes, and pointed at Allen and stated: *This man has charged me with two counts of failing to file tax returns and then used two tax returns as evidence in this court to convict me of not filing them. This is a circus.* The judge then stated: *Now I will have my say. You are incorrigible, and you are beyond rehabilitation, wherefore, I'm giving you the maximum sentence and I wish I could give you more.* This is the same man who just four years earlier admitted that I was right about the tax laws.

All of these "gentlemen" in the examples above are in violation of their oaths of office, which are made pursuant to Article VI, Clause 3 of the United States Constitution:

> *The Senators and Representatives before mentioned, and the members of the several state legislatures, and all executive and <u>judicial officers, both of the United States and of the several states</u>, shall be bound by oath or affirmation, to support this Constitution; but no religious test shall ever be required as a qualification to any office or public trust under the United States.* (Emphasis added.)

What is so alarming is that the preceding cases are the rule rather than the exception. And this situation can only grow worse, as long as we Americans keep electing those federal socialists that continue to illegally expand the power of the federal government. Extending the political march to total federal power was started by Alexander Hamilton, and unquestionably exacerbated by Abraham Lincoln.[3] The enemies of limited government have for years worked their way into positions of power so they could institute programs to further their cause—such as the intentional destruction of our culture by the dumbing down of our entire educational system. Excluding home-schooling and a few private schools, our educational system has just about been destroyed by these Hamiltonian-Lincolnites within the Department of Education, who are working hard toward that end. This is well documented by Charlotte Thomson Iserbyt in her book, *The Deliberate Dumbing Down of America*, which can be obtained through her Internet web site, www.deliberatedumbingdown.com.

All of the sound factual principles that were established by the *Founding Fathers* and *Framers* of the Constitution have been either perverted or removed altogether from federally funded schools. This includes the law schools, where the focus has been shifted from the legislature's written law to what is called case law, i.e., the written decisions of judges. A study of this case law over the years reveals that judges ever so slightly pervert the law, and then others of the same political persuasion, build on and expand that perversion until the rulings of the courts are the exact opposite of the *Framers'* intent within the Constitution, and the legislature's written law made in pursuance thereof. Of course, if a legislative act is not in pursuance of the Constitution, then, and in that case, the courts are to render it void as unconstitutional.

Both federal and state governments in the United States have what is known as separation of powers. There are three branches of government, each having distinctly separate powers. Article 1, Section 1, the very first enumerated power of the Constitution, states:

Section 1. All legislative powers herein granted shall be vested in a Congress of the United States, which shall consist of a Senate and House of Representatives.

Nowhere can you find, in either federal or State Constitutions, any power for the judiciary to make law, and that is exactly what is happening with the furtherance of, and reliance upon, case law.

A prime example of what I am talking about is the court-made so-called legal doctrine of the *separation of church and state*. Such a doctrine cannot be found in the written law, only in the case law. The First Amendment to the United States Constitution says in part:

Congress shall make no law respecting an establishment of religion, or prohibiting the free exercise thereof; . . .

To my knowledge, since the state religions of pre-revolutionary America, such as the Episcopal Church in the Colony of Virginia, there has been *no establishment of religion*, but because of observing and enforcing perverted case law, there has been plenty of *prohibiting the free exercise thereof.*

This perversion of the law is now held by the courts to be the law, regardless if it agrees with the written law or not. The Maryland Constitution only allows for a real property tax, but the Comptroller of the Treasury also collects income taxes and sales taxes. The Maryland Constitution is amended by placing the amendment on the ballot to be voted on in the general elections. In 1937, the Maryland voters turned down an amendment to allow the Comptroller to lay and collect an income tax. Three years later, in the case of *Oursler v. Tawes*, 178 Md. 471, 13 A.2d 763, the court stated:

. . . independent of constitutional provisions, and subject

243

only to the limitations placed upon it by the Federal Constitution, the power of taxation is inherent in a sovereign State, because the right to tax underlies its own constitution and is not granted by it. Stated differently, the right may be regulated and limited by constitutional mandates, but it exists without express authority in the fundamental law as a necessary attribute of sovereignty. . . . Constitutional provisions relating to the power of taxation do not operate as grants of the power; but do constitute limitations upon a power in the government thus set up, which would be otherwise without limit.

As you can see, by the time these lawyers become judges and advance their way up through the higher level of courts, their perversion becomes very persuasive to those not grounded in the written law. Eight years later, using the same logic, the citizens of Maryland had a one-cent sales tax imposed on certain items that they purchased. As the years went by, the amount of tax and the items thereon expanded.

I'm not saying that there is no lawful case law. The fact of the matter is, that there is, but it is not federal. The common law is case law, for it is the custom and usage of the people, and this is established in the courts of record within the counties of each State; and verified and settled in the highest court of each State. There is no federal common law, because there is no authority within the federal Constitution for the federal legislature to make property law, and the argument over property, and the resolution of that argument, is what makes the common law. Wherefore, the federal government has to follow the property laws of any particular State where it maintains any legal action therein. All federal law is written by the Congress, and therefore, if it would require any interpretation by a federal court, it would be void for vagueness.

Federal case law was started by federal district judges, then only in Washington, D.C., who had very little to do because of the limited federal jurisdictional powers, and they started keeping

244

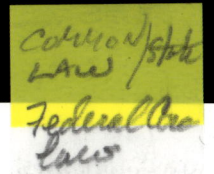

written records of the cases decided by the United States Supreme Court. The earlier volumes containing these transcripts were named for court reports that transcribed the court proceedings, such as Wall or Cranch. This type of activity made it easy for those collectivists bent on destroying our Constitutional Republic to pervert our foundation, the written law.

So we have within the legal community a gradual shift, over many decades, to a reliance on what proceeds from the mouth of judges—case law—rather than understanding and holding to the written law. This intentional shift, along with a concerted socialist political agenda within the legislative and executive branches, has made it possible to put into practice, absent written law, the Hamiltonian-Lincolnite socialist state. This malignant state has become so powerful that those judges inclined to abide by the founding principles, are afraid to do so, for personal reasons or for fear of the consequences to the Republic. Two prime examples of this are ex-federal Judge Harry Claiborne,[4] of Nevada, and Judge Robert Bork. Judge Claiborne made the federal agencies toe the line, and was wrongfully prosecuted and convicted on a complaint by the IRS, using an error made by Claiborne's C.P.A. In 1987, Judge Bork, then Federal Appeals Court Judge, was nominated by President Reagan to the Supreme Court. The Senate Nominating Committee was controlled by Hamiltonian-Lincolnites, and in order to possibly persuade them to confirm him, he stated that he would refrain from taking part in cases involving the banking system. At that same hearing, the ultra-federalist collectivist Senator Joseph Biden, from Delaware, stated something to the effect that: It took us sixty years to establish what we have and we're not going to put that in jeopardy. Bork's nomination was turned down.

In 1991, I published an extra edition of the *Save-A-Patriot Fellowship* newsletter, *Reasonable Action*. The incident that provoked the extra edition was when three judges on the Federal Court of Appeals for the Ninth Circuit rewrote a legal brief submitted by Constitutional Patriot lawyer Lowell H. Becraft, Jr., of Huntsville, Alabama, and then sanctioned him for the rewritten brief. The headline on the extra edition was: *Mr. President, Are Liars Fit To Sit As Judges?* It was circulated throughout all three branches of the federal government and some state judicial offices. It caused a stir that still exists today. Just about every time I'm a witness at a federal hearing, it is presented to me with the question asking if I published it. Of course, my response is always the same, *Yes, and it must be true, as I have never been sued for it.* That same year, to help end such tyranny as has been demonstrated in this Chapter, I composed the following Bill to be introduced in federal and state legislatures. Several members of the *Fellowship* tried, but were unable to convince any legislator to introduce it.

A BILL ENTITLED

AN ACT:
   To Prevent Government By Men Rather Than Law; and,

   To Insure That Public Policy Remains The Constitutional Prerogative Of The Legislature.

BE IT ENACTED that every judge, chancellor, magistrate and/or any other judicial officer, employed and/or appointed, in the Judicial Branch of the United States Government, by the authority derived under either Article I or Article III of the United States Constitution, who has the power to issue rulings, orders, judgments and/or decrees is required to provide a memorandum with each and every decision justifying it as to the Facts of the case, the Law of the case, and the legal Conclusion therefrom in all actions to come before that judicial official; that if the records of any court within the Judicial Branch, maintained at any place in government, show that such official, on an order, judgment, ruling and/or decree submitted for recordation has knowingly or otherwise misrepresented the law and the fact, or both, said judicial officer will be guilty of a felony. Upon conviction, such punishment shall be not less than five (5)

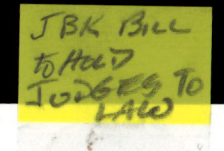

years imprisonment, $50,000.00 fine, forfeiture of all retirement benefits, and irrevocable suspension of license to practice law.

SUCH ACTION shall be brought in a court of record within the judicial branch of the United States, having jurisdiction to try criminal actions.

PROCEDURE to implement this Act:

1.   The Judicial Committee of Congress shall within 60 days after enactment of this law, prepare and order the printing of special complaint forms, for use by any citizen or resident alien, living within the geographical jurisdiction of any State of the Union, territories and possessions of the United States, to initiate this criminal action against any judicial officer of the judicial branch of government of the United States.

2.   The aforesaid citizen or resident alien shall file the aforesaid complaint with:
>   (a) the chairman of the Judicial Committee, and
>   (b) the chairman of the House Ways and Means
>   Committee.

3.   The chairman of the House Ways and Means Committee is required to cause, within 10 days of the receipt of the complaint, for the full text of it to be published in:
>   (a) the official journal(s) of Congress, and
>   (b) the largest daily newspapers in circulation within
>   the geographical boundaries of the United States.

4.   Said Judicial Committee chairman shall make the complaint a priority matter and the committee is required to appoint a special prosecutor within 30 days of receipt of the complaint.

5.   The special prosecutor is required, within 10 days of appointment, to:
>   (a) start his prosecutorial activities, and

(b) notify the complaining citizen or resident alien of his appointment:

6.   Upon completion of his investigation, not to exceed 60 calendar days, the special prosecutor shall move the Grand Jury for an indictment, or may proceed on an information.

7.   The judicial officer so charged shall not be tried within the court in which he presides.

8.   The clerk of the court of record, upon receipt of said indictment or information, shall expedite the scheduling of this action as a priority matter.

There must be an intensive confrontational education effort to revert back to the law, to bring the federal and State governments back within their respective Constitutional confines, particularly the courts. They are supposedly the guardians of *Justice*, and have to be forced into, and kept in, that role. For without their cooperation, *tyranny* cannot exist, and regretfully so, neither can *Liberty*.

Chapter 12

AVIODING the POT HOLES
in the ROAD to LIBERTY

A Constitutional Republic as strong as the United States would be nearly impossible to be overthrown by force. But if the changes are patiently instituted over decades, there is practically no resistance to these internal changes. Wherefore, the change in the American political psychology, by design, has been ever so slow. The seeds of the socialist malignancy were planted in the 1850s, the decade preceding the War Between the States, by Karl Marx and Friedrich Engels, who were at that time writing editorials for the *New York Daily Tribune*. Their Marxian principles have been advanced by wealthy and powerful individuals seeking to use this poisonous political philosophy to thwart any challenge to their wealth and power by way of the free enterprise economic system. These individuals are aided by well-meaning utopians trying to establish a world government, who believethat doing so will be the end of all wars. Some of this history was covered in Chapter VII of this book.

By the grace of God, there are always politically astute individuals who are alarmed early on and try to expose the harmful changes going on. But until the average citizen starts to suffer, there is usually no mass resistance. Of course, by that time the positions of power within the government, the establishment media and all the institutions of education have been secured by the plotters, making it very difficult for unorganized citizens to expose them and their socialist advance. The changes in the American way of life have been so gradual that to the succeeding generations which follow, the changes are thought of as the norm, and not questioned. This has been the case with such socialist schemes as Social Security and Zoning.

The biggest socialist advances, which concentrate more *de facto* power in the federal government, are almost always made in reaction to some crisis, such as a contrived war,[1] or, as of late, a terrorist attack. This tactic has been used very successfully through the ages to persuade free citizens to surrender their rights. The following was contributed to Julius Caesar but cannot be confirmed:

> *Beware the leader who bangs the drums of war in order to whip the citizenry into a patriotic fervor, for patriotism is indeed a double-edged sword. It both emboldens the blood, just as it narrows the mind.*
>
> *And when the drums of war have reached a fever pitch and the blood boils with hate and the mind has closed, the leader will have no need in seizing the rights of the citizenry. Rather, the citizenry, infused with fear and blinded by patriotism, will offer up all of their rights unto the leader and gladly so.*
>
> *How do I know? For this is what I have done. And I am Caesar.*

The actual source is unknown, but the words are frightfully true and timely.

The right is supposedly surrendered for the war effort, but when the crisis has passed, the restriction remains and the right is still compromised. Thank God, in the United States the result of this type of tactic cannot exist lawfully under our Constitution. A case in point would be the withholdings tax instituted in 1942, covered earlier in this book, supposedly for the war effort during World War II.

It took about two decades for this "patriotic" tax withholding act to be questioned openly with resistance, giving birth to the first real resistance to the Hamiltonian-Lincolnites. There were some efforts before this, but they were based mainly on lobbying efforts, amazingly, to repeal unconstitutional laws.

In 1968, A. J. Porth, a building contractor from Wichita, Kansas, openly objected to filing a Form 1040 tax return on the grounds that the filing of such return would be a waiver of his Fifth Amendment rights under the Constitution of the United States. This was reported in the *Washington Observer*, a monthly newsletter published in Washington, D.C.. The government's reaction was fast and swift. A federal judge ordered Mr. Porth to be confined for observation in a federal mental facility until he would give up this ridiculous protest. Thus, the term *tax protestor* was born. News of the incident was spread far and wide, bringing Patriots out of the woodwork, picking up the banner of *Individual Liberty*.

After reading the preceding Chapters of this book, you can see the knowledge that has been realized over the years since Mr. Porth took his stand.

In those early days we referred to ourselves as *Tax Rebels*, having very little knowledge about the federal tax code, which was generally believed to be unconstitutional. In the good old American fashion, individuals started publishing their theories in how-to booklets. The result being, just like Lexington and Bunker Hill, a lot of casualties. But as the years and knowledge progressed, the casualties were fewer and fewer. There are however, some problems: First, not every Patriot has advanced in the knowledge of the law; and secondly, there are many *wild theories* circulating around the Patriot community.

Wild theories are the most dangerous threat to the Constitutionalist Movement. They are actually more dangerous than the Hamiltonian-Lincolnites, and their dupes within the IRS, Department of Justice and the federal Courts who are constantly attacking the Patriots. Using a *wild theory* is the same as a being a lamb led to slaughter, for it makes its user wide open to attack without a defense. In short, *wild theories* are counterproductive to the *Cause of Liberty*.

The best way to identify a *wild theory* is with the written law. As stated before, the United States is a Constitutional Republic. This means that in the Executive and Legislative Branches we do not have leaders, we have elected representatives, and these representatives cannot, by law, do whatever they want. They are bound by the Constitution, the written law which enumerates the certain powers of the Executive, and which restricts the Legislature to write laws only as outlined within it. Therefore, if whatever a *theory* purports cannot be found within the written law, it is a false proposition, totally defenseless, and should be totally avoided at all costs.

There are many *wild theories* being advanced upon American Patriots. A rule of thumb is: if it sounds crazy, in all probability it is. One such crazy *wild theory* that comes to mind is: *If you use the postal zip code you owe the income tax*. Nothing could be further from the truth. This *wild theory* was so prevalent in the Patriot community some years ago, it caused a *Save-A-Patriot Fellowship* member to inquire of the Congressional Research Service in the Library of Congress if Zipcode use actually did cause its user to have a liability to pay an income tax. The following is the response:

THE LIBRARY OF CONGRESS
WASHINGTON, D.C. 20540

LAW LIBRARY
AMERICAN-BRITISH LAW DIVISION

OCT 3 1988

252

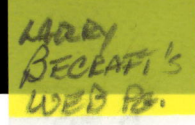

Dear Mr.

This letter is in response to your request for information concerning the legal significance of the zip codes.

The United States Postal Service handles over 147 billion pieces of mail each year. As far as we can determine, the zip codes were developed to facilitate the speed and accuracy of handling the mail in order to provide a better service. I am not sure what the zip codes have to do with jurisdiction, except to pinpoint a particular area of the country. Like paying taxes, using zip codes is voluntary and it would not be illegal not to use them. However, the result of not using zip codes would probably be a three-day delay in the delivery of one's mail. If you have additional questions, you should direct them to the Information Office, Regional Post Office, 850 Cherry Avenue, San Bruno, California 94099.

Please let us know if we can be of further assistance.

Sincerely,

Robert L. Nay
Assistant Chief

Lowell [Larry] H. Becraft, Jr., the Constitutional attorney mentioned in Chapter XI of this book, has warned for years that the Constitutional Movement is being severely compromised by *wild theories*.[2] I consider Larry to be one of the foremost researchers in the Constitutional Movement. Most of the research revelations within the Movement can be attributed to him. He has researched and debunked many of these *wild theories* and listed the results of his research on his Internet web site, The Dixieland Law Journal, http://home.hiwaay.net/~becraft/. With his permission, I am reproducing a few of the most prominent *wild theories* listed here:

The UCC Argument

Back in the early nineties, an Oregon patriot promoted the theory that "commercial law" was the foundation for all law around the world. Based upon this contention regarding commercial law, he developed the idea that an "affidavit of truth" submitted "in commerce" could create a lien which simply had to be paid. This fellow claimed that his findings were well known everywhere and that this lien process had been used for thousands of years. I obtained his memo regarding this argument and went to the law library. His contention that this "principle" manifested itself in the law was wrong; I could find nothing which supported this argument. This theory was a complete fabrication.

Did others act upon this man's ideas anyway? Leroy Schweitzer of the Montana Freemen took this patriot's ideas to heart and claimed that he created liens against public officials. Based upon these liens, Leroy started issuing sight drafts drawn upon some "post office" account and started passing them out to many gullible people who believed that such drafts were required to be paid by the feds. Not only did Leroy get into deep trouble, so did many who got drafts from him. There have been lots of people who have been prosecuted, convicted and jailed for using drafts allegedly justified by this crazy theory.

One of the most recent prosecutions of someone for using one of Leroy's drafts is Pete Stern, a patriot from North Carolina. Several years ago, Pete issued some of these drafts to the IRS. Pete has been one of the most vocal advocates of the UCC argument, "we are Brits," nom de guerre, etc. While I like Pete, still he has followed crazy arguments. Pete's federal criminal case was filed in the Western District of North Carolina and he was convicted.

As best I can tell, the popular "UCC" argument has its origins in Howard Freeman's flaky theories, the Oregon patriot's work and the "improvements" made by Leroy. The UCC argument is one of the most legally baseless ideas I have ever encountered, yet organizations like "Wrong [Right] Way Law" and people like Jack Smith continue to promote it. Here are some published cases which have correctly rejected this lunacy:

UCC
CASES

HOWARD
FREEMAN

UCC
Argument

1.   *Jones v. City of Little Rock*, 314 Ark. 383, 862 S.W.2d 273, 274 (1993)(In reference to traffic tickets, the court stated, "The Uniform Commercial Code does not apply to any of these offenses")

2.   *United States v. Stoecklin*, 848 F.Supp. 1521 (M.D. Fla. 1994)

3.   *Barcroft v. State*, 881 S.W.2d 838, 840 (Tex.App. 1994)("First, the UCC is not applicable to criminal proceedings; it applies to commercial transactions")

4.   *United States v. Greenstreet*, 912 F.Supp. 224 (N.D.Tex. 1996)(also raised flag and common law court issues)

5.   *United States v. Andra*, 923 F.Supp. 157 (D.Idaho 1996) ("The complaint filed by the plaintiff is not a negotiable instrument and the Uniform Commercial Code is inapplicable")

6.   *Watts v. IRS*, 925 F.Supp. 271, 276 (D.N.J. 1996)("The IRS's Notice of Intent to Levy is not a negotiable instrument")

7.   *United States v. Klimek*, 952 F.Supp. 1100 (E.D.Pa. 1997)(returning lawsuit complaint marked "Refusal For Cause Without Dishonor UCC 3-501" and refusing other court pleadings "for fraud" based upon UCC argument got nowhere; also raised nom de guerre and flag issues)

8.   *City of Kansas City v. Hayward*, 954 SW2d 399 (Mo.App. W.D. 1997).

A substantial part of the UCC argument was "developed" by Howard Freeman. Freeman contended that some super-secret treaty back in 1930 put this and other countries around the world in "bankruptcy" with the "international bankers" being the "creditor/rulers." Once these banker/rulers were ensconced in power, they needed some way to "toss out the old law" based upon the common law, and erect commercial law as the law which regulated and controlled everything. Roosevelt and his fellow conspirators then set to work and developed a plan to achieve the destruction of the "common law" and the erection of commercial law. This was accomplished by the decision in the Erie Railroad case in 1938. According to this theory, Erie RR banished the common law, leaving in its place only commercial law via the UCC. Freeman also alleged that lawyers were informed of this "takeover" by the "international bankers" and that they were required to take a secret oath to not tell the American people about the takeover. Of course, as the direct result of this change in the law from common law to commercial law, no court could ever cite a case decided prior to 1938. (See more complete explanation of this concept here). . . .

But there are tremendous flaws in this argument. I do not challenge the fact that big international bankers are economically powerful and that such power enables them to secure favorable legislation. However, I do disagree with the "secret treaty" contention. Back in the 1930s and indeed all the way up to about 1946, all treaties adopted by the United States were published in the U.S. Statutes at Large. As a student of treaties, I looked for this secret treaty and could not find it, and I had access to complete sets of all books containing treaties, especially those in the Library of Congress in DC. The major premise of this argument is this contention regarding the secret treaty, which even the proponents of the argument cannot produce. Their argument, "I cannot produce this secret treaty, but believe me anyway," simply is unacceptable to me as I want proof.

The advocates of this argument also contend that the Erie RR case was the one which banished the common law and erected commercial law in its place. The problem with this contention is that Erie RR does not stand for this proposition. This was a personal injury case; Thompkins

was injured while walking along some railroad tracks as a train passed. Something sticking out of the train hit Thompkins and injured him, hence his suit for damages. Please read this case of *Erie R. Co. v. Tompkins,* 304 U.S. 64 (1938), which stands for the proposition that federal courts must follow the common law of the state where the injury occurred. How this case is alleged to declare the exact opposite escapes me, but in any event, Erie RR does not support the contention of the UCC advocates.

To prove that Erie RR changed the law, it is alleged that no court can cite a case decided prior to 1938. This is perhaps the simplest contention to disprove, achieved just by reading cases (which apparently the UCC activists do not do). All my life I have read cases which cited very old cases and I have never seen such a sharp demarcation where the courts did cite pre-1938 cases before 1938 and then ceased afterwards. Here are just a few post-1938 cases which cite pre-1938 cases, the constitution, the Federalist Papers and lots of other old authority:

INS v. Chadha, 462 U.S. 919 (1983)
New York v. United States, 505 U.S. 144 (1992)
Printz and Mack v. United States, 521 U. S. 898 (1997)

When you scan these cases, please note the parentheses like "(1997)" above for Richard Mack's case. This denotes the year any particular case was decided. You can easily see that these recent cases do in fact cite cases decided as far back as 1798. The contention that pre-1938 cases are not cited is nothing but lunacy, believed by folks like Dave DeReimer, a "redemption process" advocate.

This argument also contends that the States of this nation were placed in "bankruptcy" via the "secret treaty." If this were true, why did the Supreme Court decide in 1936 that states and their subdivisions could not *bankrupt? See Ashton v. Cameron County Water Improvement Dist., 298 U.S. 513, 56 S.Ct. 892 (1936).*

Finally, I must inform you that neither I nor any other lawyer I know has ever taken the "secret oath" as alleged by this argument. When I was sworn in as an Alabama lawyer in September, 1975, it was on the steps of the Alabama Supreme Court down in Montgomery in front of God, my parents and everybody else. I swore to uphold and protect the United States and Alabama Constitutions. Nothing in that oath could remotely be the alleged "secret oath." I have also been admitted to practice before the U.S. Supreme Court, and the U.S. Courts of Appeals for the 2nd, 3rd, 4th, 5th, 6th, 7th, 8th, 9th, 10th and 11th Circuits; I did not take the "secret oath" when I was admitted to practice before these courts, nor when I was admitted to practice before several U.S. District courts. I have not taken any other oath and I know that the only oath most other lawyers have taken is the same. But I do not doubt that some lawyers are members of other secret societies who may have taken oaths of which I am unaware.

My advice is that if you hear anyone making some argument about the UCC, run away as fast as you can. The argument is crazy.

Next Larry exposes the *wild theory* fallacy of turning printing styles into "law." Amazingly, it's done completely without any legislative acts:

"Nom de Guerre": Names in CAPS

Some advocates of this argument identify its source: a book written by a man named Berkhimer. Allegedly, in this book, the author states that a "nom de guerre" is a war name symbolized by a given name being written in capital letters. I have tried to find this passage in this book but have been unable to do so. *The argument contends that because of events in 1933, we have been made "enemies" and government indicates our status as enemies by the nom de guerre.* If this is true, then why have the styles of the decisions of the United States Supreme Court since its establishment been in caps? This argument has gotten lots of people in trouble. For example, Mike Kemp of the Gadsden Militia defended himself on State criminal charges with this argument and he was thrown into jail. I have not even seen a decent brief on this issue which was predicated upon cases you can find in an ordinary law library.

In any event, *several courts have rejected this argument:*

1. *Jaeger v. Dubuque County*, 880 F.Supp. 640 (N.D.Iowa 1995)
2. *United States v. Heard*, 952 F.Supp. 329 (N.D.W.Va. 1996)
3. *Boyce v. C.I.R.*, 72 T.C.M. 1996-439 ("an objection to the spelling of petitioners' names in capital letters because they are not 'fictitious entities'" was rejected)
4. *United States v. Washington*, 947 F.Supp. 87, 92 (S.D.N.Y. 1996)("Finally, the defendant contends that the Indictment must be dismissed because 'Kurt Washington,' spelled out in capital letters, is a fictitious name used by the Government to tax him improperly as a business, and that the correct spelling and presentation of his name is 'Kurt Washington.' This contention is baseless")
5. *United States v. Klimek*, 952 F.Supp. 1100 (E.D.Pa. 1997)
6. *In re Gdowik*, 228 B.R. 481, 482 (S.D.Fla. 1997)(claim that "the use of his name JOHN E GDOWIK is an 'illegal misnomer' and use of said name violates the right to his lawful status" was rejected)
7. *Russell v. United States*, 969 F.Supp. 24, 25 (W.D.

Mich. 1997)("Petitioner * * * claims because his name is in all capital letters on the summons, he is not subject to the summons"; this argument held frivolous)

8. United States v. Lindbloom, 97-2 U.S.T.C. 50650 (W.D. Wash. 1997)("In this submission, Mr. Lindbloom states that he and his wife are not proper defendants to this action because their names are not spelled with all capital letters as indicated in the civil caption." The CAPS argument and the "refused for fraud" contention were rejected)

9. Rosenheck & Co., Inc. v. United States, 79 A.F.T.R.2d (RIA) 2715 (N.D. Ok. 1997)("Kostich has made the disingenuous argument the IRS documents at issue here fail to properly identify him as the taxpayer. Defendant Kostich contends his 'Christian name' is Walter Edward, Kostich, Junior and since the IRS documents do not contain his 'Christian name,' he is not the person named in the Notice of Levy. The Court expressly finds Defendant WALTER EDWARD KOSTICH JR. is the person identified in the Notice of Levy, irrespective of the commas, capitalization of letters, or other alleged irregularities Kostich identifies as improper. Similarly, the Court's finding applies to the filed pleadings in this matter")

10. United States v. Weatherley, 12 F.Supp.2d 469 (E.D.Pa. 1998)

11. United States v. Frech, 149 F.3d 1192 (10th Cir. 1998)("Defendants' assertion that the capitalization of their names in court documents constitutes constructive fraud, thereby depriving the district court of jurisdiction and venue, is without any basis in law or fact").

More recently, Jon Roland of The Constitution Society web site wrote the following about this argument:

Typographic Conventions in Law
Jon Roland, Constitution Society

One of the persistent myths among political dissidents is that such usages as initial or complete capitalization of names indicates different legal entities or a different legal status for the entity. They see a person's name sometimes written in all caps, and sometimes written only in initial caps, and attribute a sinister intent to this difference. They also attach special meanings to the ways words may be capitalized or abbreviated in founding documents, such as constitutions or the early writings of the Founders.

Such people seem to resist all efforts to explain that such conventions have no legal significance whatsoever, that they are just ways to emphasize certain kinds of type, to make it easier for the reader to scan the documents quickly and organize the contents in his mind.

They also seem to go to enormous lengths looking for dictionaries or court rules to tell them what such typography means, without ever seeming to find what they are looking for, other than the actual usages themselves in important court cases.

Well, there is an authoritative reference, the one used by courts and lawyers all over the world. It is The Bluebook: A Uniform System of Citation, compiled by the editors of the Columbia Law Review, the Harvard Law Review Association, the University of Pennsylvania Law Review, and The Yale Law Journal, 16th ed. 1996. Copies can be obtained from any law book store or by writing The Harvard Law Review Association, Gannett House, 1511 Massachusetts Av., Cambridge, MA 02138.

To explain how typographic conventions originated, and what they mean, I am reminded of the story of the first -grader whose teacher became alarmed by the crayon drawings of one of her students. She called in the school counselor and she became alarmed, so she called in a child psychologist, who also became alarmed in turn. Fearing for the mental health of the child, they called in her parents.

The parents, now themselves concerned about their child, arrived at the meeting. "What happened?" the father said. The school staff persons showed his daughter's art work to him and to his wife. The father looked the drawings over, and said, "Look pretty good to me. I couldn't do that well at that age."

"But the colors!" the teacher said. "She does everything in black, grey, and brown!" said the counselor. "It seems morbid," said the psychologist.

So the father said, "Why don't we ask my daughter?" The school staff looked aghast at this audacious suggestion, but, not having any better ideas, they asked the little girl to come in.

She saw her parents, and the school staffers, all gathered around her art work, looking concerned, and became a bit concerned herself. But her father knew what to say. "Hon, your teachers want to know why you are drawing everything in black, grey, and brown."

"I gave most of my crayons to the other kids when they used theirs up", she said. "Black, grey, and brown are the only colors I have left."

Lawyers continued to hand-write legal documents long after typewriters were invented. As a profession, they tend to be the last to adopt new technology. When things were hand-written, they had only a few ways to highlight words. They could use block printed characters instead of cursive, or they could underline. Typesetters converted the block printed characters to all caps, sometimes with

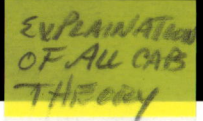

different font sizes, and the underlined words to italics.

As lawyers and legal staff began to use typewriters, they could not conveniently underline, and they didn't have italic fonts, so putting words in all caps was about the only way they had to show emphasis. Judges began rewarding lawyers (or so they thought) with better decisions if they put some words, like the names of parties, in all caps, to make it easier for overworked judges to quickly scan through many pages of pleadings and make sense of them.

Then computers came along. People started using them to produce legal documents. But a lot of them only had capital letters on their printers, or did not distinguish between upper and lower case. Programs in COBOL are examples of this. It was also found that it was easier to read words printed in all caps on forms, and to distinguish the newly printed words from the pre-printed words on the forms.

In the meantime, there were advances in typesetting typography. People became able to print special symbols, bold face, different fonts and sizes, superscripts, underlined, and colors. And with that came demands for using differences in typography to highlight words in legal documents, including treatises, law review articles, briefs, etc.

Now we have personal computers and laser printers that can do anything the typesetter can do, and legal workers are now under pressure to produce nicely composed legal documents according to the same conventions that typesetters are asked to use.

This explosion of choices could have led to confusion, so the various courts have established rules for how they

Basically, they have settled on three font styles: upper-and-lower case Roman, Italics, and Roman all-caps with larger point size for initials. Of course, if these are saved as ASCII text files, the Italics are lost, and the all-caps only show up as a single point size. Sometimes, to show Italics, as a legacy of underscoring, the words to be italicized are surrounded by underscore characters, as we do in the text above in the text version of this article.

The Bluebook calls for different typographics for the same kinds of things in different places. For example, a case cite like _Marbury v. Madison_ would be italicized in the body of a law review article, but not in a footnote. Why? Who knows. It doesn't have to make sense. It's what they do. If you submit it using different conventions, the editors will change it to their journal's conventions.

The important thing to remember, however, is that there is no legal significance to the typography of a name, other than how well it distinguishes one object from others with which it might be confused. It is the object that matters. A misspelling is a "scrivener's error." Doesn't change anything. Just needs to be corrected. Caps, complete or initial, don't mean anything. Just whatever the writer thought would aid the reader to get through the document quickly and with a minimum of confusion.

Constitution Society, 1731 Howe Av #370, Sacramento, CA 95825 Tel. 916/568-1022, 916/450-7941VM

The nom de guerre position is one rabidly advocated by Wrong Way Law. It is all based upon hype and emotions; the speakers who advocate this argument know how to

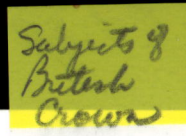

push the emotional "hot buttons" at patriot pep rallies. I have reviewed the "best" briefs regarding this issue and they are all trash. Yet I continue to see people call themselves "John, of smith," "John: Smith," etc., and I just simply conclude that such parties have attended a Wrong Way Law seminar and have accepted a pack of lies. Further, it is remarkable that all the people who believe this idea have never checked it out; they just accept it because some patriot guru claimed it was correct.

The last *wild theory* from Larry's web site that we're going to review reverses the outcome of the War for Independence:

Simple facts regarding the "we are subjects of the British Crown" issue

Several years ago, some folks developed an argument that "we are still subjects of the British crown" and started promoting it. You are free to believe that argument, which will waste your time. Here is a simple refutation of that argument:

1. The Articles of Confederation provided as follows:

"Article II. Each state retains its sovereignty, freedom, and independence, and every Power, Jurisdiction and right, which is not by this confederation expressly delegated to the United States, in Congress assembled."

2. Our country and the British Crown signed the Treaty of Peace on September 3, 1783, the first provision of which reads as follows:

"His Britannic Majesty acknowledges the said United States, viz, New-Hampshire, Massachusetts-Bay, Rhode-Island and Providence Plantations,

Connecticut, New-York, New-Jersey, Pennsylvania, Delaware, Maryland, Virginia, North-Carolina, South-Carolina, and Georgia, to be free, sovereign and independent States; that he treats with them as such; and for himself, his heirs and successors, relinquishes all claims to the government, proprietary and territorial rights of the same, and every part thereof."

See also Nov. 30, 1782 Provisional Treaty and Jan. 20, 1783 Treaty of Cessation of Hostilities.

Does this 1783 Peace Treaty still exist? All one needs to do to confirm this is to check out a government publication entitled "Treaties in Force" which can be found in any good library, especially a university library. Under the list of our treaties with Great Britain and the United Kingdom, you will find that this 1783 treaty is still in effect, at least a part of it: "Only article 1 is in force." Art.1 was the section of this treaty acknowledging our independence. The War of 1812 resulted in modifications of this treaty and so did later treaties.

3. The courts have not been silent regarding the effect of the Declaration of Independence and the Treaty of Peace. For example, the consequences of independence were explained in Harcourt v. Gaillard, 25 U.S. (12 Wheat.) 523, 526-27 (1827), where the Supreme Court stated:

"There was no territory within the United States that was claimed in any other right than that of some one of the confederated states; therefore, there could be no acquisition of territory made by the United States distinct from, or independent of some one of the states.

"Each declared itself sovereign and independent, according to the limits of its territory.

266

"[T]he soil and sovereignty within their acknowledged limits were as much theirs at the declaration of independence as at this hour."

In M'Ilvaine v. Coxe's Lessee, 8 U.S. (4 Cranch) 209, 212 (1808), the Supreme Court held:

"This opinion is predicated upon a principle which is believed to be undeniable, that the several states which composed this Union, so far at least as regarded their municipal regulations, became entitled, from the time when they declared themselves independent, to all the rights and powers of sovereign states, and that they did not derive them from concessions made by the British king. The treaty of peace contains a recognition of their independence, not a grant of it. From hence it results, that the laws of the several state governments were the laws of sovereign states, and as such were obligatory upon the people of such state, from the time they were enacted."

In reference to the Treaty of Peace, this same court stated:

"It contains an acknowledgment of the independence and sovereignty of the United States, in their political capacities, and a relinquishment on the part of His Britannic Majesty, of all claim to the government, propriety and territorial rights of the same. These concessions amounted, no doubt, to a formal renunciation of all claim to the allegiance of the citizens of the United States."

Finally, in Inglis v. Trustees of the Sailor's Snug Harbor, 28 U.S. (3 Peters) 99, 120-122 (1830), the question squarely arose as to whether Americans are "subjects of the crown," a proposition flatly rejected by the

Court:

"It is universally admitted both in English courts and in those of our own country, that all persons born within the colonies of North America, whilst subject to the crown of Great Britain, were natural born British subjects, and it must necessarily follow that that character was changed by the separation of the colonies from the parent State, and the acknowledgment of their independence.

"The rule as to the point of time at which the American antenati ceased to be British subjects, differs in this country and in England, as established by the courts of justice in the respective countries. The English rule is to take the date of the Treaty of Peace in 1783. Our rule is to take the date of the Declaration of Independence."

In support of the rule set forth in this case, the court cited an English case to demonstrate that the English courts had already decided that Americans were not subjects of the crown:

"The doctrine of perpetual allegiance is not applied by the British courts to the American antenati. This is fully shown by the late case of <u>Doe v. Acklam</u>, 2 Barn. & Cresw. 779. Chief Justice Abbott says: 'James Ludlow, the father of Francis May, the lessor of the plaintiff, was undoubtedly born a subject of Great Britain. He was born in a part of America which was at the time of his birth a British colony, and parcel of the dominions of the crown of Great Britain; but upon the facts found, we are of opinion that he was not a subject of the crown of Great Britain at the time of the birth of his daughter. She was born after the independence of the colonies was recognized by the crown of Great

Britain; after the colonies had become United States, and their inhabitants generally citizens of those States, and her father, by his continued residence in those States, manifestly became a citizen of them.' He considered the Treaty of Peace as a release from their allegiance of all British subjects who remained there. A declaration, says he, that a State shall be free, sovereign and independent, is a declaration that the people composing the State shall no longer be considered as subjects of the sovereign by whom such a declaration is made."

Notwithstanding the fact that English and American courts long ago rejected this argument, I still encounter e-mail from parties who contend that this argument is correct. For example, just recently I ran across this note which stated:

"In other words, the interstate system of banks is the private property of the King... This means that any profit or gain anyone experienced by a bank/thrift and loan/employee credit union ?? any regulated financial institution carries with it ?? as an operation of law ?? the identical same full force and effect as if the King himself created the gain. So as an operation of law, anyone who has a depository relationship, or a credit relationship, with a bank, such as checking, savings, CD's, charge cards, car loans, real estate mortgages, etc., are experiencing profit and gain created by the King ?? so says the Supreme Court. At the present time, Mr. Condo, you have bank accounts (because you accept checks as payment for books and subscriptions), and you are very much in an EQUITY RELATIONSHIP with the King."

This note also alleged that George Mercier, who wrote an article apparently popular among those who believe the "contract theory" of government, was a retired judge, which is false. Just because you read it on the Net does not make it true.

One of the advocates of this flaky idea is David Gould ("Goul") who has a web site named "The Amazing Vision of David Gould," where he promotes this trash. In the summer of 1999, Goul joined a couple of e-mail lists which I receive and started blasting this theory in a series of e-mail notes. According to Goul, one of the reasons "we are Brits" is because the King of England via a treaty in 1782 loaned the United States funds to engage in the war against him; Goul maintains that the fact that the King was loaning money to us to fight him really shows that even today we are still subjects of the Crown. In reply, I pointed out that the treaty he mentions was really a French loan agreement where the United States borrowed money for the Revolution from the King of France, not the King of Great Britain. I sent out a series of e-mail notes which refuted everything that Goul declared and it did not take long before Goul stopped his nonsense.

However, my belief that I had corrected Goul and educated him about an incorrect legal argument proved erroneous. I have examined his web site recently and he has only become more virulent in his argument that we are Brits . . . What makes him particularly dangerous is the fact that he blends religion with his arguments. I absolutely dislike people who combine Christianity with false legal arguments; I dislike people who hold my religion up to disrepute by associating it with nutty ideas.

I have one final note regarding this issue. Recently, the US Supremes in <u>JP Morgan Chase Bank v. Traffic Stream (BVI) Infrastructure Ltd</u>, ___ U.S. ___ (June 2002)

*rendered its decision in this case and any reading of it
should permanently gut this "we are Brits" insanity.*

In addition to verifying an alleged *theory* by the research of statutes, there is also the need to understand different jurisdictions. In other words, at one time it was alleged that if you had a drivers license you had a liability to pay an income tax. The major flaw in such a *theory* is that the traffic code and the tax code are two separate jurisdictions. In all my years on the police force in Baltimore, and all my years participating in the Constitutional Movement, I have never come across any provision of the traffic code imposing a tax, or, on the other hand, the tax code imposing traffic requirements or infractions. It is the same with the U.C.C. (Uniform Commercial Code) covered above. The provisions of this code deal with commercial paper under State laws, where the federal tax code is under federal jurisdiction. The only connection that there could be between the two, is that in some States the statutes for filing tax liens are within the U.C.C., and the IRS would have to follow those statutes to file a federal tax lien within a county in that State.

There have been *wild theories* over the years that have been debunked, and because so many Patriots were injured by their use, abandoned. But as time went by, I have witnessed how some new guru happens upon one of these *theories* and revives it, sucking into their trap the new, inexperienced Patriot. Wherefore, it is meaningful to cover some other such *theories* here to possibly prevent further damage to the movement and unsuspecting Patriots.

A debunked *wild theory* that seems to keep coming back in various scenarios is the 14th Amendment citizen.

As discussed within this book, from the beginning of the Constitutional Republic there have been individuals that have banded together to work tenaciously to take the federal government beyond its enumerated powers at the expense of the several States —*Hamiltonian-Lincolnites* known as federalists. Counter to this, there have been those known as *Jeffersonian-Democrats*, individuals fighting to hold the federal government strictly to the written provisions of the Constitution, fighting for what is known as *States Rights*.[3] This struggle crashed head-on with the election of Abraham Lincoln to the presidency. A certain number of the southern States seceded from the union of States known as the United States, an action which is not prohibited by the Constitution. After the secession of these States, Lincoln gave some military orders that actually caused an outbreak of violent hostilities, and then he ordered the invasion of Virginia, at that time a State of the Confederate States of America.

After the cessation of hostilities, and the collapse of the Confederate States of America in 1865, the Congress passed an Act to amend the Constitution by adding the 13th Amendment to abolish slavery, and it was ratified by the States that remained within the union of States:

> *Section 1. Neither slavery nor involuntary servitude, except as a punishment for crime whereof the party shall have been duly convicted, shall exist within the United States, or any place subject to their jurisdiction.*

> *Section 2. Congress shall have power to enforce this article by appropriate legislation.*

As the former States of the Confederate States of America re-entered the Union of States, they were forced to agree to the ratification of this Amendment.

Now that the slaves were free, there was two problems that needed to be solved. According to the provisions of the Constitution, only those slaves that were born within the States were citizens; and the slave States had laws forbidding slaves the right to vote.

There are only two ways that anyone can become a citizen of

the United States: The first by birth, and the second by naturalization, and the latter requires the taking of a test. The great majority of the freed slaves were not capable of taking a test; wherefore, Congress passed an Act to make all the former slaves citizens, giving them the right to vote. The problem with the enactment of this law was that Congress had no Constitutional authority to enact it. So in 1866, Congress passed the 14th Amendment to the Constitution to insure that the before-mentioned unlawful Act, and other unlawful Acts involving the freed slaves, would have Constitutional authority, thereby making them lawful. To my knowledge, what would have been the proper question of the re-enactment of these laws after the ratification was never addressed. In 1868, the 14th Amendment was ratified by all the States, and states in pertinent part:

> *Section 1. All persons born or naturalized in the United States, and subject to the jurisdiction thereof, are citizens of the United States and of the state wherein they reside. No state shall make or enforce any law which shall abridge the privileges or immunities of citizens of the United States; nor shall any state deprive any person of life, liberty, or property, without due process of law; nor deny to any person within its jurisdiction the equal protection of the laws.* (Emphasis added.)

With a little bit of knowledge, and a whole lot of imagination, some promoters of wild theories contended that this Amendment made Americans have dual citizenship, citizens of the State in which they resided, and citizens of the United States subject to the jurisdiction of Washington, D.C. They further concluded that, being subject to the jurisdiction of Washington, D.C., American citizens were subject to the liability of an income tax. They advocated that the remedy to rectify this wild fairytale was to renounce your U.S. Citizenship, and that would leave you to be only a citizen of the State in which you reside.

It is needless to say, many a good, well-meaning Patriot, who

273

bought into this outrageous foolhardiness, suffered severely, both in physical incarceration and loss of property. I had an occasion some years ago to talk to an assistant U.S. attorney in Los Angeles, California, and she told me that there were so many individuals in California renouncing their U.S. citizenship, that she was thinking about starting deportation proceedings. I do not believe she ever did, as I never heard any more about it.

During the 1980s, some gurus were advocating that all dealings with the federal government, no matter what, were contractual. The Preamble to the Constitution states:

> *We the People of the United States, in Order to form a more perfect Union, establish Justice, insure domestic Tranquility, provide for the common defense, promote the general Welfare, and secure the Blessings of Liberty to ourselves and our Posterity, do ordain and establish this Constitution for the United States of America.*

Because the first words in the Constitution are *We the People*, these gurus determined that citizens actually contracted with the federal government, and therefore, federal taxes were contractual. They also concluded that Social Security was contractual, and the use of Post Office services such as the zip code subjected the user to federal jurisdiction. Therefore, their obvious remedy was to revoke the contract and avoid the tax. Of course, their presentation had a very elaborate *theory*, convincing many that it was so.

Back in the 1980s, a lady in California declared that *land patents* were the highest form of land titles, and that they even defeated mortgages. Later on, others added that they defeated property taxes also. Nobody advocating this *wild theory*, nor those blindly applying its proposed use, ever bothered to research why land patents even existed, or what the land patent's original use was.

Large land areas of North and South America were claimed

by European monarchs and pronounced to be their colonies. The English monarch claimed the majority of eastern North America to belong to England. In order to take physical control of the land, he gave to certain of his subjects *land grants* to establish colonies. Wherefore, these *land grants* describing the land area to be possessed were recorded in the capitol of each colony. As the holder of the *land grant* would divide and redistribute the land to others, there was a written document describing the new landholder, and the land he so possessed. This document became known as a *land deed*, or a *deed to real property*, and was recorded in the county within the colony, in which the land existed, in that county's courthouse. *Land grants / Land Patents*

At the time of the Revolution, there were thirteen original colonies, and at the time of the establishment of the Constitutional Republic, there existed only the thirteen original States. All the land therein was occupied by the *land grant* and *land deed* process. In the third administration, President Jefferson negotiated and instigated the Louisiana Purchase from France, obtaining a large part of what is now the western United States. This land was not acquired by any *land grant* from a monarch. And when it was redistributed to citizens of the United States, it was done so by patent, a *land patent* which was recorded in the territory or the State, as the case may be. Every distribution and recording after that, just like the *land grant*, was by a *land deed*. That is why there are no *land patents* to be found in the thirteen original States.

There is no act of Congress to be found that authorizes the use of *land patents* to cheat the holder of a mortgage, authorize the exemption from lawful State real property taxes, nor is there any authority found within the Constitution for Congress to pass such an act.

In the early 1980s, a Maryland man happened to come across a Delaware corporation named the IRS. Right away he jumped to the conclusion that this was the federal Internal Revenue Service, and published his "discovery." It spread like wildfire throughout the Patriot community. If he, or any of his followers, would have taken the time to investigate to make sure they were right, they would have discovered that this corporation was an accounting firm established in 1933, and no longer in existence. The very same thing occurred in the mid-1990s. There was a new Nevada corporation entitled IRS, Inc. As soon as it was circulated through the Patriot community that this corporation was the federal Internal Revenue Service, I called the Nevada Secretary of State, and he instantly informed me that beyond a shadow of a doubt, this was not the federal Internal Revenue Service, just an accounting firm that thought the name would bring them business.

Back in the early 1980s, not getting justice in the federal and State courts, some Patriots theorized that they, being *We the People*, had a right to establish their own court system, and entitled it The One Supreme Court. They claimed it was a common law court, because it got its jurisdiction from the common law. They started trying Patriots and finding them not guilty before the federal and/or State court and then the Patriot would invoke the Constitutional provision of double jeopardy. This, of course, failed and sort of died off without any real serious injury to anyone. But it was revived again some years later, and became more forceful in trying to carry forth its edicts and orders. Then it was taken more seriously and some of the participants got some serious time in the federal prison system. What these well-meaning Patriots overlooked was the fact that there is no such authorization either in the federal Constitution, or any of the State Constitutions. Thus, in essence, these unwitting Patriots were committing a revolutionary act against the United States, an act no different than the one committed by the *Founding Fathers* in 1774. When Governor Lord Dunmore ordered the Virginia Colonial Legislature, the House of Burgesses in Williamsburg, Virginia, shut down, the *Founding Fathers* went to the Apollo Room in the Raleigh Tavern in Jamestown, Virginia and reconvened the legislature. The contemporary Patriots are very fortunate that they were not charged with sedition.

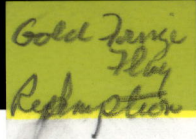
Gold Fringe
Flag
Redemption

There are also those who contend that if a courtroom flies an American flag with gold fringe around its edge, then that court is an admiralty court, and does not have jurisdiction over domestic matters such as tax cases. This, of course, has no basis in fact, and it cannot be verified anywhere except in the minds of those individuals.

Some of these *wild theories* are not only dangerous for the duped Patriot using them, but through the Patriot's belief in the *theory,* have caused financial harm to other Americans. One such *theory* is called the Redemption Process.

Larry Becraft explains the Redemption Process thusly:

> *In essence, . . . everyone's birth certificate constitutes ownership in "America, Inc." and we all have stock in this corporation, which stock is represented by these birth certificates (see Lodi v. Lodi, 173 Cal.App.3d 628, 219 Cal.Rptr. 116 (1985), where similar arguments were rejected; and Dose v. United States, 86 U.S.T.C. 9773 (N.D.Iowa 1986) ("Petitioner * * * informs the Court of [his] 'notorious recission of [his] social security number' and recission of his birth certificate, which documents had previously made him a 'member of Corporate America (commune)' converting him into 'a slave of the commune subject to the regulation and control of the Federal Government' * * * the fact that Dose has attempted to rescind his social security number and birth certificate by sworn affidavit is irrelevant * * *")). According to Roger [Elvick, the originator of the theory], the big banks and other financial institutions regularly trade in these birth certificates, buying and selling them to others. Of course, according to this new argument, you can do the same thing.*

Larry continues with an example of what happened to a Patriot who believed this *theory* and put it into practice:

277

So what is going to happen? I bet that those who advocated using "acceptance for value" to refuse criminal process like an indictment or information will be charged with obstruction of justice, and they will be tied into a giant conspiracy of those who told others to send in drafts drawn on the U.S. Treasury. This stupidity will just be another instance where the freedom movement will be held up to the press and the rest of America as a bunch of crackpots, nuts and fruitcakes, and "dangerous" ones at that.

Have people already gotten into trouble by using the "redemption process" sight drafts? Hyla Clapier is a sweet, little old lady from Idaho. She was convinced last year by the redemptionists to try to buy a car with one of those "redemption process" sight drafts drawn on the U.S. Treasury. Her effort brought her an indictment, trial and conviction. If you wish to study the details of her case, simply read her docket sheet posted on the U.S. District Court of Idaho's web site. In late April, 2000, I received a call from an Ohio newspaper reporter and was informed that a man in his local community had attempted to buy 8 Cadillacs with those sight drafts. I was also informed that the man was being prosecuted for several felonies. Is the "redemption process" sight draft effort anything but another crackpot idea? I think not.

The last *wild theory* that I will address was hatched by a man whom, a couple of years ago, I had the misfortune to spend two days with, at the end of which I questioned my own sanity. Eric Madsen contends that an Act of Congress, dated February 21, 1871, created the corporate United States. In other words, according to Eric, there are two United States governments, the one created by the Constitution of the United States, and the other secret corporate United States created in 1871, which took the place of the former. The corporate United States government is running the country, and the dispossessed government created by the Constitution is in some sort of holding pattern, a *limbo*. Because of this Act of Congress, the State governments are also corporations, with the State's Constitutional government also in limbo. Therefore, the corporate State governments are holding elections electing individuals to the State and federal corporate governments, thus causing a void in the Constitutional government's offices.

Because of these circumstances, according to Eric, he held an election and was elected governor of the Constitutional State of Colorado by one vote being cast—his—and later, following the same election process, he was elected to the "Constitutional United States government's Senate." He is advocating that others follow this process in other States, and I have heard that some Patriots have done so. I asked Eric why he did not take his seat in the Senate, and he responded that when the time is right, he will.

The major flaw in Eric's *theory* is that the Act of February 21, 1871, did not create a corporate U.S. Government, but rather, a municipal corporation which was the first Washington, D.C. municipal government.[4] Therefore, Eric's *theory* loses its foundation and thus fails factually.

There are several *wild theories* that are not being covered within this book. As stated above, the best way to check out any *theory* that may be presented to you is by examining the appropriate jurisdictional statute, if indeed one exists. A good rule of thumb is to reject any *theory*, if the argument for it starts with a statement like "I believe," or "it appears to be." When it comes to law, "I believe," or "it appears to be," are just not good enough.

Even though there are scam artists circulating in the Patriot community, taking advantage of Patriots' ignorance of the workings of the law, I do not believe that all these individuals coming up with these *wild theories* are scam artists. From my observations and discussions with some of these individuals, I have concluded that they are in a state of denial, not wanting to accept the fact of the raw tyranny that is emanating from our courts (some of which was covered in Chapter 11 of this book). I can understand that it is hard for some individuals to accept the fact that Americans can turn their backs on the principles of *Liberty*, which are the foundation of this great Constitutional Republic, merely for expediency in government. God help us!!

Part V

THE LONG ROAD BACK

Chapter 13

SAVE-A-PATRIOT FELLOWSHIP

The Republic did not arrive at this present dangerous political and financial state of affairs haphazardly. As illustrated herein, it was brought to this condition by people who foster an alien political philosophy, and who use that philosophy as a way to amass power and wealth. They have been able to accomplish this power grab by taking advantage of the ignorance of the people—those who hold political office and know not what they are doing; those who have recognized that something is wrong, but do not really know how to combat it; and those who have recognized that something is wrong and are indifferent to it, because to act may interfere with the comfort of their lifestyle.

I personally woke up to the fact that things were not right back in 1963. Before that, even as a boy of 16 years, I suspected something was wrong in the way Senator Joseph McCarthy was being attacked and interfered with in trying to root out the enemies of the Republic. The obvious sham of the Bay of Pigs invasion caused me to search in earnest, and I have spent the last thirty-eight years trying to learn how to combat the problem. Being the type of person that approaches things logically, and tries to benefit from prior mistakes, I have traveled through many political activities.

I first became involved in an organization that promoted educational books on the worldwide communist movement, and its infiltration into government agencies. It mainly advocated letter writing to political office holders as a solution. It did not take long to see that this was not very productive, and actually counter-productive, in that many of its members became very frustrated and inactive.

I also took a very active role in political election campaigns, spending what were for me large sums of money, but that turned out to be a big waste of money and time; as many of us have found out over the years, professional politicians will tell you anything to get elected. Even the politicians who try to keep their promises are in such a minority that they turn out to be nothing more than voices crying in the wilderness. Even worse, due to their ignorance of the Constitution, this minority, while fighting unlawful, unconstitutional bills and treaties, act as though the passage of these acts and treaties would lawfully change the functions of the government.

My political education really began with my entrance into what is known by the public as the *Tax Protest Movement*. Through this activity, my attention was truly drawn to the U.S. Constitution, some federal statutes, U.S. Supreme Court decisions, and some fundamental principles of law. I received instruction in the police academy in Baltimore on basic law, which, with my experience gained on the police force, was very helpful in keeping me from falling into the *wild theory* trap. But, as many of us have found out, the best teacher is necessity. When you throw down a gauntlet at the feet of the IRS and the Department of "Justice," your hunger for education begins in earnest.

I can recall telling my wife—now a seasoned veteran of forty-six years, but then, still a young wife of seven years struggling with four young children—that someday I would probably go to jail. But going to jail would be a sign that I was becoming successful in my struggle for the *Cause of Liberty*. I can also recall her looking at me saying, "Right. OK," as she turned her attention back to our four preschool children. In 1975, in order to

284

gain attention to our educational effort, I publicly challenged the Baltimore District Director of the IRS and the U.S. Attorney for the District of Maryland to prove me wrong on my contentions about the U.S. Constitution and the federal income tax. WBAL-TV, Channel 11 in Baltimore, offered prime-time coverage and contacted the before-mentioned gentlemen, who, in turn, declined to appear. I appeared on the six o'clock evening news, and talked about what was in reality my then limited knowledge of the federal income tax. On the following April 15th, 1976, Special Agent James Reed, and Special Agent Clifford Earp, of the Baltimore IRS District Office, came to my house to read me my rights, and after a five year investigation, my prophecy to my wife came true.

After my sentencing, being convicted of two counts of *failure to file*, for which I received the maximum sentence of one year on each count and a $5,000 fine on each count to run consecutively, the IRS Publicist for the Baltimore Office, Dominic LaPonzina, had the network media waiting for me outside of the Federal Courthouse. The one question asked of me, which stands out in my mind was: *"What now, Mr. Kotmair, now that you have been convicted and received the maximum sentence?"* I answered with, *"I'm proud to be in service for my country, and you are all invited to the Holiday Inn up the street to help me celebrate at the banquet in my honor tonight."* With that I walked away, looking back at Dominic LaPonzina, who did not seem too happy with the results of his big press event. That night the banquet was covered by all the local television news media, and I was given numerous awards for my efforts in the *Cause of Liberty*. Patriots came from all over the country to participate. I was told that the Judge and the U.S. Attorney were not too happy about being upstaged.

In 1973, after being abused in a civil suit I filed against two IRS agents in the Federal District Court in Baltimore, and also in the 4th Circuit Court of Appeals, it became apparent that justice would not come by the courts. It became clear that the only way back to ensuring that the government would observe and stay within its Constitutional bounds was to educate the public and thus force it back through the resulting grassroots political action.

I organized a Maryland *Committee of Correspondence*, hoping to emulate Samuel Adams, who successfully used the same tactic exactly two hundred years before, causing the first political connection with other Founding Fathers, in other colonies. The idea was to hold meetings and eventually connect with other similar committees within the State of Maryland and other States of the Union, to bring about the needed grassroots political movement. Successful contact was made with other Patriots hoping to achieve the same purpose. In the winter of 1980, Tom Junker of New York City and John Murphy and Ferd Watson of Collingswood, New Jersey, arranged for a meeting to be held in the Christian Admiral Hotel, in the seaside resort of Collingswood. The hotel was owned by the Rev. Dr. Carl McIntire,[1] and being closed down for the season, he graciously re-opened it and even served us meals at his own expense. Representatives came from clear across the United States, making this first effort at linking Patriot organizations together a success.

The organization that was formed was called *The Patriot Network*, and there were four directors selected to operate it: George Meyers of Racine, Wisconsin; Tom Junker of Queens, New York; Robert Clarkson of Anderson, South Carolina, and myself, from Westminster, Maryland. Clarkson and I were to be the first fulltime directors, with Meyers and Junker joining us when the need arose. The headquarters was in Clarkson's home in Anderson, and I was to travel the country, lecturing to the various groups, and in doing so, attempt to bring them into *The Patriot Network*.

Having experience with the courts during my tenure as a police officer, and in my Patriot efforts, I was not too keen on the services agreed upon. The effort was to have a legal defense fund, and select the best possible criminal cases—that should, due to the circumstances, be easy to win—and support them financially; this being the big-win theory, or the fast-result theory. The first case to be selected was mine, as I was indicted just before the

286

Collingswood meeting, and because of some prior Patriot activity, I was one of the subjects of the infamous FBI-IRS COINTELPRO operation in the late 1960s and early 1970s. The theory was that this would give me every right to assert the 5th Amendment on an IRS 1040 tax return. Well, as stated above, the powers-that-be would not allow such a victory, and it did not happen.

Several months later, the organizational name *Patriot Network* was changed to the *National Patriot Association*. George Arlen of Dallas, Texas, replaced Robert Clarkson as a director, and the headquarters were moved to a property that one of the Directors bought in Arkansas for that purpose. At every directors' meeting, I would stress that the emphasis should be changed from the big-win theory to the support of the Patriot and his/her family. I would argue that there was enough evidence to show the corrupt practices and collusion between the Department of Justice, IRS and the judiciary, especially in tax cases. I would cite the documented jury rigging in my criminal tax trial, and argue that the big-win theory only makes the defense lawyers richer. I pointed out that the main cause of desertions in George Washington's Continental Army was related to the soldiers worrying about their personal family problems, and this movement cannot survive unless the Patriot has some means to look out for their families. All of this was to no avail.

My wife and I continued to travel and lecture on behalf of *National Patriot Association*, until my appeal was denied and I was ordered to report to the prison camp in the Maxwell Air Force Base, in Montgomery, Alabama in August, 1982.

During the next seventeen months and five days—a two year sentence, less time off for good behavior and for working in the camp and on the Air Force Base—I had plenty of time to formulate my logistical plan for the Patriot Constitutional Movement.

I would be remiss here if I did not relate to the reader some of my experiences while a resident at Camp Maxwell. I was only there a couple of days when I was summoned by the camp captain, who acknowledged the fact, without any prompting from me, that I was a political prisoner. He related that he knew my background as a police officer, that his secretary was leaving in a couple of months, and he offered the position to me. I respectfully thanked him and declined. A few days after that, I was summoned by the camp staff recreational officer, who was also the camp union representative, and upon my arrival at the recreational building, he summoned me into his office and stated that he wanted to know everything I knew about the tax laws and the Constitution. This man worked with me the entire time that I was interned in Camp Maxwell. We set up a weekly Constitutional class as part of the camp recreational program, and brought in speakers. This man was a *black* man from the State of Georgia, and a true Patriot in every sense of the word. His brother later became a member of the Fellowship. The only downside to this whole experience was the separation from my wife and family, which was harder on my wife, as most of her activities ended upon my internment.

At that time, the law only allowed the accumulation of one hundred and eighty days, free and clear, off any sentence for "good time" and "camp time." Due to the length of my sentence I accumulated two hundred and three days; wherefore, upon my release in January of 1984, it was required that the first twenty-three days of my release would be in the status of "as if on parole." I was required to report into the parole office at the federal courthouse in Baltimore within three days of my release. I arrived home with enough time that first day to report in and did so. The parole officer requested that I stay out of the newspapers, off radio and television shows for the next twenty-three days. He stated that at the end of that time, he would forward me a letter acknowledging that I was no longer under the jurisdiction of the Attorney General of the United States. As I was going out the door to his office, he called and asked: "What about the $10,000 fine?" I asked him if he wanted it in Kotmair Reserve Notes,[2] and his reply was: "Get out of here." Twenty-three days later, he mailed the letter, and twelve days after that, I made the first mailing for the recruitment of Patriots to join the *Save-A-Patriot Fellowship* to a list of names that I gathered while touring the U.S.A. for *The Patriot Network* and the *National Patriot Association*. The recruitment package included an application and the *Fellowship* plan that I formulated while at the federal prison camp. This plan, which was rejected by the other directors of *The Patriot Network* and the *National Patriot Association*, is still successfully operating today, eighteen and a half years later.

The *Fellowship* plan is straight-forward in its application, and explained in the Fellowship agreement thusly:

> *Simply put, Fellowship members pledge to reimburse other members for losses of cash or property incurred by illegal confiscations. This is done by spreading reimbursement costs to all the members. For example, suppose that after a valiant and stubborn struggle through the phases of the legal maze, a member were to lose his vehicle to an illegal seizure. Let's value the vehicle at 9,000 Federal Reserve Notes (commonly called "dollars"). If there are 10,000 members participating in the Fellowship, S.A.P. would verify the loss and apportion the liability at a rate of 90 cents per member. PRESTO! Mr. or Ms. Member Patriot suffers NO loss and his friends' fear of possible IRS retaliation is gone! Real-life examples such as this have convinced "closet" Patriots to join the S.A.P. Fellowship in droves! Welcome to the Constitutional Revivalist Movement!*
>
> *The surest and safest protection of funds is to keep them in the hands of the members. The only money to be sent to S.A.P. Headquarters is the annual 70 FRNs (cash) or a totally blank Postal Money Order can be sent by certified mail. S.A.P. maintains no bank account, so checks or money orders made out to "S.A.P." can't be endorsed and cashed. The membership fee is used for the administrative needs of S.A.P.—staff, rent, phone, printing, postage, etc. After verification by Headquarters of losses to claimant*

member; you send payments DIRECTLY to the claimant (or their beneficary)! S.A.P. merely verifies that all members have met their assessment obligations by a simple procedure.

Payment For Incarceration. There are still occurrences when a Patriot is criminally tried, convicted and jailed. This is a most difficult financial burden to individually shoulder. Therefore, it is the stated policy of the Fellowship to assess for the beneficiary of each incarcerated Patriot 25,000 FRNs per calendar year, during the period of incarceration. To the best of our knowledge, there have never been more than 30 Patriots in jail after conviction at any one time. At this rate, and assuming that all were covered S.A.P. Fellowship members, this protection would cost 10,000 members 75 FRNs for all those jailed. If there are 80,000 members participating, it would only be 9.38 FRNs each for 30 beneficiaries.

The figure of "80,000" is in line with a 1984 federal estimate of the number of participants within the so-called Tax Patriot segment of the Constitutional Revivalist Movement. Using this figure as our goal for total Fellowship participation, we could increase the incarceration payoff amount to 100,000 FRNs each per calendar year and it would only cost each member 37.50 FRNs to support the 30 jailed members With this kind of hard-cash protection, Americans will not only lose their fear of the IRS, but will almost be standing in line to go to jail!!! Even IRS agents could not resist such an offer!

In other words, remove the financial threat to the average American citizen, and the IRS' house of cards will collapse!—AND LIBERTY WILL ABOUND!!

In 1984, the year the *Fellowship* plan was written, 100,000 FRNs was a lot of money. Inflation has shrunk the viability of this scenario, and it was replaced with the *Victory Express*, which will be covered later on in this Chapter.

The original *Fellowship* plan above did not include any coverage for criminal prosecutions, the logic being that such coverage would enrich lawyers at the membership's expense. One of the *Fellowship* members in Alaska asked if I, as the Fiduciary of the *Fellowship*, had any objection to him starting such coverage and soliciting membership to it from *Fellowship* members and others. I responded that I had none and published his effort, *The Patriot Defense Fellowship (PDF)*, for the membership. Within the year, circumstances made it impossible for him to continue his participation and he requested that the *PDF* become part of the *Save-A-Patriot Fellowship*. It was presented to the *Fellowship* membership, and on their concurrence, it was made optional for S.A.P. Fellowship members, and remains so today.

The following is the published *Statement of Purpose* for the *Save-A-Patriot Fellowship*:

> *The Save-A-Patriot Fellowship is a 1st Amendment association dedicated to seeing that IRS and other government personnel obey the law, and that the government, in meeting its exigencies, may not extend its activities beyond the law.*
>
> *The Fellowship actively promotes the study of the law and the assertion of one's rights in accordance with the law. It does not "protest" or "object" to any tax, income or otherwise, and is NOT a "tax protest" organization. However, Fellowship members believe that many Internal Revenue Service (IRS) employees routinely misapply and illegally enforce the provisions of the law and that the public must find a way to hold them within the law. To that end the Fellowship educates the public, shows in its publications what the law actually says, and attempts to clarify the limitations of various tax laws as was intended by Congress. The Fellowship does not advocate or condone unlawful resistance, protest, or other like actions.*
>
> *However, as law-abiding citizens, we will not condone*

illegal threats, intimidation or acts of violence by government employees who exceed their authority under the law. The Fellowship has researched and developed legal defenses to help prevent this and to protect our Liberty and Property.

The Fellowship believes that this has become necessary because too many government bureaucrats have been relying on unlawful and un-American tactics such as fear and intimidation to keep the public "in line" in order to perpetuate their own private agendas. They have used and continue to use the news media to plant stories suggesting that resistance is useless and reprisal is swift and financially painful. These "reminders" and a lifetime of conditioning make it difficult for most people to assert their rights. However, S.A.P. Fellowship members have joined together to help remove the risk by pledging to assist one another!

To our knowledge, there is no insurance company willing to buck the system and insure Patriots against criminal acts of government agencies or their employees. Creating and operating a conventional insurance company would have been impossible. The bureaucrats would have insisted on our submission to the dictates of the Insurance Commission. In no time at all, we would have been expending funds fighting legal actions just trying to survive. It would have also been necessary to protect such funds from the searching eyes of the IRS and other government agencies.

There was only one totally logical answer: a Fellowship that gives the Patriot insurance-like protection, hence Save-A-Patriot!

The *Fellowship* has a membership-only 24-page newsletter entitled *Reasonable Action*, which is its main tool for disseminating news within the Constitutional Revivalist Movement and for educating its members on the facts about the laws revealed by its research. The articles appearing on its pages represent the state-of-the-art in legal understanding of the United States system of income taxation. You will not find any groundless "far-out" theories. You will find thoughtful, provocative articles, discussions and opinions that are grounded in fact and logic. The editors strive to ensure the accuracy of all the articles, insisting that the authors give references, so that the reader may verify the accuracy himself. Education is the key to throwing off the imaginary chains of IRS bondage!

In addition to the *Reasonable Action* newsletter, the Fellowship also publishes a 4-page newsletter entitled the *Liberty Tree*, which accompanies the member's monthly statement. This newsletter contains the latest *Fellowship* news and political commentary beneficial to the membership.

For the first three years, the *Fellowship* consisted only of the membership assistance programs. In 1987, a casework department was added to handle IRS correspondence received by the membership. Within a matter of a few months, a paralegal department was added, making the *Fellowship* a full-service Patriot organization. Since that time, thousands of cases have been handled for the membership by the two departments.

In response to a written invitation to the Commissioner of the Internal Revenue Service, asking him to show whether the educational information disseminated by the *Fellowship* was correct or incorrect, the IRS raided the *Fellowship* offices and the home of the Fiduciary on December 10, 1993. They seized whatever cash they found, all the computers, computer files and all the filing cabinets containing the paper copies of all the correspondence to and from the IRS on behalf of our members.

The day before the raid, in response to a subpoena, I was before a federal grand jury in Sioux Falls, South Dakota, supposedly testifying at an inquiry about one of the *Fellowship* members. Not long into the proceedings, it became evident that the U.S. Attorney present was trying to indict me. I suspected something was wrong after I tried three times to quash the subpoena for the reason that all I could testify to was information about the correspondence to the IRS on the member's behalf, which was already in the government's possession. I stated this in my petition to quash to the court and the U.S. Attorney's response contained an affidavit from the investigating IRS Special Agent that contained a lie. When I pointed this out to the court in my motion to reconsider, the court completely ignored it and ordered me to appear. Wherefore, I came prepared to defend myself and expose the wrongdoings of the government. My appearance took about an hour and a half, and the U.S. Attorney was ill-equipped to dispute and combat my testimony. Needless to say, I was not indicted, and the paralegal, who accompanied me with a Writ of Habeas Corpus, just in case it was needed, and I just made it back to the airport in time to make the last flight out to Baltimore. The next day, it became evident what the whole grand jury affair was about. The IRS raid would have been devastatingly successful for them if they could have released to the press that I was indicted by a federal grand jury. Thank God for giving us the foresight to suspect and then combat their diabolical plan.

As stated earlier in the book, the *Fellowship* and I filed an action in the Federal District Court in Baltimore for the return of the property, which the court ordered. When the property was returned, it was evident that none of it was touched For instance, the construction duct tape the IRS used on the drawers of the filing cabinets was still intact, and there was no sign of the computers being tampered with, giving evidence that this effort was to destroy the *Fellowship* rather than a criminal investigation of me. After several hearings and three years, the court ruled in favor of the *Fellowship*. The decision of the court is posted on the *Fellowship's* Internet web site.

In 1997, in order to further dispel any IRS fear campaigns and enhance the *Fellowship* recruitment efforts, the *Victory Express* program was instituted. This, in essence, is a revised version of the Membership Assistance Program. The *Victory Express* merely changes what each member will be assessed to a minimum of 10 FRNs, regardless of the size of the claim, and no matter how large the membership becomes.

An example would be, if the membership were only 1,000, the member having and making a valid claim would presumably receive 10,000 FRNs (10 FRN minimum x 1,000 members), say for the loss of a car valued at 9,000 FRNs. This would actually be a profit of 1,000 FRNs for the loss of the car.

The goal is membership of 100,000 members, presumably expecting each claim will pay 1,000,000 FRNs!—whether the member loses a home or is incarcerated in a federal prison camp for 6 months for "willful failure to file." And, as stated in the Membership Handbook:

> . . . unlike the lottery, he won't have to wait 20 years! 97% of the population won't earn a million FRNs during their entire lives, let alone for 6 months of their time! Some members may even wish for multiple sentences, since the incarceration assessments are for any portion of a year, each! Because of adverse publicity, federal judges will be hard-pressed to sentence Patriots to serve time in federal prison camps.

> When the membership reaches 100,000, IRS agents will begin to defect their positions en masse. With no "hired guns" to extort the public, the welfare state will collapse along with the Federal Reserve Bank and the evil-doers can be brought to Justice.

> Under the new "VICTORY EXPRESS," Mr. Freeman's friends can assert their constitutional rights and obey the Law as written without fear of the IRS. As Americans by the hundreds of thousands join the Constitutional Revival Movement, the despotic house of cards will collapse—and LIBERTY WILL BE RESTORED!!!

Of course, we also understand that without education, any victory would be short-lived. For, as stated before, IGNORANT AND FREE CAN NEVER BE. Wherefore, the *Fellowship's* main effort will always continue to be education. We have faith in the American character, and believe that once the average American understands how we have drifted from the concept and precepts of *Freedom* and *Liberty*, they will reject this socialist scheme that has been deliberately thrust upon them.

To these ends, speaking on behalf of all the *Fellowship* members, I am taking this opportunity to invite you, the reader, and all men and women of good conscience to join the *Fellowship* and become involved in its efforts to save the Republic by the dissemination of the truth to our fellow Americans. For just as the *Founding Fathers* believed, once informed, statesmen will arise from the population to serve the Republic and their fellow Americans through the observance of the Constitution, no matter what obstacle may stand in their way.

The following is the *Fellowship's* contact information:

Save-A-Patriot Fellowship
Post Office Box 91
Westminster, Maryland 21158

Telephone Number: 410-857-4441
Facsimile: 410-857-5249
Internet Address: www.save-a-patriot.org

Be sure to let us hear from you. For together we can put an end to the destruction of our Republic!!

Chapter 14

LOOKING BACK
OVER OUR SHOULDER

The Problem:

In the last 226 years, there has been a slow, piecemeal change from a union of States (whose founders recognized that the creation thereof was by the Grace of God, and the continuance thereof would depend upon the keeping of His Word) to an imperial state that is struggling to take the place of God. This is nothing more than the continuation of the age-old struggle that began as a Luciferian rebellion in the heavens and manifested itself here on earth in the Garden of Eden.[1]

After man's fall in Eden, history has recorded the early struggle of this rebellious influence that tempted and consumed the minds of man with very few exceptions. One exception was a man named Noah, and his obedient family. In order to check this widespread evil rebellion, God made a covenant with Noah, and saved him and his family along with certain of the living creatures, to continue their kind from a worldwide flood in an Ark made according to specifications God gave to Noah.

It is also recorded that after the time of the flood, the rebellion resumed, and those who held to the worship of God were saved and taken out of bondage that they had fallen into in Egypt. They were given a selected piece of land on which to flourish under

His Law, which He gave to Moses. The fall of this civilization established by God came by the rejection of His Governmental Plan in favor of a king who supposedly would take care of them and assume their responsibilities. As explained in Chapter 1, God's Plan allowed total freedom from secular governmental control.

Not giving up on His freewill creation, God sent a Messiah, His Son, to make the perfect sacrifice, whereby all man had to do was believe on His Son and accept the fact that it was the perfect sacrifice to be saved.[2] This really caused a problem for the Luciferian rebellion. For as this new phenomenon spread, it shook the very foundations of Lucifer's corrupt worldly institutions, which, of course, did not believe in the curtailment of secular governmental control.

The very center of the Luciferian world, Rome, could not stop or co-exist with the followers of the Messiah, the Christians. This presented a real problem for the Luciferian governmental institutions, which combined religious and civil authorities. Such a combination of authority allowed the control of every aspect of the entire population to benefit the Luciferian rulers, who were, and are, in most cases, his dupes, beguiled by their lust for greed and power. The Christians brought an outside influence that if not stopped, could cause the downfall of such a governmental system. The nonexistence of the state church is dangerous to the existence of any monarch or dictator, denying to him the total control of the populace.

An effort was made by the Roman Caesars to discourage the spread of Christianity by submitting them to extreme deadly brutality in the Roman Arena. But because these Christians had an unending belief in the hereafter in heaven as their reward, these despicable, gory atrocities did not work, and Christianity continued to spread rapidly.

Emperor Constantine came into power in 305 A.D., and solved the problem by ending the persecution of the Christians and offering financial restitution to the family survivors of those who lost their lives in the Roman Coliseums. Constantine was not converted to Christianity at that time. History tells us that at that time his personal devotions were made to the pagan gods, Mars and Apollo.[3] With his recognition of the Christian Church, Constantine turned what was a problem into an asset, making Christianity an instrument of Imperial policy.[4]

Constantine

On May 20, 325, Constantine summoned church leaders to the First Ecumenical Council, over which he presided, instituting his precepts to be used as church law.[5] The church became known as the Holy Roman Catholic Church, and the dominant religion of the Roman Empire. Over time, the study of the New and Old Testaments was discouraged, and in time, become virtually nonexistent. Rituals of various pagan religions were incorporated to replace the study of the Scriptures.

As the Roman Empire declined, the political power went from the emperors to the popes of the Church, who dominated all of the rulers of Europe, ushering in what became known as the *Dark Ages*, discouraging scientific advances and literacy for the commoners and upper classes alike. A threat came to the pope's domination in 768 when Charles the Great, who was known by his historical name Charlemagne, became king of what is now France, West Germany and the Netherlands. Even though he was of

Charlemagne

the Roman Catholic faith (no other organized religion existed at that time in Europe), he rejected the pope's secular dominance. He established an "academy" group of scholars, and embarked on a program of cultural reformation. This renaissance effort was short-lived, as Charlemagne succumbed to the traditional authority of the pope on Christmas Day, 800 A.D., by accepting the crown and title of Emperor of the Roman Empire from Pope Leo. Thus the secular and religious dominance of the popes resumed without any serious interruption, until what was to become known as the Great Reformation.

On October 31, 1517, Martin Luther, a Roman Catholic Augustinian monk, theology professor at Wittenberg University, and a priest at the City Church in Wittenberg, Germany, nailed 95 Theses entitled: *Disposition of Doctor Martin Luther on the Power and Efficacy of Indulgences* to his Roman Catholic Church superiors, condemning the sale of indulgences. His reasons for doing so are taken from his document as follows:

> *Out of love for the truth and the desire to bring it to light, the following propositions will be discussed at Wittenberg, under the presidency of the Reverend Father Martin Luther, Master of Arts and of Sacred Theology, and Lecturer in Ordinary on the same at that place. Wherefore he requests that those who are unable to be present and debate orally with us, may do so by letter.*

This was the first real threat to the combined secular-religious governmental dominance since the Messiah's establishment of Christianity, which was side-tracked due to Constantine's efforts, but was now on the verge of being revived.

Luther, a prominent scholar of the day, translated the Scriptures into the German language, and discovered some alarming discrepancies between its content and that of the teachings of the Roman Catholic Church under the popes since Constantine. In addition to that, he objected to representatives of the Vatican selling indulgences (to finish building St. Peter's Basilica in Rome), representing to the purchasers, in so many words, that they bought a tickets to Heaven. The price for Letters of Indulgence varied according to the crime: Robbing a church and

MartinLuther

perjury—9 Ducats; (an Austrian gold coin) and murder—8 Ducats.

The Theses called for open public debate, instead of just among scholars. For his efforts, in the year 1521, Luther was excommunicated from the Roman Catholic Church and declared a heretic. Pressured by some German princes to give him a hearing, the German emperor, Charles V, invited Luther to the Imperial Diet of Worms. The emperor and the Vatican had hoped that once there he could be made to recant and quell the religious and political storm caused by the widespread circulation of the Theses. Instead of recanting, Luther became more steadfast in his stand, declaring at the Diet:

> *Unless I am convinced by Scripture and plain reason— I do not accept the authority of the popes and councils, for they have contradicted each other—my conscience is captive to the Word of God. I cannot and I will not recant anything, for to go against conscience is neither right nor safe. God help me. Amen.*

Luther left Worms without being arrested, possessing a letter giving him twenty-one days safe travel time. After he and the princes that supported him left, the emperor signed a *Wormser Edikt* (Imperial Act) declaring him an outlaw, making it possible for anyone to kill him without punishment. The Vatican and the emperor fully understood the political implications of this Reformation of the New Testament and of the availability of the Bible to the public.

Friedrich the Wise

On his way back to Wittenberg, Luther was allowed to be kidnapped and hidden at Wartburg, Germany by the German prince, Elector Friedrich the Wise, who believed Luther was unjustly persecuted, not having been convicted of a crime. The kidnapping ruse also protected the prince from being charged with harboring an outlaw.

The next year, 1522, Luther came out of hiding and began preaching and organizing the Reformation movement, which naturally brought about political changes as well as religious. He did this even though his life was in danger. But the danger ended that year when the Second Imperial Diet of Nuremburg declared the banishment of Luther as unenforceable. This reprieve, however, was short-lived, for in 1524, the Third Imperial Diet of Nuremburg renewed the banishment. But by that time, the Reformation movement had spread so fast and become so powerful throughout the whole of Europe that the renewed banishment was unenforceable and meaningless; for the enforcement of it would most certainly have unintended consequences.

Luther advocated the education of the population through the use of schools operated and administered by the Reformation Christian churches. In 1534, Luther published the Bible in German, and it was soon translated into other languages and spread like wildfire all over Europe, putting it, for the first time, into the hands of aristocrat and commoner alike, the very thing that the Vatican prevented from happening for centuries. Thus, a large wedge was driven between the secular and religious authorities, dealing a serious blow to the Luciferian government philosophy.

As the Reformation grew, it started to split up and give birth to different but similar doctrines, all having the common thread of Salvation by Grace, believing in Christ's Sacrifice. With the spread of these teachings, dormant for some 1200-odd years, not only was the Vatican's domination of the ruling aristocracy of Europe in trouble, the whole aristocratic system itself started to be questioned, even by some of those within that class. One of the main verses of the Reformation from the New Testament strikes at the very heart of that Vatican-aristocratic alliance, and for the first time since the establishment of *God's Theocracy*, leads the minds of men to the concept of *Individual Liberty*.

For in it the righteousness of God is revealed through faith to faith; as it is written, "The just will live by faith."

Yes, the Reformation started a religious and political movement that shook the very foundations of the Roman religious-secular feudal governmental establishment from which it has never recovered. This renaisscance infected aristocrats and commoners alike. It even struck the royal family in England. The son of Queen Elizabeth I, Sir Francis Bacon (1561—1626), was among those who picked up and kept the *Torch of Liberty* burning after the death of Martin Luther on February 18, 1546.

Sir Francis Bacon

Bacon was very active in the English Parliament and had the distinction of being a member of both the House of Lords and the House of Commons. Through those Chambers, he fought the control the English government had through subsidies. He knew, as many in the U.S. Congress don't seem to know, that government "money" is not the answer to the problems of the marketplace. He declared: *Truth can never be reached by just listening to the voice of an authority.*[6] Even though the Reformation was well under way, such thoughts were not dominant in the early 1600s in Europe, and one had to be very careful discussing limited government without an aristocracy. In order to advance such notions, Bacon resurrected the Rosicrucian Mystery School and the Freemasons, giving new life and purpose to these secret fraternal societies to advance the previously mentioned Baconian philosophy[7]—a philosophy that would give birth to the eradication of the aristocracy and the feudal system of government, in favor of self-government by citizens themselves. He introduced measures in Parliament to alter the language of the law so that it could be understood by the commoner. He is recorded as having told Parliament: *Laws are made to guard the rights of the people, not to feed lawyers.* He pushed for American colonization in Parliament, and as Lord Chancellor of England, was in charge of overseeing that colonial effort.[8] A member of his secret society,

Sir Walter Raleigh (1554—1618), was believed to have planted the seeds of the Baconian philosophy in the colonies. It is also believed that the real reason for Raleigh's execution was that he would not reveal any information about the Rosicrucian Society membership.[9]

John Locke

John Locke (1632—1704), the famous English philosopher, was influenced by the works of Bacon.[10]   As did Bacon, Locke also had some control over the development of the American colonies.   In 1696, a Board of Trade was established and Locke was appointed to it. Among its responsibilities, the Board oversaw the English colonial governments.   Even though his health was failing, Locke remained on the Board until 1700. He was its most influential member, and had a strong influence on the political attitudes of many of the *Founding Fathers*, particularly Samuel Adams, the *Father of the American Revolution*.

There is evidence that George Washington, Benjamin Franklin, and Thomas Jefferson were connected to Bacon's refurbished secret societies, the Freemasons and Rosicrucians.[11] The secret codes of the Rosicrucians, a means of communication between its members, have been found in Jefferson's writings,[12] and Jefferson personally sealed up the "repositories" of the Bacon Group in Colonial America, and buried it in a vault made for that purpose in the Burton Church yard in Colonial Williamsburg.[13] (Manly Hall, and his wife Marie, made an effort to excavate for this treasure, but were frustrated by the Rockefellers. The Halls had the churchyard scanned by a penetrating radar device and it indicated the location of the copper vault.   There was an effort in 1991 to organize an illegal dig for 1992, by Marsha Middleton, a friend of Marie Hall, but there has been no report of whether it took place.)

By the Grace of God, and the resolve of Bacon, Raleigh, Locke and certain Patriots of the American Revolution, a manmade government implementing *God's Governmental Plan* was established for the first time in the history of the world. Evidence that this was the intent of the Revolution is found in the first two paragraphs of the Declaration of Independence, drafted by Thomas Jefferson and adopted by the Continental Congress:

> *When in the Course of human events, it becomes necessary for one people to dissolve the political bands which have connected them with another, and to assume among the powers of the earth, the separate and equal station __to which the Laws of Nature and of Nature's God entitle them__, a decent respect to the opinions of mankind requires that they should declare the causes which impel them to the separation.*
>
> *We hold these truths to be self-evident, __that all men are created equal, that they are endowed by their Creator with certain unalienable Rights, that among these are Life, Liberty and the pursuit of Happiness.—That to secure these rights, Governments are instituted among Men, deriving their just powers from the consent of the governed.__—That whenever any Form of Government becomes destructive of these ends, it is the Right of the People to alter or to abolish it, and __to institute new Government, laying its foundation on such principles__ and organizing its powers in such form, as to them shall seem most likely to effect their Safety and Happiness.* (Emphasis added.)

In other words, every man is equal, meaning free from domination by other men, either personally or by the use of government force. Wherefore, under these circumstances, the only lawful function of government is the protection of life and property; for when government exceeds this Plan, it just naturally discriminates between citizens.

Of course, the establishment of the American Constitutional Republic was not the end of the struggle between God's Governmental Plan and Lucifer's. Simultaneously, with the signing of the Declaration of Independence, Lucifer was preparing his counterattack through a Jesuit-educated professor of civil law at the University of Ingolstadt, Adam Weishaupt, who was a Jewish "convert" to the Roman Catholic Church. Weishaupt's organized effort was called the Order of the Illuminati (enlightened ones),[14] and the plan was to offset the spread of the Reformation, and subsequently the American Revolution, by the organization of a

Adam Weishaupt

world government under the control of members of the Illuminati.[15] After a few failures to organize a world government— the first of which came in 1814, immediately after the Napoleonic Wars, with the Congress of Vienna, and another with the League of Nations in 1919—partial success was obtained in 1948 with the United Nations.

The practice of the Luciferian governmental plan is not honesty or forthrightness. As was discussed in earlier chapters, there were those holding positions of influence within the Revolution and in the Constitutional Republic that started to undermine it immediately. The most influential of these Luciferian dupes was Alexander Hamilton, and as shown in Chapter 6, he was not beyond lying, treachery, and sedition to bring about a dominant federal government at the expense of the several States, and subsequently, the free citizens. He organized and led the Federalist political party and put it at the disposal of powerful bankers, aiding them further with the establishment of the unconstitutional First Bank of the United States, chartered in 1791. But as was also shown, the Baconian torchbearer and champion of God's Governmental Plan, Thomas Jefferson, led the opposing political party, the Democratic-Republicans, and put down this Luciferian rebellion by politically causing the inability of the Federalists in Congress to re-charter the Bank in 1811.

Even though, as explained in Chapter 5, the *Framers* of the Constitution intended to prohibit the use of paper money, they

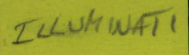

neglected to take into consideration the misuse of the deposit reserves by banks to support their private bank notes. One of the main reasons that Hamilton gave for the First Bank of the United States was the regulation of the deposit reserves of the State-chartered banks.

The second champion of the Reformation and subsequent American Constitutional Republic was President Andrew Jackson. He understood fully the greedy and power-hungry bankers that controlled the Second United States Bank, chartered in 1816, that would in effect help destroy the intended purpose of this government. Jackson was elected in 1829 and vetoed the Act of Congress to re-charter the Bank in 1832, thus again spoiling the second attempt to scuttle *God's Governmental Plan* by the Luciferian dupes and conspirators, through control of the Republic's money system.

The real and present danger to *God's Governmental Plan*, as enacted by the *Founding Fathers*, came with the Inauguration of Abraham Lincoln to the office of president of the Republic in 1861. Lincoln openly declared that his political views were that of the Hamiltonian-Federalists, later to become known as the Whigs. He also, by his actions in the office of president, demonstrated very little knowledge of the Constitution, or any regard for his oath of office to uphold and defend it against all enemies, both foreign and domestic. In fact, he became a domestic enemy with his acts of sedition, and his administration set the precedence for the state of governmental anarchy that exists today. The year 1861 can truly be called the high water mark of the Constitutional Republic as *God's Governmental Plan*.

Even though the Constitution is still intact as the *Framers* wrote it (other than for the 11th and 17th Amendments), the administrations of Lincoln and subsequent presidents have violated it whenever it suited them. This precedence came about by the total destruction of the Confederate States of America, whose political views were more in line with Jefferson's Democratic-

Republicans—later to become known as Democrats. In order to obfuscate this historical fact, the revisionist historians have set the actual cause of the "Civil" War as slavery, and nothing could be further from the truth. The true facts regarding Lincoln's seditious acts and the cause of the War are set out as follows:

1. Lincoln's political career, and the speeches he made while running for the Presidency, indicated that he had strong federalist views, and thus would favor the industrial Northern States' tariff advantage over the Southern States. The commodities that the Southern States were forced to take in trade from their European trading partners had a high tariff placed on them, which could be considered an unconstitutional export tax on the cotton traded. This tariff, set in place by the dominance in Congress of the industrial North, was destroying the economy of the Southern States because of its serious effect on the cost-profit ratio on the cotton.

2. There is no provision within the Constitution of the United States that prevents a State from seceding, or leaving the union of States. Lincoln arrested certain members of the Maryland Legislature without probable cause because their vote, if cast, would cause Maryland to secede from the union of States. Therefore, this act, without the authority of the Constitution, was a violation of his oath of office and an obvious seditious act.

3. The Constitution only allows for *calling forth the Militia to execute the Laws of the Union, suppress Insurrections and repel Invasions* (Article 1, Section 8, Clause 15). After certain Southern States seceded from the Union of States and formed a government, modeled after the original Confederacy of the United States, Lincoln agitated to cause a war, by deploying the U.S. fleet of war ships to blockade the port of Charleston, South Carolina. In addition, after three promises to vacate Fort Sumter in Charleston harbor, he failed to keep those promises, and instead ordered the commanding officer, Colonel

Anderson, not to vacate the fort, and increased the number of war ships deployed to blockade the harbor. Considering these overt acts to be acts of war, the army of the Confederate States of America fired on Fort Sumter. The firing on Fort Sumter cannot be considered an attack on the United States, since the Fort was the territory of the Confederate States of America being unlawfully occupied by the army of the United States.

4. Lincoln also violated the intent of Article 1, Section 8, Clause 15 of the Constitution by ordering the Army of the United States to invade the Confederate States of America, and committing these troops to battle in Manassas, Virginia. Therefore, this act, without the authority of the Constitution, is a violation of his oath of office and an obvious seditious act.

5. Lincoln persuaded the Congress to pass *Legal Tender Acts* that created *bills of credit* (paper money), which he signed into law. *Bills of credit* were deliberately barred within the Constitution drafted by the Framers, and ratified by the Union of States. In all, there were two *Legal Tender Acts*: The Act of July 17, 1861, which issued the *Demand Notes*, and the Act of July 11, 1862, authorizing *United States Notes*, which are still in existence today. Therefore, these acts, without the authority of the Constitution, are violations of his oath of office and obviously seditious.

6. Lincoln signed into law two National Bank Acts passed by Congress, for the purpose of creating an unlawful system of national banks, creating an unlawful uniform national currency, and creating an active secondary market for Treasury securities to help finance the war. Therefore, these acts, without the authority of the Constitution, are violations of his oath of office and obviously seditious.

7. The policies of Lincoln caused the arrest of more than 38,000 political prisoners without probable cause, who were incarcerated for the duration of the war without any official

charge or trial, simply because it was believed that their release would possibly be prejudicial to prosecuting the war.[16] In addition, Lincoln banished Ohio Congressman Vallandigham from the United States, and shut down over 300 newspapers for criticizing his unconstitutional acts. Secretary of War Stanton was quoted as telling a visitor: "If I tap that little bell, I can send you to a place where you will never again hear the dogs bark." The Raleigh, North Carolina *News and Observer* wrote after the war: "It is to the honour of the Confederate government that no Confederate secretary could touch a bell and send a citizen to prison."[17] Therefore, these acts, without the authority of the Constitution, are violations of his oath of office and obviously seditious.

8. Lincoln's establishment of a permanent federal internal tax is not unconstitutional, but it does violate the intent of the *Framers*, who implemented *God's Plan for Taxation* as described by His Son in the Bible.[18] He signed into law Acts of Congress creating the Office of the Commissioner of Internal Revenue, and making the commodities of alcohol, tobacco, and firearms the subject of a permanent excise tax, setting the stage for the financial support of a federal government of ever-increasing size.

The biggest lie that the revisionist historians tell about this War of Northern Aggression is that it was fought to end slavery, and that Lincoln was the champion of that cause. The true historical facts give evidence to the contrary. For instance, in 1861, Major General John C. Fremont, commanding the Western Department of the Army of the United States, issued a proclamation freeing the slaves of slave owners who were believed to support the Confederate States of America. When this became known to Lincoln, he removed Fremont and declared the proclamation void.[19] Lincoln also reversed a similar proclamation issued by Major General David Hunter, Commander of the Department of the South.[20]

For obvious reasons, Lincoln was the first President to need bodyguards. The Pinkerton Detective Agency was hired to protect him, and evolved into the Secret Service, which is now part of the Department of the Treasury. Interestingly enough, every President since Lincoln has needed such protection.

The administrations that followed Lincoln did not make any corrections regarding the unconstitutional use of paper money and permanent internal taxation. To the contrary, they all exercised them, and increased even further the usurped federal powers. Theodore Roosevelt violated Article 1, Section 8, Clause 17, with the creation of National Parks and the National Park Service to regulate them. The march to fulfill the *enlightened ones'* dream picked up steam in the Wilson administration, with the establishment of the Federal Reserve Bank and the making of its private bank notes legal tender. Wilson was under the influence of the Rockefeller interests, who headed up the American branch of the Illuminati known as the Council on Foreign Relations (CFR). The CFR was behind Wilson's failed attempt to enter the United States into a world government—the League of Nations—in 1919.

The Hamiltonian-Lincolnite president that really set the stage for Lucifer's world government, described in the Book of Revelation within the Bible, was Franklin Delano Roosevelt. Roosevelt was a true *federalist* in every sense of the word. He used the financial depression, staged by the Rockefellers and their financial associates within the CFR, to launch the federalist *New Deal*, which brought about the following:

1. The *Administrative Procedures Act*, which aided and made possible the creation of all sorts of federal agencies, and changed the jurisdictional relationship between the citizens and the government;

2. The *Social Security Act*, which made it possible for citizens to be numbered, and for the Internal Revenue Service to keep records on those numbered citizens;

3. The *Victory Tax Act* and the subsequent *Current Tax Payment Act*, which created the withholding of a wage tax that

was needed to support the tax-and-spend inflation created by Congress in conjunction with the Federal Reserve Bank; and,

4. Even though the United States' entry into the *United Nations* followed Roosevelt's administration in 1948, it was conceived within the Roosevelt Administration, and its Charter drafted by the *New Deal* convicted communist traitor Alger Hiss, under the direction of *New Dealer* President Harry S. Truman.

Alger Hiss

Barring none, each succeeding presidential administration since Roosevelt has moved the United States closer to surrendering its sovereignty to a world government run by the *enlightened ones* of the *New World Order*. Every president since Truman, envolved our Republic in numerous unconstitutional undeclared "wars" that were fought under the direction of the *United Nations*. President George Herbert Walker Bush on March 6, 1991, stated the following to the Congress:

> *Now, we can see a new world coming into view. A world in which there is the very real prospect of a <u>new world order</u>. In the words of Winston Churchill, a "world order" in which "the principles of justice and fair play. . . protect the weak against the strong . . . " <u>A world where the United Nations, freed from cold war stalemate, is poised to fulfill the historic vision of its founders</u> [Roosevelt and Hiss]. A world in which freedom and respect for human rights find a home among all nations.* (Emphasis added.)

President Clinton ordered members of the military engaged in United Nations' wars to wear the uniform of the United Nations, and Specialist Michael G. New was dishonorably discharged for refusing to do so. Clinton also sanctioned the *Combat Arms Survey*, which was dispensed to a contingent of several hundred U.S. Marines on May 10, 1994, at Twenty Nine Palms, California.

Navy Lt. Commander Guy Cunningham administered the survey. One of the questions asked was:

> *I would swear to the following code: 'I am a United Nations fighting person. I serve in the forces which maintain world peace and every nation's way of life. I am prepared to give my life in their defense.'*

Another question was:

> *The U.S. government declares a ban on the possession, sale, transportation, and transfer of all non-sporting firearms. A thirty (30) day amnesty period is permitted for these firearms to be turned over to the local authorities. At the end of this period, a number of citizen groups refuse to turn over their firearms. Consider the following statement: I would fire upon U.S. citizens who refuse or resist confiscation of firearms banned by the U.S. government.*

It is not hard to see where this type of activity is leading.

Lincoln arrested and imprisoned citizens *without probable cause*. Clinton authorized the killing of 82 men, women, and children in Waco, Texas, on April 19, 1993, *without probable cause*. His Attorney General, Janet Reno, gave the reason for the attack, which took these lives, as alleged child abuse within the Branch Davidians' Compound. Evidently, according to the Clinton administration, the solution to alleged child abuse is to kill the children to stop the alleged abuse. Which, by the way, was investigated by local law enforcement and found to be unfounded.

President George W. Bush, in the name of fighting terrorism, is busily setting in place a police state that would put the Gestapo and the KGB to shame; asking Americans to surrender their God-Given Rights for a fantasy of being secure, by the acceptance of admittedly unconstitutional police powers. Being an ex-police officer, I can truthfully state that it is a very rare occasion when a police officer is present to stop the commission of a crime. Police take reports of criminal acts and investigate the same. Because of this fact, the *Founding Fathers*, in their wisdom, and their quest for *individual freedom*, gave us the *Second Amendment* to the Constitution for self-protection and to prevent the government from violating its intended purpose—as outlined in the *Declaration of Independence* and some of the Constitutions of the original thirteen States. The *Maryland Declaration of Rights* within the State Constitution is most explicit on this point:

> *Art. 44. That the provisions of the Constitution of the United States, and of this State, apply, as well in time of war, as in time of peace; and any departure therefrom, or violation thereof, under the plea of necessity, or any other plea, is subversive of good Government, and tends to anarchy and despotism.*

And:

> *Art. 6. That all persons invested with the Legislative or Executive powers of Government are the Trustees of the Public, and, as such, accountable for their conduct: Wherefore, whenever the ends of Government are perverted, and public liberty manifestly endangered, and all other means of redress are ineffectual, the People may, and of right ought, to reform the old, or establish a new Government; the doctrine of non-resistance against arbitrary power and oppression is absurd, slavish and destructive of the good and happiness of mankind.*

Hopefully, the federal and state governments can be brought back within their respected *lawful jurisdictions* through educational means, and we can avoid the need to resort to such an extreme *duty* as outlined by the *Founding Fathers*.

Backtracking

George Washington

I dwell on this prospect with every satisfaction which an ardent love for my country can inspire, since there is no truth more thoroughly established than that there exists in the economy and course of nature an indissoluble union between virtue and happiness; between duty and advantage; between the genuine maxims of an honest and magnanimous policy and the solid rewards of public prosperity and felicity; since we ought to be no less persuaded that the propitious smiles of Heaven can never be expected on a nation that disregards the eternal rules of order and right which Heaven itself has ordained; and since the preservation of the sacred fire of liberty and the destiny of the republican model of government are justly considered, perhaps, as deeply, as finally, staked on the experiment entrusted to the hands of the American people.

First Inaugural Address, April 30, 1789

Now having some understanding of the problem, and where these Hamiltonian-Lincolnites and CFR-Illuminati Internationalists (also known as the Bilderbergers) are trying to take us, it is time to put into place counteractivities to force the federal and state governments back within their proper Constitutional jurisdictions. In order to do this we have to examine the strategy that has been used to bring us to this predicament that lovers of *Individual Liberty* are in today.

Since the enumerated powers of the federal government, within the Constitution are mainly foreign and virtually void within the States, and since the State governments have sufficient legal remedies, both criminal and civil, to maintain justice and protect

Individual Rights, there was no need for any expansion of governmental powers for either the federal or State governments. Wherefore, this near-perfect structure could not be successfully attacked from without, which Lincoln admitted,[21] but rather there had to be a delusion created that, over time, would cause citizens to unconsciously be alienated from it.[22] And the beginning of this delusion is exactly what Lincoln and his fellow federalists of that period initiated.

They were successful in causing a large segment of the population to accept the *illusion* that the "Union" formed by the States, was somehow paramount to the States themselves, and consequently, in their minds (for it does not exist within the Constitution), the Union of States became an "indivisible nation." Theoretically, the servant became the master, thus reversing the principles of *Liberty* established by the *Founding Fathers*. Citizens started thinking of themselves more as Americans rather than Virginians, or Marylanders. It must be remembered that General Robert E. Lee left the Army of the United States and took a commission in the Army of the Confederate States of America, because in his words: *His duty was to the State of Virginia*.

Robert E. Lee

This point can be somewhat substantiated by the language within the opinion of the Supreme Court case of *Gibbons v. Ogden*, 22 U.S. 1, (1824). The legislature of the State of New York passed an Act giving the inventor of the steamboat, Robert Fulton, exclusive commercial use of the waterways between Elizabethtown, New Jersey and New York City. A steamboat competitor, Thomas Gibbons, sued for injunctive relief against the State of New York. The case went to the U.S. Supreme Court and was decided on March 2, 1824, and the opinion was written by then-Chief Justice John Marshall. In the opinion, Marshall proves the point that I am laboring to make, that the United States is not a nation, but rather a Union of States having the services of a federal government, which is lawfully under the control of all the States collectively. The following is a paragraph taken from Marshall's opinion:

> *This act demonstrates the opinion of Congress, that steam boats may be enrolled and licensed, in common with vessels using sails. They are, of course, entitled to the same privileges, and can no more be restrained from navigating waters, and entering ports which are free to such vessels, than if they were wafted on their voyage by the winds, instead of being propelled by the agency of fire. The one element may be as legitimately used as the other, for every commercial purpose <u>authorized by the laws of the Union</u>; and the act of a State inhibiting the use of either to any vessel having a license under the act of Congress, comes, we think, in direct collision with that act.* (Emphasis added.)

John Marshall

Marshall was a *federalist*, but even he properly recognized the fact that the country of the United States of America was the States united.

During the post-war *reconstruction period* within the Southern States, there actually was federal dominance, which catered to this false public perception of an indivisible union with a dominant central government.

The perception of federal dominance continued with the expansion and development of the western territories. Before becoming States, much of the western territories were governed by the military, and the remainder by federally appointed governors, judges, and U.S. marshals. Hollywood depicts this historical period in such a way as to give the impression that the federal authority is somehow superior to State law.

Wherefore, one of the first steps back to secure our *Individual Liberties* is to have an understanding of the jurisdictional limits given the federal government by the Constitution and then teach other Americans accurately of that fact.

Once the institutions of the Federal Reserve Bank and Federal Reserve Board were put in place by the Hamiltonian-Lincolnites, the CFR-Illuminati internationalist bankers started to use this new-found power to manipulate the money and credit supply to cause the conditions that brought about the New York Stock Exchange crash in 1929. Standing in readiness for this event, Franklin Delano Roosevelt and his hand-picked socialist candidates all campaigned under what they called the *New Deal* for America. Of course, the "Old Deal" was limited government and *Individual Liberty*. Thus the stage was set for American citizens to accept faith in government rather than in God to supply their personal needs. This was the beginning of the moral decadence in America, which manifested itself some thirty years later in the 1960s.

The Federal Reserve System, if not destroyed, will cause a financial destruction of the Constitutional Republic which will be beyond repair. Hopefully, in the alternative, education and the resulting participation of the American public can bring pressure on the federal politicians to force the Department of Justice to bring charges of fraud against the Federal Reserve Bank principals and the Federal Reserve Board members, while simultaneously seizing all of its assets. This would eradicate the great majority of the fraudulent national debt, and curtail the ability of Congress to foolishly squander the Republic's assets.

The mainstay of the *New Deal* was the *Social Security* program, from which sprang the majority of the bloated federal bureaucracy. As explained in Chapter 8 of this book, citizens are not required to have *social security numbers*, nor are they subject to the social security laws. This booklet was published and disseminated by the then-new *Social Security Administration* to entice Americans to participate in this *socialist* program:

It would be a major step to ending this *socialist threat* to educate Americans that they are not really subject to participating in, nor using the numbers connected with, *social security programs*. This would at first cause a problem due to the majority of the population's participation in *social security programs*, and the perceived notion that retirement benefits will be lost. But because these programs are voluntary for citizens, not all those participating will bail out for fear of losing the accumulated credits toward benefits. I'm not saying that it would not be without any financial pain for those who stay in the programs, because most of the younger workforce would bail out if they knew how to get their employer to stop withholding it from their wages. And the only way employers will stop such withholding will be if the law as written becomes general knowledge; for the fear of federal retribution has become so great that most would rather violate their fellow Americans' Rights than take the chance of confronting the IRS and the Department of Justice. So the best way to overcome this problem is for all informed citizens to make an all-out effort to correctly learn and spread the word about the requirements of the *social security* laws, which are discussed in sufficient detail in Chapter 8 of this book.

Another significant attack on citizens' Rights and the concept of government established by the *Founding Fathers* came in 1922, when CFR member, and future president, Herbert Hoover[23] then the Secretary of Commerce, introduced the concept of *zoning*. Hoover promoted Zoning through a government publication entitled: *Zoning Primer, An Advisory Committee on Zoning*, which he made available through the Department of Commerce in Washington, D.C. Karl Marx, in his *Communist Manifesto,* cited the following ten planks (steps) needed in setting up a *godless-socialist-federal-state*:

Karl Marx

    1. *Abolition of property in land and the application of all*

rents of land to public purposes.

2. *A heavy progressive or graduated income tax.*
3. *Abolition of all rights of inheritance.*
4. *Confiscation of the property of all emigrants and rebels.*
5. *Centralization of credit in the hands of the State, by means of a national bank with State capital and an exclusive monopoly.*
6. *Centralization of the means of communications and transportation in the hands of the State.*
7. *Extension of factories and instruments of production owned by the State, the bringing into cultivation of waste lands, and the improvement of the soil generally in accordance with a common plan.*
8. *Equal liability of all to labor. Establishment of industrial armies especially for agriculture.*
9. *Combination of agriculture with manufacturing industries, gradual abolition of the distinction between town and country, by a more equitable distribution of population over the country.*
10. *Free education for all children in public schools. Abolition of children's factory labor in its present form Combination of education with industrial production.*

Notice that the very first step is the control of property. *Liberty* and *Property* are inseparable.

The Supreme Court's six-to-three decision in *Village of Euclid, Ohio v. Ambler Realty Co.*, 272 US 365 (November 22, 1926), declared *Zoning* to be Constitutional: *provided it reasonably relates to the public health, safety and welfare.* This raises the question: Where did the Supreme Court find such authority within the Constitution for their ruling?

A word search of the Constitution reveals that the word *health* cannot be found; the word *safety* can only be found once, and then it has nothing to do with general living conditions. It

321

states in Article 1, Section 9, Clause 2:

> *The Privilege of the Writ of Habeas Corpus shall not be suspended, unless when in Cases of Rebellion or Invasion the public Safety may require it.*

I really believe the Supreme Court was actually stretching it a wee bit with the word *safety*. Of course, it really comes down to the way you look at it. Surely *zoning* is *rebellious* as to the intent of the Constitution and your *secured Rights* to *property* contained therein, and surely it has to be admitted that *Zoning* is an invasion of *private property*.

The word *welfare* can only be found once within the Constitution, and once within the Preamble to the Constitution. In the Constitution it is found in Article 1, Section 8, Clause 1:

> *The Congress shall have Power To lay and collect Taxes, Duties, Imposts and Excises, to pay the Debts and provide for the common Defence and general Welfare of the United States; but all Duties, Imposts and Excises shall be uniform throughout the United States;*

This raises the question of: What does the raising of taxes for the support of a lawfully authorized function of the federal government have to do with the police powers of a village in the State of Ohio? The same question could be asked of the use of the word *Welfare* in the Preamble as follows, except that the purpose of the Preamble is just to express the *intent* of the Constitution and has *no legal effect*, thus cannot be put to the purpose used by the Court.

> *We the People of the United States, in Order to form a more perfect Union, establish Justice, insure domestic Tranquility, provide for the common defence, promote the general Welfare, and secure the Blessings of Liberty to ourselves and our Posterity, do ordain and establish this Constitution for the United States of America.*

The associate justice who wrote the Opinion for the Supreme Court's 6-to-3 decision in *Euclid v. Ambler Realty Co.*, George Sutherland, stated within the majority Opinion:

> *The board [of zoning appeals] is given power in specific cases of practical difficulty or unnecessary hardship to <u>interpret the ordinance in harmony with the general purpose and intent</u>, so that the public health, safety and general welfare may be secure and <u>substantial justice done.</u>* (Emphasis added.)

When they embark on journeys outside the land of authorized jurisdictions (the *protection of life and property*), government has to discriminate, and interpret vague laws as the men involved see fit.

The most alarming statement in Sutherland's Opinion is his confession that he, and the other five justices voting with him, are placing themselves above the law because they believe it necessary to do so. He excuses this SEDITION as follows:

Sutherland

> *Such regulations are sustained, under the complex conditions of our day, for reasons analogous to those which justify traffic regulations, which, before the advent of automobiles and rapid transit street railways, would have been condemned as fatally arbitrary and unreasonable. And in this there is no inconsistency, for, while the meaning of constitutional guaranties never varies, the scope of their application must expand or contract to meet the new and different conditions which are constantly coming within the field of their operation. In a changing world it is impossible that it should be otherwise. <u>But although a degree of elasticity is thus imparted</u>, not to the meaning, but <u>to the application of</u>*

constitutional principles, statutes and ordinances, which, after giving due weight to the new conditions, are found clearly not to conform to the Constitution, of course, must fall.[24] (Emphasis added.)

So in the minds of these jurists, the enumerated provisions of the Constitution should be stretched or ignored when justices of the Supreme Court see fit to do so, to serve an end that they think is needed, in total disregard of the *Separation of Powers* and the *Amendment* process found within the Constitution. The fruit of such logic is SEDITION and TYRANNY. For in the free society that the *Founders* gave us, *property* is a most essential element. For without our total control of it, there is no *Liberty*. Of course, this Right cannot be used to infringe on another's Rights. However, such a principle does not extend to any State or county government to enforce its arbitrary judgment, or, as in many historical cases, its corrupt purposes. From the inception of the Constitutional Republic until 1926, controversies over one's property Rights were appropriately handled in the States' civil courts.

The reasons given for the enactment of *zoning* are no longer viable. In this modern age, factories and commercial establishments no longer desire to locate in residential areas. They are locating instead in industrial parks, malls, and shopping centers. Businesses on Main Street and residential areas die for lack of parking for automobiles. *Zoning* really manifested itself after World War II, and spread into rural areas in the 1960s. Property is controlled to such a degree that in order to occupy one's property, the zoning department is requiring the attainment of a use-and-occupancy permit before doing so, and threatening heavy fines for not doing so.

Like *zoning*, State *license* laws, in most cases, are of questionable jurisdiction; and have been used to further establish unreasonable and unlawful government controls. Black's Law Dictionary, 5th Edition, defines *license* generally as:

324

The permission by competent authority to do an act which, without such permission, would be illegal, a trespass, or a tort.

Unlike *zoning, license* laws have been around since the beginning of the Constitutional Republic and even before. Really, other than for the purpose of taxation, a *license*, in my opinion, has no reason to exist in our Union of Republics. Not arguing the difference between a driver and traveler, does a driver's license make anyone a better or safer driver?—of course not. In the same vein, does a license to carry a gun make the individual carrying that gun more responsible?—again, of course not. In the mid-1950s through the mid-1960s, I was a police officer carrying a loaded handgun at all times. Now, supposedly, as a civilian I need a license to do so. Was I a different person than I am now, because I did that particular type of work?—of course not, but if I'm caught carrying a loaded handgun, they will charge me with violating some unconstitutional criminal law.

Being state jurisdictions, both *zoning* and *license* laws are condoned, supposedly, under the *police powers* of the States. The term *police powers* is a fairly vague term. If it is applied and interpreted as the lawful function of government found within the Declaration of Independence (*protection of life and property*), there is no danger to our *Individual liberties*. However, as expected, the courts do not stop there. The rulings of the courts in regards to the *police powers* of the State are reflected in the definition found in Black's Law Dictionary, 5th Edition:

> **Police power.** *An authority conferred by the American constitutional system in the Tenth Amendment, U.S. Const., upon the individual states, and, in turn, delegated to local governments,* through which they are enabled *to establish a special department of police;* adopt such *laws and regulations as tend to prevent the commission of fraud and crime,* and secure generally the comfort, safety, morals, health,

325

and prosperity of its citizens by preserving the public order, preventing a conflict of rights in the common intercourse of the citizens, and insuring to each an uninterrupted enjoyment of all the privileges conferred upon him or her by the general laws. (Emphasis added.)

First, nowhere within the Tenth Amendment can there be found any authority for the States to do anything. The Amendment states very clearly:

The powers not delegated to the United States by the Constitution, nor prohibited by it to the States, are reserved to the States respectively, or to the people.

Also, as you can see, there is no provision therein to establish any police department other than the county sheriff, according to the principles of a *republican* form of government.[25] And finally, laws and regulations do not prevent crime; they only punish those who violate laws and regulations.

Black's definition of *police powers* continues:

The power of the State to place restraints on the personal freedom and property rights of persons for the protection of the public safety, health, and morals or the promotion of the public convenience and general prosperity. The police power is subject to limitations of the federal and State constitutions, and especially to the requirement of due process. Police power is the exercise of the <u>sovereign right of a government to promote order, safety, health, morals and general welfare</u> within constitutional limits and is an essential attribute of government. Marshall v. Kansas City, Mo., 355 S.W.2d 883. (Emphasis added.)

In our Constitutional Republic, governments are not sovereign; the only sovereigns are the citizens themselves.

Governments are merely representatives of the people, and are restricted to only those enumerated powers, written within the respective Constitutions, which actually serve the interest of the *sovereign citizens*. Under these circumstances, the State governments can only act to protect *life* and *property*, which in turn *promotes the general welfare*. But when the courts add words like *health*, *morals*, and *general welfare*, the problems begin, and are exacerbated by overly zealous State legislatures passing unconstitutional laws, which in turn prompt bureaucrats to take advantage of the ignorance of the general public. This problem is admitted by the U.S. Supreme Court in the case cited as the landmark case on the subject:

> *There are, however, certain powers, existing in the sovereignty of each state in the Union, somewhat <u>vaguely termed police powers, the exact description and limitation of which have not been attempted by the courts</u>. Those powers, broadly stated, and without, at present, any attempt at a more specific limitation, relate to the safety, health, morals, and general welfare of the public. Both property and liberty are held on such reasonable conditions as may be imposed by the governing power of the state in the exercise of those powers, and <u>with such conditions the 14th Amendment was not designed to interfere</u>. Lochner v. People of State of New York, 198 U.S. 45 (1905).* (Emphasis added.)

This is a perfect example of Hamiltonian-Lincolnite judicial legislation. Here we have, in 1905, six men claiming to have the power to reverse the relationship, established by the *Founding Fathers,* between government and the American citizen; admittedly replacing it with some *vague* and *undefined police powers* of the State, even in unspecified disregard of an amendment to the Constitution of the United States.

Zoning and *licenses* are not paramount on the list to save the Constitutional Republic, but they are contributing factors, and should be ended to prevent further unlawful expansion of both state and federal governments. To this end, the average American will have to be properly educated on the subject.

In 1892, *The Youth's Companion* magazine innocently published the following words for students to repeat on Columbus Day of that year. The gesture was most likely well-meaning, and believed to be patriotic, but in actuality it perpetuated the myth about the national government advanced by the Hamiltonian-Lincolnites:

> *I pledge allegiance to my Flag and the Republic for which it stands—one nation indivisible—with liberty and justice for all.*

Reciting this pledge became very popular, and it evolved into a general practice for children to recite it at the beginning of the school day.

At the first National Flag Conference in Washington D.C., on June 14, 1923, the following changes were made to it:

> *I pledge allegiance to the Flag of the United States and the Republic for which it stands—one nation indivisible—with liberty and justice for all.*

In 1942, the *New Deal* Congress officially recognized the above pledge, and in 1954, Congress added the words *under God*, which is its official wording today:

> *I Pledge Allegiance to the flag of the United States of America and to the Republic for which it stands, one Nation under God, indivisible, with liberty and justice for all.*

It would be naïve to believe the pledge of allegiance to the flag is harmless. This deep-rooted practice instills in our youth false and alien principles about our Constitutional Republic that stay with them the remainder of their lives. As written, it gives the insidious message that the federal government is superior to the State governments by using the term *one Nation*. And with the history of the "Civil" War, as written by the revisionists, taught in all the schools, it is generally believed that the union of States is *indivisible*, being merged into *one Nation*. As explained before within this book, nothing could be further from the truth, as it cannot be found within the Constitution. And last, but not least, oaths of Allegiance are meaningless when pledged to an object such as a *flag*, and cannot be rectified by the addition of the word *Republic*. For a *Republic* is the type of government created by the *Constitution*, which in itself would not require an *Oath of Allegiance*. By law, all *Oaths of Allegiance* are to be made to the *Constitution* of the United States, and to the *Constitution* of the State in which the citizen resides. Wherefore, to correct this possibly and most likely innocent, but seditious error, I propose the use of the following pledge of allegiance:

> *I Pledge Allegiance to the Constitution of the American States united, and to the Republic which it created, implementing God's governmental plan for man, and asking His blessing for its observance, which will provide Liberty and Justice for all.*

Failure to make such corrections only contributes to the misinformation and confusion that have facilitated the advances of the Hamiltonian-Lincolnites.

If we do not relate the events that have taken place during our lifetime to the next generation, then of course that generation will be ignorant of them. We cannot count on the history that is being taught within our schools, for the school's curriculum has been influenced by the unlawful financial aid of the Hamiltonian-Lincolnites within the federal government. Wherefore, the present generation now entering the work force is of the mindset that everyone earning a wage has to have a *social security number*, employers have to have an *employer identification number*, or there has to be some sort of *taxpayer identification number* before any business whatsoever can be contracted. This mindset definitely complements the public attitude needed for an entry into a cashless society and world government.

Franklin Delano Roosevelt took the first steps towards a cashless society with the 1933 *Gold Reserve Act*, which took the United States off the gold standard, and the 1942 *Victory Tax Act*. The *Gold Reserve Act* recalled all of the gold certificates in circulation, and refused the redemption of United States currencies in gold to everyone domestically, except the Federal Reserve Banks. The Act allowed the Federal Reserve Banks to keep gold certificates and redeem them, and other U.S. currencies, in gold bullion. The Act also made Federal Reserve Notes *legal tender* for the first time. Before the Act, the Notes' *payment obligation* stated:

> This space contained a photograph of Franklin Delano Roosevelt, and was removed for the reasons given in footnote 26 of this Chapter

REDEEMABLE IN GOLD ON DEMAND AT THE UNITED STATES TREASURY OR IN GOLD OR LAWFUL MONEY AT THE FEDERAL RESERVE BANK

And, after the Act:

THIS NOTE IS LEGAL TENDER FOR ALL DEBTS, PUBLIC AND PRIVATE, AND IS REDEEMABLE IN LAWFUL MONEY AT THE UNITED STATES TREASURY, OR AT ANY FEDERAL RESERVE BANK

With the signing of the *Gold Reserve Act*, Roosevelt removed, for want of a better word, honest U.S. currency, gold certificates, and made the dishonest money, Federal Reserve Notes, *legal tender*, forcing their acceptance in the American marketplace.

The *Victory Tax Act* created the climate for the notorious propaganda slogan: *Pay Your Fair Share.*

Thirty years later, John F. Kennedy took the second step needed for a cashless society by signing on June 4, 1963, an act of Congress abolishing silver certificates. In March 1964, the Secretary of the Treasury halted redemption of silver certificates in silver dollars.

The final transition from government-issued currency to privately issued currency was taken in the Nixon administration. The following was copied from the United States Treasury Internet web site:

> *Both United States Notes and Federal Reserve Notes are parts of our national currency and both are legal tender. They circulate as money in the same way. However, the issuing authority for them comes from different statutes. United States Notes were redeemable in gold until 1933, when the United States abandoned the gold standard. Since then, both currencies have served essentially the same purpose, and have had the same value. Because United States Notes serve no function that is not already adequately served by Federal Reserve Notes, their issuance was discontinued, and none have been placed into circulation since January 21, 1971.*

After the separation from England, all the country's fiat paper money was issued by the States themselves. The *Framers* then corrected the inflationary abuse of paper currency and gave us honest money within the mandates of the Constitution and the resulting Coinage Acts. Lincoln gave us unconstitutional paper money, and Wilson, Roosevelt, Kennedy and Nixon turned over the issuance of fiat paper money to the private Federal Reserve Bank. Now, the present Hamiltonian-Lincolnites and CFR-Illuminati international financiers are taking advantage of the electronic revolution in the transition to a cashless society.

The following quote from the Times of London is attributed to a member of the Rothschild banking family in response to the issuance of the United States Notes in 1862:

If that mischievous financial policy which had its origin in North America should become indurated down to a fixture, then that government will furnish its own money without cost. It will pay off its debts and be without a debt. It will become prosperous beyond precedent in the history of the civilized governments of the world. The brains and wealth of all countries will go to North America. That government must be destroyed or it will destroy every monarchy on the globe.[27]

The Rothschild family is one of the present-day stockholders of the Federal Reserve Bank.[28]

Every presidential administration since Lincoln has in some way, either knowingly, or through manipulation, aided these international financiers. The membership lists of the CFR have contained the names of government officials ever since its creation, and so does the international version of the CFR, the Bilderbergers, which meets every year to decide the fate of the world, to their personal advantage.

I'm not saying that every individual in government service is a conspirator; it would be ridiculous to even think so. No rational person wants their family and/or their fellow citizens to be injured. What I am saying is that American citizens have been conditioned to accept a police state and the surrender of their sovereignty to it. They have lost sight of, and have no idea of, the meaning of *Individual Liberty*. They have as a "nation" accepted, either willingly, unwillingly, or ignorantly, the Marxian principle of *from each according to his ability, to each according to his need*. In other words, forcibly taking from the haves to give to the have-nots, with the influential taking the lion's share before anything gets to the have-nots.

Wherefore, if you desire for youself, your children, and their children to have the blessings of the *Gifts of God*, expounded and claimed by the *Founding Fathers*, then the events that we have *backtracked* must be reversed, and courts must be made to apply the law as written.

A Call To Action:

If ye love wealth better than liberty, the tranquility of servitude better than the animating contest of freedom, go home from us in peace. We ask not your counsels or arms. Crouch down and lick the hands which feed you. May your chains set lightly upon you, and may posterity forget that ye were our countrymen.

Samuel Adams
Father of the American Revolution.

The facts contained in this book are true. If you have any doubts, for your own sake, and that of your family, I implore you to verify them for yourself. They are part of the factual knowledge that I have accumulated in my thirty-nine year journey in search of the truth of what was going wrong within our land of *Liberty*.

The greedy enemies of *Individual Liberty* are far advanced in their plans for a cashless society and a slave state within a world government, but it is not too late to stop them. They were further along in the South American country of Brazil in 1965, when an educational effort by small businessmen saved that country. The small businessman can also be a very important player in the salvation of our Constitution and Republican form of government, by educating his employees and refusing to force them into the servitude of the socialist *employment tax*.

Once educated, citizens should join political parties and become influential in helping *Liberty-loving* statesmen obtain office to bring about the corrections needed. This will not be done overnight. We have to be patient and not panic in this late hour. Remember, the quarterback that keeps his composure and does not panic during the two-minute drill is the most successful in winning the football game. One of the main tools that can and should be used to this end is talk radio. With the constant barrage of lies being fed to the public through the establishment media, it has been my experience that the public is very responsive to the truth when they hear it in a verifiable form.

Talk radio is feasible and affordable, when we work together. I have had experience in broadcasting talk radio through my affiliation with *Liberty Works Radio Network*, which was started and operated by some of the *Save-A-Patriot Fellowship* members. The response to the *Liberty*-oriented message broadcast over it was very gratifying. It is a fact that talk shows which have a federalist-socialist host (commonly known as liberals) do not fare very well, while the hosts who call themselves conservatives (who, in most cases, only give lip service to the real meaning of *Individual Liberty*) are the most successful. All the signs indicate that we should be successful in achieving our goals.

All that is left for us to do is band together to get the job done. With this in mind, if you're not already a member, I invite you to consider joining the *Save-A-Patriot Fellowship*. For the *Fellowship* has the knowledge, gained through years of experience, to help keep you from being sidetracked, neutralized, or possibly injured along the way. It is impossible to stand alone against such an influential foe, BUT WHEN WE ARE GATHERED TOGETHER IN JESUS' NAME, WE HAVE HIS PROTECTION AND BLESSING—I HAVE ALSO EXPERIENCED THAT. With all of this in our favor, we are sure to *pierce the illusion* that has been used to beguile American citizens.

Notes:

Part I: *The Framers' Intent*

Chapter 1: *God's Governmental Plan for Mankind*

1. Charlotte Thomson Iserbyt, *The DeliberateDumbing Down of America*, (Bath, ME:3D Research Co., 1999).
2. Gary Allen, *None Dare Call It Conspiracy*, (Seal Beach, CA: Concord Press, 1972).
3. Signers of the Declaration of Independence.
4. The attendees of the Constitutional Convention of 1787 who drafted the United States Constitution.
5. The form of government and divine law given to Moses for the benefit of the Israelites.
6. John Locke, *The Second Treatise of Civil Government*, 3d ed., (London: A.&J. Churcghill, 1690).

Chapter 2: *The Bibical Tax Plan*

1. *Rom.* 13:7.
2. *Matt.* 22:21.

Chapter 3: *The Form and Structure of Our Government*

1. W. Cleon Skousen, *The Naked Capitalist*, (Salt Lake City: privately published, 1970).
2. In Art. 1, Sec. 8, Cl. 9, Congress has the power "To constitute tribunals inferior to the supreme Court." Although Congress has the power to create these courts, the power of the courts are still enumerated within Art. 3.
3. James Madison in *Federalist Nos. 47—51*.
4. U.S. Constitution, Art. 2, Sec. 2, Cl. 1.

5. Article 1, Section 8, Clause 12.
6. Article 1, Section 1
7. Article I, Section 2, Clause 3.
8. Article I, Section 7, Clause 1.
9. *Corpus Juris Secundum*, 1956 ed., Vol 16, § 73, *Constitutional Law*.

Chapter 4: *The Federal Taxing Authority*

1. Reported in detail in Edward A. Ellison, Jr., J.D. and John W. Kurowski, *Prosperity Restored by the State Rate Tax Plan*, (Baltimore, MD: Free State Constitutionists Media Publishing, 1985).
2. *Madison's Notes on the Constitutional Convention of 1787*, Formation of the Union of the American States, 69th Cong, 1st sess, H. Doc. No. 398, 581.
3. Luther Martin stated in his communication to the legislature of Maryland in January, 1788; . . . *that the general government ought not to have the power of laying direct taxes . . .*
4. *Thomas v. United States*, 192 U S 363
5. Hamilton in *Federalist No. 36*.
6. Hamilton in *Federalist Nos. 12—13* and *30—36.*
7. *Internal Revenue Manual,* Chapter 1100 at § 1111.31.
8. There is verified evidence to prove that the 16th Amendment was not ratified by the required number of States. See Bill Benson, *The Law That Never Was*, (South Holland, IL: Constitional Research Asssociates, 1985).
9. *Black's Law Dictionary*, 5th Ed.: *vagueness doctrine.* Under this principle, a law which does not fairly inform a person of what is commanded or prohibited is unconstitutional as violative of due process.

Part II: *The Money System Established by the Framers*

Chapter 5: *What is Money?*

1. Rev. Charles E. Coughlin, *Money! Questions and Answers*, (The National Union for Social Justice, 1936).
2. Webster's Third International Dictionary, s.v. "scrip": (c) A paper currency or token issued for temporary use in an emergency. Noah Webster 1828 *America Dictionary of the English Language* defines "scrip": A small writing, certificate or schedule; a piece of paper containing a writing. "Bills of exchange cannot pay our debts abroad, till scrips of paper can be made current coin."—John Locke.
3. Ibid.
4. F. Tupper Saussy, *The Miracle On Main Street*, (Sewanee, TN: Spencer Judd Publishers, P.12).
5. *Formation of the Union of the American States*, 69th Cong., 1st sess., H.Doc. 398, 109.
6. Ibid,. 60.
7. Bold indicates that the words were italicized by the author.
8. Ibid., 556 & 557.
9. Ibid., 557.
10. Ibid., 557.
11. Ibid., 627 and 628.
12. *Federalist No. 44.*

Chapter 6: *Why do We Use Paper Money Today?*

1. The Statutes at Large 1 (April 2nd, 1792): 250.
2. Adrienne Kock and William Peden, eds., *The Life and Selected Writings of Thomas Jefferson* (New York: Random House, 1993), 125—126.
3. Harvard Classics (1910) vol.43 (1910), 222.
4. *Formation of the Union of the American States*, 69th Cong., 1st sess., H. Doc. 398, 166.
5. *4 Wheat* beginning at 401.
6. *Erie Railroad. Co. v. Tompkins*, 302 US 671. 82 L Ed

518.

7. Black's Law Dictionary, 5th ed., s.v. '*simplex dictum*": a mere assertion; an assertion without proof.

8. *America*, vol. 6, Library of Congress, 111.

9. Charles A. Beard and Mary Ritter Beard, A Basic *History of the United States*, (NY: Doubleday, Doran, 1944), 291.

10. James Madison, *Journal of the Federal Convention*, vol.1, 264—265.

11. Coughlin, *Money!*, 100.

12. Ibid p. 170 through 172.

13. *Legal Tender Act*, 12 Statutes at Large 12 (1862): 345, sec. 1.

14. Emanuel M. Josephson, *The "Federal" Reserve Conspiracy & Rockefeller Their "Gold Corner"* (New York: Chedney, 1968), 19.

15. J. LaurenceLaughlin, *The Federal Reserve Act: Its Origin & Its Problems* (NY MacMillen, 1933).

16. Emanuel M. Josephson, *The "Federal" Reserve Conspiracy & Rockefeller Their "Gold Corner"* (New York: Chedney, 1968), 41.

17. Felix Warburg was the chief of espionage and intelligencefor Kaiser Wilhelm's Germany.

18. J. LaurenceLaughlin, *Report to the Indianapolis Monetary Commission*.

19. President Wilson campaigned for office promising to keep the United States out of World War I, but once in office did everything in his power to enter the War, while Rockefeller increased his wealth supplying the war effort.

20. Sterling E. Edmunds, *The Roosevelt Coup D'Etat of 1930—40* (available from Boise, ID: Gospel Ministries Publications).

21. Edwin T. Layton, "And I Was There" Pearl Harbor and Midway - Breaking the Secrets, (NY: William Morrow, 1985).

22. See Beardsley Ruml, *Taxes For Revenue Are Obsolete*,

Part III: *Are the Provisions of the Internal Revenue Code Constitutional?*

Chapter 7: *Subtitle A, Income Taxes*

1. Resident aliens have the same rights and privileges as citizens, except they cannot vote or hold political office.
2. *Mark Eisner v. Myrtle H. McComber*, 252 US 189, Decided March 8, 1920.
3. *Title 5, United States Code*, § 301 will be discussed when we examine Subtitle C.
4. This tax is covered in detail in Part III of Chapter 8, *Subtitle C, Employment Taxes*.
5. *Internal Revenue Code* § 991 defines DISC as a Domestic International Sales Corporation.
6. *Internal Revenue Code* § 922 defines FSC as a foreign sales corporation that was created or organized under the laws of any foreign government.
7. Sections 901 through 970 are Part III of Subchapter N, *Income from sources without the United States*.
8. Whittaker Chambers, a self-confessed communist spy, named White as an underground communist contact during a hearing before Congress.

Chapter 8: *Subtitle C, Employment Taxes*

1. Webster's Third New International Dictionary, s.v. "inflation": An increase in the volume of money and credit relative to available goods resulting in a substantial and continuing rise in the general price level.
2. Ruml, *"Taxes For Revenue Are Obsolete."*
3. Randolph Paul, "The Current Tax Payment Act," June 14, 1943, source Records Group 56, National Archives,

College Park, MD. Mr. Paul was the General Counsel, Treasury Department.

4. Employment taxes were contained in Chapter 9 of the *Internal Revenue Code* of 1939, and were changed to Chapter 21 through 25 in the 1954 and 1986 *Internal Revenue Codes.*

5. From the Internal Revenue Service web site March 4, 2002: ITIN is a tax processing number for certain nonresident and resident aliens, their spouses and dependents. The ITIN is only available to individuals who cannot obtain a social security number (SSN).

6. Person is used here as it is defined in § 7701(a)(1) of the *Internal Revenue Code.*

Chapter 9: *Subtitle F, Procedure and Administration—Assessment Authority*

1. According to the IRS manual, three-digit CP codes are to be used for businesses; two-digit CP codes are designated for individuals.

2. *Thomas v. United States*, 192 U. S. 363.

3. Duties and imposts are terms commonly applied to levies made by governments on the importation or exportation of commodities. Cooley, *Const. Lim.* 7th ed., 680.

4. This was verified by the Congressional Research Service and made public by Barbara B. Kennelly, a member of Congress from the State of Connecticut, on January 24, 1996, in a letter to a member of the *Save-A-Patriot Fellowship,* and published in the *Fellowship's* newsletter, *Reasonable Action.*

5. The entire *Internal Revenue Code.*

Chapter 10: *Subtitle F, Procedure and Administration—Enforcement of Title*

Part IV: ...and "Justice" for All

Chapter 11: *The Department of Justice & the Federal Courts*

1. *Black's Law Dictionary* 5th Edition, from the Latin meaning *we command*.
2. Evidence sufficient in law to raise a presumption of fact or to establish the fact in question unless rebutted, *Webster's Third International Dictionary*.
3. See Thomas J. DiLorenzo's, *The Real Lincoln: A New Look at Abraham Lincoln, His Agenda, and an nnecessary War (Roseville, CA: Prima Publishing, 2002)*.
4. Harry's vindication by the Nevada Supreme Court can be found at *State Bar of Nevada v. Claiborne*, 756 P.2d 464 (Nev. 1988).

Chapter 12: *Avoiding the Pot Hole in the Road To Liberty*

1. Major General Smedley Butler, U.S.M.C., *War Is A Racket*, by: Major General Smedley Butler, U.S.M.C. (New York: Round Table Press, 1935).
2. There are many examples of wild theories to be found on Larry's web site, http://home.hiwaay.net/~becraft/. If you have been exposed to a legal argument about taxation that sounds a bit out of the ordinary, visit his web site and see if it is listed.
3. States' Rights are not the same as Individual Rights. States' Rights are the Constitutional powers given to the States by the federal and State Constitutions. Whereby, any encroachment by the federal government upon these powers would be an unlawful act.
4. Because the U.S. Constitution only allows Washington, D.C. to be the seat of government, the validity of a Washington, D.C. city government is extremely

questionable. Constitutionally, the District of Columbia can only contain the seat of government and not have any inhabitants or private businesses.

Part V: *The Long Road Back*

Chapter 13: *The Save-A-Patriot Fellowship*

1. Dr. McIntire died on March 19, 2002, at the age of 95. He fought for half a century to warn the American public of the socialist threat, broadcasting over 600 radio stations, and according to the *Philadelphia Inquirer*, losing millions of dollars fighting federal agencies trying to stop his effort.
2. Kotmair Reserve Notes were redeemable by the author in hot air and poppycock, just like Federal Reserve Notes, and in the early days of the movement, used them to pay the IRS. Their actual use was to help dispel fear for potential Patriots.

Chapter 14: *Looking Back Over Our Shoulders*

1. *Isa.* 14:12—15.
2. *John* 3:16-21.
3. Hans A. Pohlsander, *De Imperatoribus Romanis*, An Online Encyclopedia of Roman Emperors: Constantine I (306 - 337 A.D.), available at www.roman-emperors.org.
4. Ibid.
5. Ibid.
6. William T. Smedley, *Mystery Of Francis Bacon* (1910), A biography of Francis Bacon, avail;able at www.hiddenmysteries.com/freebook/bacon/bacontoc7. Ibid.html
8. Alfred Dodd, *Francis Bacon's Personal Life-Story (London: Century Hutchinson Ltd., 1986).*
9. Manly P. Hall, *America's Assignment with Destiny* (Los Angeles: Philosphical Research Society, 1973).

10. Will Durant, *The Story of Philosophy*: The Lives and Opinions of the Greater Philosophers (NY: Simon & Schuster, 1926).

11. Linda S. Schrigner, *"Bacon's 'Secret Societies'—The Ephrata Connection*. Available at www.geocities.com/ Athens/Acropolis/2216/Ephrata_Presentation/ Ephrata_Bibliog.htm.

12. Hall, *America's Assignment with Destiny*.

13. Ibid.

14. John Robinson, *Proof of a Conspiracy to Destroy All Governments and Religions, 3d ed., (Philadelphia: T. Dobson,*1789).

15. Myron Fagan, *Thirst For Justice — The Illuminati*. Available at www.prolognet.qc.ca/clyde/illumin.htm

16. Nat G. Rudulph, *"Why America Lost the 'Civil War.'"* Available at www.dixienet.org.

17. Ibid.

18. *Book of Matthew*: Chapter 17, verses 24-27.

19. Bennie J. McRae, Jr., *Major Generals John C. Freemont and David Hunter versus President Abraham Lincoln* (Trotwood, OH: LWF Communications, n.d.). Available at www.coax.net/people/lwf/fhl_pol.htm

20. Ibid.

21. Lincoln's address before the Young Men's Lyceum of Springfield, Illinois, University of Rochester 1838 Douglass Project.

22. Ibid.

23. *Annual Report 1991/92*, The Council On Foreign Relations, Pratt House, New York.

24. Being a naturalized citizen from England, the seditious sophistry Sutherland expounds can be understood.

25. Under a Republican form of government, all official authority is invested in elected officials only.

26. A photograph of F.D.R. dressed in royal robes with a crown displaying a dollar sign on his head appeared in a book published in October 2002, entitled *Grandmère: A Personal History Of Eleanor Roosevelt*, written by his

grandson David B. Roosevelt and published by Warner Books, New York. The photograph's caption, found on page 166, stated:

> *My grandfather had a sense of humor. In this never-before published photograph (left) FDR is depict as the "Imperial President"*...

The photograph, as well as the whole book, is copyrighted. A request was made to usethe photograph but there was no response and, therefore, it could not be used.

27. R.E. Search, *Lincoln Money Martyred*, (Frankston, TX: Hidden Mysteries Books, n.d.), originally published in 1935.

28. The owners of the Federal Reserve Bank stock certificates are listed on the *Save-A-Patriot Fellowship* web site: *www.save-a-patriot.org.*

Acknowledgments

This book would be incomplete without giving recognition and thanks to those faithful _Save-A-Patriot Fellowship_ employees that spent so much time converting my scribbling into understandable English. They are listed in alphabetical order: _Dick Greb, Deborah Hoeldtke, James Kerr_ and _Bonnie Nobile_.

Also, many thanks to my grandson, _Neil Dunty_, for his superb drawing of the "Emperor Without Clothes" used on the front cover.

Index

B

Babylon — 11, 42

Bacon, Sir Francis — 303, 304

Baltic Mining Company — 33

Baltimore, Maryland — i, 54, 108, 139, 147, 177, 197, 198, 199, 239, 240,271, 284, 285, 288, 294

Baltimore City Police Department, Baltimore, Maryland — i, ii

Bank of England — 42

Bank of the United States — 52, 53, 54

Bay of Pigs — i, 283

Beast in Revelation — 46

Beauregard, Pierre Gustave Toutant (general) — 64

Becraft, Lowell [Larry] H. Jr. — 245, 253, 258, 265, 277

Bee, Bernard E. (General) — 64

Belgium — 107

Benson Linda (Social Security Adminstration) — 198

Berkhimer, — 258

Bible — 4, 310, 311

Biden, Joseph (senator) — 245

Bilderbergers — 315, 332

Bills of Credit — 62, 68

Blaskopf, Lawrence — 191

Board of Tax Appeals — 140

Board of Trade — 304

Bonaparte, Napolean — 12

Bork, Robert (judge) — 245

Boston, Massachusetts — 10, 241

Boyle, Terrence W. (judge) — 196, 214 , 215, 216, 218, 219, 220, 221, 222, 223, 224, 225, 227, 228, 229, 230, 231, 233, 234, 235, 236, 237

Branch Davidians — 313

Brazil, South America — 333

British Bankers Association — 65

British Crown — 265

British Monarchy — 11

Brooklyn, New York — 28

Bunker Hill — 251

D

J

K

Marx, Karl — 249, 320
Maryland — i, iii, 28, 54, 59, 199, 202, 240, 243, 244, 266, 286
Maryland Committee of Correspondence — iii, 286
Maryland Constitution — 193, 243
Mason, George (colonel) — 45, 46
Massachusetts, Boston — 10, 241
Massachusetts Bay Colony — 265
Maxwell Air Force Base — iii, iv, 287
May, Francis — 268
McCarthy, Joseph (senator) — 283
McCulloch, James — 54, 55, 56, 57, 60, 61
McIntire, Rev. Dr. Carl — 286, 344
Mercer, John Francis — 45
Mercier, George — 270
Messiah — 298, 300
Meyers, Grorge — 286
Middleton, Marsha — 304
Miller, James (judge) — 240, 241
Miller Group — 232
Minutemen — ii
Montana Freeman — 232, 254
Montgomery, Alabama — 61, 258, 287

Morris, Governeur Robert — 45, 51
Moses — 121, 298, 337
Muench, George — 198,199
Murphy, John — 286
Mussolini — i

N

Napoleonic Wars — 306
National Parks — 311
National Patriot Association — iii, iv, 287, 289
Ness, Elliot — 154
Netherlands — 107, 299
Nevada — 245
New, Michael G. — 312

O

P

Z